Instant Pot Cookbook #2019

600 Most Wanted Instant Pot Recipes

for Your 3 Quart Instant Pot Pressure Cooker

(Instant Pot Mini Duo Recipes)

Jennifer Stephenson

Legal & Disclaimer

The information and contents herein are not designed to replace or take the place of any form of medical or professional advice and are not meant to replace the need for independent medical, financial, legal or other professional advice or services, as may be required. The content and information in this book have been provided for educational and entertainment purposes only.

The content and information in this book have been compiled from reliable sources and are accurate to the author's best knowledge, information, and belief. The author cannot guarantee this book's accuracy and validity and cannot be held liable for any errors and/or omissions. Further, changes will be periodically made to this book when needed. It is recommended that you consult with a health professional who is familiar with your personal medical history before using any of the suggested remedies, techniques, or information in this book.

Upon using the contents in this book, you agree to hold harmless the author from and against any damages, costs, and expenses, including any legal fees potentially resulting from the application of the information provided You agree to accept all risks associated with using the information presented inside this book.

Table of content

Introduction

A mini instant pot is an amazing appliance for food lovers. This appliance is perfect for the small family who needs smaller-sized meals. It is the perfect appliance for a couple or for 4-6 servings. A mini instant pot is a multitasking electric pressure cooker which helps you to cook various types of dishes, a smaller version of the instant pot. It works like a pressure cooker, slow cooker, rice cooker and steamer.

A mini instant pot is used to cook food quickly without compromising its nutritional value. The mini instant pot has versatile cooking functions, so you can cook various meals in a single pressure cooker like breakfast, stew, snacks, soups desserts and main course meals, such as vegetarian, chicken, meat and seafood. It suits couples or small size families, running on a microprocessor, which makes it safe and convenient. A mini instant pot requires minimal space in the kitchen due to its compact size, while its microprocessor automatically adjusts intensity and heating duration, keeping an eye on both pressure level and temperature. A mini instant pot comes with 11 pre-programmed cooking functions: Rice, Bean/Chili, Porridge, Soup/Broth, Slow cook, Meat/Stew, Keep Warm, Sauté/Searing and Yogurt. Its pressure settings are Normal, More and Less, with + and – settings for time.

Chapter 1 Close Contact Mini Instant Pot

Smart and Safety Features

- A mini instant pot is high-efficiency compared to other appliances' energy usage.
- A mini instant pot comes with multiple pre-programmed cooking functions, including a 4-hour pressure cooking capacity, and slow cooking capacity between 30 minutes and 20 hours.
- It comes with an LED display, which gives you a modern cooking experience, along with its high-quality stainless-steel body.
- It has a safety lid lock, which prevents accidental opening of the pressure cooker during high pressure.
- Includes a temperature regulator, which helps to prevent the burning of ingredients.
- Auto shutdown if the pressure exceeds its safety level.
- A lid position sensor helps to prevent the pot form operating if the lid is in an unsafe position.

How to Use Mini Instant Pot

- Plug instant pot into power and switch on, then open lid.
- Add ingredients you want to cook into pot area, then gently stir.
- Close lid and select function.
- Set cooking time and temperature, as per ingredients.
- When cooking time is over, release pressure and open lid.
- Enjoy your delicious meal.

A mini instant pot needs less time to achieve pressure because it's smaller. A mini instant pot cooks food faster then the larger model, so it saves energy as well as time.

Benefits of Mini Instant Pot

1. A mini instant pot requires less liquid for cooking a meal. While large pot requires 1 ½ cups liquid, a mini pot requires just 1 ¼ cup of liquid for cooking a meal. Cooking juices also come from your ingredients, meaning it requires less liquid to achieve pressure.

2. A mini instant pot saves time and energy. It cooks faster than any traditional cooking method, saving up to 70 percent of other cooking methods' energy. It cooks food on high pressure, which helps to save cooking time.

3. A mini instant pot offers you versatile cooking options. You can cook various types of meals in a single pot, like breakfast recipes, eggs, yogurt and oatmeal. You can make risottos and pasta dishes, as well as soups, stew, cake, pies, etc.

4. A mini instant pot's safety features make it one of the safest appliances to use. Its pressure and temperature sensing technology help to regulate inside pressure and temperature, preventing instances of burning ingredients or causing other damage.

5. Pressure cooking helps kill harmful micro-organisms. A mini instant pot cooks food under high pressure, creating a temperature above boiling. This kills all harmful micro-organisms, such as fungi, bacteria and viruses.

6. A mini instant pot helps preserve nutrients in food. Mini instant pot requires less water compared to other cooking methods, the result of which means less vitamins and minerals dissolve in water. A mini instant pot is quick, evenly distributing steam throughout the cooking process. Due to this, your food is not oxidized and maintains its natural color and flavor.

Mini Instant Pot Different Cooking Functions/Buttons

1. **Keep Warm/Cancel:** This button is used to cancel the current cooking program. Your mini instant pot will go to standby mode, while the Keep Warm function keeps your food warm, maintaining its temperature between 145°F to 172°F.

2. **Sauté:** This button functions just like your frying pan. Your pressure cooker lid must be open at the time of sautéing to maintian the program's integrity. You can also adjust the temperature using the Less, Normal and More settings.

3. **Soup:** Use this to cook various types of soups and broth. Default cooking time for this function is 30 minutes under high pressure.

4. **Manual:** This function is used to adjust manual pressure, temperature and time setting, with the help of the +/- buttons. Default manual mode is set to high.

5. **Slow cook:** This converts your mini instant pot into a slow cooker. The default time is set at 4 hours for slow cooking, but you can use +/- buttons to adjust the time up to 20 hours. When using slow cooking function, always remember to set the valve to Venting, as that allows steam to escape as your dish cooks.

6. **Steam:** You can use the stem function for steaming veggies, seafood, and many other things. The steam function is also great for reheating food. When using this function, always keep valve switched to Sealing. The default time for this function is 10 minutes at high pressure.

7. **Porridge:** This function is used to prepare oatmeal and porridge, as well as various types of grains. Its default time setting is 20 minutes at high pressure.

8. **Yogurt:** Used this to make various types of yogurts. The default time for this function is set at 8 hours. You can increase or decrease time using the adjust buttons.

Mini Instant Pot Tips

1. **Use the Right Amount of Liquid:** Always use the right amount of liquid recommended by the recipe. A mini instant pot requires less liquid compared to a larger model. If large instant pot requires 1 ½ cup of liquid for cooking, the mini instant pot requires only 1 ¼ cup of liquid. The right amount of liquid helps to cook food evenly.

2. **Preheat liquid:** To save cooking time, preheat your liquid in the pot, as you would a sauce. Use the Sauté mode for preheating liquid. Add meat and simmer for a few minutes before pressure cooking to save time later on.

3. **Use appropriate accessories:** Always use the accessories that come with your mini instant pot for cooking. If you use unsuitable accessories in the pot, there are chances to melt or burn inside the pot during cooking.

4. **Use Keep Warm function:** This function is used to keep your food at a safe temperature until it is ready to serve. It maintains food temperature between 145°F to 172°F by default.

5. **Use the sauté button for reducing excess liquid:** After you finish cooking, should your sauces be too thin, the Sauté button is used to boil off the excess liquid.

6. **Brown the meat:** If you want to increase the flavor in your dish, you should brown the meat before pressure cooking. To brown your meat, use Sauté mode.

7. **Follow instruction manual:** Always follow the instructions carefully to avoid mishaps and misadventures.

Mini Instant Pot Cautions

1. Always seal the pot properly before you start cooking. Check the lid is placed and locked properly.

2. Do not open the lid before depressurizing. After the pot finishes cooking, open the pressure valve to depressurize the pot. If you feel the lid is hard to open, it means that there is still some pressure inside the pot.

3. Stay away from the steam release valve. Do not expose any body part over the valve, as it may cause serious burns.

4. Fill the instant pot with enough liquid and ingredients before closing lid. Always keep in mind that amount of food and liquid inside the pot should not exceed the third line.

5. If you want to add thickening agents, such as arrowroot powder or cornstarch, add it after completing your cooking, as it makes the liquid thick. Due to this, pressure cannot build properly inside the pot.

6. Always check that the sealing ring was in good condition. If you find any damage, do not use the cooker until the seal has been replaced.

7. Don't forget to turn off the Keep Warm button after you finishing cooking to avoid overcooking your food.

8. Always clean your instant pot after you finish cooking. Follow the instruction manual how to clean the pot properly to avoid damaging it.

9. Always keep pot out of children's reach, whether the pot is hot or not.

Chapter 2 Instant Pot Breakfast Recipes

Mini Breakfast Frittata

(Servings: 3|Cooking Time: 10 minutes)

Ingredients:
- 6 eggs
- ¼ cup cheddar cheese, shredded
- ¼ cup milk
- ½ small onion, chopped
- ½ bell pepper, chopped
- 1 small potato, peeled and chopped
- 4 bacon slices, chopped
- ½ tsp. black pepper
- ½ tsp. sea salt

Directions for Cooking:
1. Take three ceramic ramekins and place bacon on the bottom of each ramekin.
2. Add chopped vegetables on top of bacon.
3. In a bowl, whisk eggs with pepper and salt. Pour egg mixture over vegetables.
4. Sprinkle shredded cheddar cheese on top.
5. Cover each ramekin with aluminum foil.
6. Pour 1 cup water into instant pot and place trivet in pot. Place ramekins on trivet.
7. Cover instant pot with lid and cook on manual high pressure for 10 minutes.
8. Quick release pressure then open the lid.
9. Remove ramekins from the instant pot and set aside to cool completely.
10. Serve and enjoy.

Nutrition information per serving:
Calories: 367; Carbohydrates: 14.9g; Protein: 25g; Fat: 23g; Sugar: 3.6g; Sodium: 1093mg

Delicious Baked Oatmeal

(Servings: 12|Cooking Time: 60 minutes)

Ingredients:

- 2 eggs
- ½ cup unsweetened chocolate chips
- 2 tsp. baking powder
- 3 cups quick oats
- 1 cup milk
- 1 tsp. vanilla
- ½ cup peanut butter
- ½ cup brown sugar
- 2 tbsp. butter, melted
- ½ tsp. salt

Directions for Cooking:

1. Spray 7" baking pan with cooking spray and set aside.
2. In a large mixing bowl, whisk eggs with brown sugar and butter until mixed.
3. Add vanilla and peanut butter and mix well.
4. Now add milk and whisk until well combined.
5. In a separate large bowl, add all dry ingredients less chocolate chips and mix until combined.
6. Pour egg mixture into the dry ingredients mixture and mix until fully combined.
7. Add chocolate chips and fold well.
8. Pour 1 ½ cups water into instant pot then insert trivet into pot.
9. Pour batter into the prepared baking pan and cover with aluminum foil.
10. Place baking pan on top of the trivet. Seal instant pot with lid and select high pressure for 60 minutes.
11. Quick release pressure then open the lid.
12. Remove pan from the instant pot and set aside to cool completely.
13. Serve and enjoy.

Nutrition information per serving:
Calories: 270; Carbohydrates: 26g; Protein: 8.3g; Fat: 15.1g; Sugar: 8.1g; Sodium: 187mg

Sweet Pumpkin Bread

(Servings: 16|Cooking Time: 60 minutes)

Ingredients:

- 2 eggs
- ½ tsp. vanilla
- ¼ cup maple syrup
- 1 ¼ cups pumpkin puree
- ¼ cup sugar
- 1 tsp. pumpkin pie spice
- 1 tsp. baking soda
- 2 cups instant oatmeal

Directions for Cooking:

1. Add all ingredients into the blender and blend until smooth.
2. Spray 7" baking pan with cooking spray. Pour batter into the prepared baking dish and spread evenly.
3. Cover baking pan with aluminum foil.
4. Pour 1 ½ cups water into instant pot, then place trivet into the pot. Place baking dish on top of the trivet.
5. Seal instant pot with lid and select manual high pressure for 60 minutes.
6. Quick release pressure then open the lid.
7. Remove pan from the instant pot and set aside to cool completely.
8. Cut bread into the slices and serve.

Nutrition information per serving:
Calories: 78; Carbohydrates: 15.1g; Protein: 2.3g; Fat: 0.3g; Sugar: 6.9g; Sodium: 89mg

Apple Blueberry Quinoa

(Servings: 4|Cooking Time: 1 minute)

Ingredients:

- 1 ½ cups quinoa, rinsed and drained
- ¼ cup pistachios, chopped
- 1 cup plain yogurt
- 1 cup apple juice
- ¾ cup apple, grated
- 1 tbsp. honey
- ¼ cup raisins
- 1 cinnamon stick
- 1 ½ cups water
- ¼ cup blueberries

Directions for Cooking:

1. Add quinoa, cinnamon stick and water into instant pot.
2. Seal pot with lid and select manual. Set timer for 1 minute.
3. Allow pressure to release naturally for 10 minutes, then release using quick release method.
4. Fluff quinoa with spoon and transfer into the mixing bowl. Remove cinnamon stick from quinoa.
5. Once quinoa is completely cool, add raisins, apple juice, grated apple and honey. Stir well to combine.
6. Place quinoa in refrigerator for 1 hour.
7. Add yogurt and stir well. Top with blueberries and pistachios.
8. Serve immediately and enjoy.

Nutrition information per serving:
Calories: 397; Carbohydrates: 71.8g; Protein: 13.8g; Fat: 6.6g; Sugar: 25.5g; Sodium: 73mg

Perfect Steel Cut Oats with Currants

(Servings: 4|Cooking Time: 30 minutes)

Ingredients:

- 1 cup steel cut oats
- 1 tbsp. maple syrup
- ¼ cup dried currants
- 1 tbsp. butter
- ¼ tsp. salt
- 3 ¼ cups water

Directions for Cooking:

1. Add butter into instant pot and set on Sauté mode.
2. Once butter is melted, add oats, maple syrup, currants and salt. Stir for 2-3 minutes or until oats are toasted.
3. Add water and stir well.
4. Seal pot with lid and select manual high pressure for 10 minutes.
5. Allow pressure to release naturally for 10 minutes, then release using quick release method.
6. Stir well and serve.

Nutrition information per serving:
Calories: 120; Carbohydrates: 18.2g; Protein: 2.8g; Fat: 4.2g; Sugar: 3.7g; Sodium: 169mg

Gluten-Free Breakfast Porridge

(Servings: 2|Cooking Time: 3 minutes)

Ingredients:

- 1 tbsp. honey
- 2 tsp. coconut oil, melted
- 1 cup water
- ½ cup unsweetened shredded coconut
- ½ cup pecan halves
- ¼ cup pepitas shelled
- ½ cup cashews

Directions for Cooking:

1. Add all ingredients except honey, coconut oil and water into the blender and blend until mixture looks like almond meal.

2. Transfer blended mixture into instant pot. Add honey, coconut oil and water; Stir well.
3. Seal pot with lid and select Porridge mode. Set timer for 3 minutes.
4. Quick release pressure then open the lid.

5. Stir well and serve.

Nutrition information per serving:
Calories: 748; Carbohydrates: 31.8g; Protein: 15.3g; Fat: 63.9g; Sugar: 13.8g; Sodium: 154mg

Healthy Breakfast Cinnamon Oatmeal

(Servings: 4|Cooking Time: 5 minutes)

Ingredients:
- 1 cup oats
- 3 tbsp. butter
- 2 tbsp. brown sugar
- 1 cup apple, peeled and diced
- 2 ½ cups water
- 1/8 tsp. cinnamon
- 2 tbsp. raisins

Directions for Cooking:
1. Add butter into instant pot and set on Sauté mode.

2. Once butter is melted, add raisins, cinnamon, apples, brown sugar, oats and water. Stir well.
3. Seal pot with lid and select manual high pressure for 5 minutes.
4. Quick release pressure then open the lid.
5. Stir well and serve.

Nutrition information per serving:
Calories: 214; Carbohydrates: 29.6g; Protein: 3.1g; Fat: 10.1g; Sugar: 13.1g; Sodium: 69mg

Creamy Oatmeal

(Servings: 2|Cooking Time: 13 minutes)

Ingredients:
- 1 cup steel cut oatmeal
- 1 tsp. maple syrup
- ½ tsp. vanilla
- 3 cups unsweetened almond milk

Directions for Cooking:
1. Set instant pot on Sauté mode. Add oatmeal and sauté for 2-3 minutes.
2. Add almond milk and stir well.
3. Seal pot with lid and select manual high pressure for 10 minutes.

4. Allow pressure to release naturally, then open lid.
5. Add maple syrup and vanilla, and stir well.
6. Top with fresh berries and serve.

Nutrition information per serving:
Calories: 227; Carbohydrates: 33.1g; Protein: 6.9g; Fat: 7.9g; Sugar: 2.5g; Sodium: 273mg

Cinnamon Cornmeal Porridge

(Servings: 4|Cooking Time: 12 minutes)

Ingredients:
- 1 cup cornmeal
- ½ cup condensed milk
- ½ tsp. nutmeg
- 1 tsp. vanilla
- 2 cinnamon sticks

- 1 cup milk
- 4 cups water

Directions for Cooking:
1. Add milk and 3 cups water into instant pot. Set on Porridge mode for 6 minutes.

2. In a bowl, add cornmeal and remaining cup water. Mix until combined.
3. Transfer cornmeal mixture into instant pot.
4. Add nutmeg, vanilla and cinnamon sticks. Stir well.
5. Cover pot with lid and select manual high pressure for 6 minutes.
6. Release pressure naturally, then open lid.
7. Add condensed milk and stir well.
8. Serve and enjoy.

Nutrition information per serving:
Calories: 268; Carbohydrates: 47.5g; Protein: 7.5g; Fat: 5.8g; Sugar: 24g; Sodium: 95mg

Traditional Pumpkin Pie Oatmeal

(Servings: 4|Cooking Time: 13 minutes)

Ingredients:
- 2 cups rolled old fashioned oats
- ½ cup maple syrup
- ½ tsp. vanilla
- 1 tsp. pumpkin pie spice
- ½ cup pumpkin puree
- 1 ¾ cup milk
- 2 cups water

Directions for Cooking:
1. Pour 1 cup water into instant pot. Set pot on Sauté mode to boil water.
2. Meanwhile, in a pyrex dish, mix together add oats, maple syrup, vanilla, pumpkin pie spice, pumpkin puree, milk and remaining water. Cover dish with aluminum foil.
3. Press the cancel button. Place trivet into the pot, and Pyrex dish on top of the trivet.
4. Seal pot with lid and select manual high pressure for 8 minutes.
5. Release pressure naturally for 5 minutes, then quick release.
6. Open lid carefully. Remove dish from the instant pot and set aside to cool completely.
7. Stir well and serve.

Nutrition information per serving:
Calories: 360; Carbohydrates: 66.5g; Protein: 10.9g; Fat: 5.9g; Sugar: 30.4g; Sodium: 59mg

Savory Breakfast Grits

(Servings: 6|Cooking Time: 15 minutes)

Ingredients:
- 1 cup milk
- 2 ½ cups water
- 1 cup cheddar cheese, shredded
- 4 tbsp. butter, melted
- 1 cup grits

Directions for Cooking:
1. Pour 2 cups water into instant pot then place a trivet inside.
2. In a baking dish, mix together 2 tablespoons of butter, water and grits. Cover dish with aluminum foil and place on top of the trivet.
3. Seal pot with lid and cook on manual high pressure for 15 minutes.
4. Quick release pressure then open the lid.
5. Remove dish from the instant pot. Transfer grit mixture to the large mixing bowl. Add milk and cheese to the grit mixture and stir until cheese is melted.
6. Serve and enjoy.

Nutrition information per serving:
Calories: 184; Carbohydrates: 6.2g; Protein: 6.5g; Fat: 15g; Sugar: 2.4g; Sodium: 251mg

Spinach Bacon Frittata

(Servings: 4|Cooking Time: 15 minutes)

Ingredients:

- 6 eggs
- ¼ cup bacon, cooked and chopped
- ½ cup tomato, chopped
- 1 cup fresh spinach
- ½ tsp. Italian seasoning
- 2 ½ tsp. heavy cream
- ¼ tsp. pepper
- ¼ tsp. salt

Directions for Cooking:

1. In a bowl, whisk eggs with spices and heavy cream.
2. Spray 7" baking pan with cooking spray.
3. Add bacon, tomato and spinach to the pan. Pour egg mixture over bacon mixture.
4. Cover pan with aluminum foil.
5. Pour 1 ½ cups water into instant pot, then place trivet into pot.
6. Place baking pan on top of trivet. Seal instant pot with lid and cook on manual high pressure for 15 minutes.
7. Quick release pressure then open the lid.
8. Serve and enjoy.

Nutrition information per serving:
Calories: 120; Carbohydrates: 1.9g; Protein: 9.2g; Fat: 8.5g; Sugar: 1.2g; Sodium: 276mg

Fluffy Pancake

(Servings: 2|Cooking Time: 17 minutes)

Ingredients:

- 1 egg
- 1 ½ tbsp. olive oil
- 1 ¼ cups buttermilk
- ¾ tsp. baking soda
- ¾ tsp. baking powder
- 3 tbsp. sugar
- 1 cup all-purpose flour

Directions for Cooking:

1. In a large mixing bowl, mix together flour, baking soda, baking powder and sugar.
2. Add buttermilk, oil and eggs, and whisk until well combined.
3. Spray 7" spring-form pan with cooking spray. Pour batter into the prepared pan.
4. Pour 1 cup water into instant pot, then insert trivet into pot.
5. Place pan on top of trivet. Seal pot with lid and cook on low pressure for 17 minutes.
6. Quick release pressure then open the lid carefully.
7. Remove pan from the pot and set aside to cool completely.
8. Slice and serve.

Nutrition information per serving:
Calories: 480; Carbohydrates: 74.1g; Protein: 14.3g; Fat: 14.7g; Sugar: 25.7g; Sodium: 668mg

Cheese Mushroom Frittata

(Servings: 2|Cooking Time: 15 minutes)

Ingredients:

- 4 eggs
- 1 ½ cups water
- 2 Swiss cheese slices, cut into 4 pieces
- 4 oz. mushrooms, sliced
- 1/8 tsp. white pepper
- 1/8 tsp. onion powder
- 2 tsp. heavy cream
- ¼ tsp. salt

Directions for Cooking:

1. In a bowl, whisk eggs with spices and heavy cream.
2. Spray 7" baking pan with cooking spray. Add sliced mushrooms to pan and pour egg mixture over mushrooms.
3. Arrange cheese slices on top of mushroom and egg mixture. Cover pan with aluminum foil.
4. Pour 1 ½ cups water to the instant pot then insert trivet into pot. Place pan on top of the trivet.
5. Seal pot with lid and cook on manual high pressure for 15 minutes.
6. Release pressure using quick release method.
7. Serve and enjoy.

Nutrition information per serving:
Calories: 262; Carbohydrates: 18.5g; Protein: 20.5g; Fat: 18.5g; Sugar: 2.1g; Sodium: 478mg

Banana Nut Oatmeal

(Servings: 4|Cooking Time: 3 minutes)

Ingredients:

- 1 banana, chopped
- ¼ cup walnuts, chopped
- 1 tsp. honey
- 2 cups milk
- 2 cups water
- 1 cup steel cut oats

Directions for Cooking:

1. Add milk, water and oats to the instant pot, and stir well.
2. Seal pot with lid and select manual high pressure for 3 minutes.
3. Allow pressure to release naturally, then open lid.
4. Add walnuts, banana and honey to the oats. Stir well.
5. Serve and enjoy.

Nutrition information per serving:
Calories: 218; Carbohydrates: 28.8g; Protein: 8.9g; Fat: 85g; Sugar: 10.8g; Sodium: 63mg

Delicious Berry Oatmeal

(Servings: 2|Cooking Time: 4 minutes)

Ingredients:

- 4 oz. fresh berries
- ¼ tsp. cinnamon
- ½ tsp. vanilla
- 2 tbsp. honey
- 1 cup almond milk
- 15 oz. coconut milk
- 1 cup steel cut oats

Directions for Cooking:

1. Spray instant from inside with cooking spray.
2. Add all ingredients to pot and stir well. Seal pot with lid and select manual high pressure for 4 minutes.
3. Allow pressure to release naturally, then open lid.
4. Stir well and serve.

Nutrition information per serving:
Calories: 594; Carbohydrates: 60.3g; Protein: 9.3g; Fat: 37.5g; Sugar: 25.9g; Sodium: 36m

Cinnamon Mash Banana Oats

(Servings: 2|Cooking Time: 4 minutes)

Ingredients:

- 2 bananas, sliced
- ½ tsp. cinnamon
- 1 cup milk
- 1 cup water
- 2/3 cup rolled oats

Directions for Cooking:

1. Spray instant pot with cooking spray.
2. Add all ingredients to the instant pot and stir well. Cover pot with lid and cook on manual high pressure for 4 minutes.
3. Quick release pressure then open the lid.
4. Mash banana chunks with a fork and stir well.
5. Serve and enjoy.

Nutrition information per serving:
Calories: 271; Carbohydrates: 51.9g; Protein: 8.9g; Fat: 4.7g; Sugar: 20.2g; Sodium: 64mg

Flavored Avocado Kale Oats

(Servings: 2|Cooking Time: 10 minutes)

Ingredients:

- ½ cup steel cut oats
- 2 green onions, sliced
- ½ avocado, diced
- 1 tbsp. tahini
- 1 tsp. tamari
- 4 tbsp. nutritional yeast
- 1 tbsp. miso paste
- 1 cup frozen kale, chopped
- 1 cup water
- 1 cup unsweetened almond milk

Directions for Cooking:

1. Add oats, almond milk and water into instant pot. Stir well.
2. Cover pot with lid and select manual high pressure for 8 minutes.
3. Allow pressure to release naturally for 6 minutes, then release using quick release method.
4. Set pot on Sauté mode. Stir in nutritional yeast, tamari, tahini, miso paste and kale, and cook for 2-3 minutes.
5. Top with green onions and avocado.
6. Serve immediately and enjoy.

Nutrition information per serving:
Calories: 354; Carbohydrates: 36g; Protein: 17.7g; Fat: 18.6g; Sugar: 1.9g; Sodium: 616mg

Brussels Sprouts with Bacon

(Servings: 4|Cooking Time: 6 minutes)

Ingredients:

- 1 lb. Brussels sprouts, trimmed and halved
- 2 tsp. orange zest
- ½ cup water
- ½ cup orange juice
- 2 bacon slices, diced
- 1 tbsp. olive oil

Directions for Cooking:

1. Add olive oil to the instant pot and set on Sauté mode.
2. Add bacon and sauté for 3-5 minutes or until crisp.

3. Add water and orange juice. Deglaze the instant pot.
4. Add Brussels sprouts and stir well.
5. Seal pot with lid and cook on manual high pressure for 3 minutes.
6. Release pressure using quick release method. Open lid carefully.
7. Garnish with orange zest and serve.

Nutrition information per serving:
Calories: 145; Carbohydrates: 13.9g; Protein: 7.6g; Fat: 7.9g; Sugar: 5.1g; Sodium: 249mg

Healthy Apple Dates Oatmeal

(Servings: 2|Cooking Time: 4 minutes)

Ingredients:
- ¼ tsp. vanilla
- ¼ tsp. cinnamon
- 2 dates, chopped
- 1 apple, chopped
- ½ cup water
- ¼ cup instant oatmeal

Directions for Cooking:
1. Add all ingredients to the instant pot and stir well.
2. Cover pot with lid and cook on manual high pressure for 4 minutes.
3. Allow pressure to release naturally for 5 minutes, then release using quick release method. Open lid carefully.
4. Stir well and serve.

Nutrition information per serving:
Calories: 122; Carbohydrates: 28.9g; Protein: 1.9g; Fat: 0.9g; Sugar: 17g; Sodium: 4mg

Delicious Blueberry Oatmeal

(Servings: 4|Cooking Time: 3 minutes)

Ingredients:
- 1 cup steel cut oats
- 1 tbsp. brown sugar
- 3 cups milk
- 1 cup blueberries
- 1/8 tsp. cinnamon
- Pinch of salt

Directions for Cooking:
1. Add all ingredients into instant pot and stir well to combine.
2. Seal pot with lid and cook on manual high pressure for 3 minutes.
3. Allow pressure to release naturally, then open lid.
4. Stir well and serve.

Nutrition information per serving:
Calories: 198; Carbohydrates: 30.4g; Protein: 9g; Fat: 5.2g; Sugar: 14.2g; Sodium: 127mg

Blueberry French toast Casserole

(Servings: 4|Cooking Time: 25 minutes)

Ingredients:
- 4 French bread slices, cut into pieces
- 1 cup blueberries
- ½ tsp. cinnamon
- ½ tsp. vanilla
- ¼ cup brown sugar
- 2 eggs
- 1 cup milk
- ¾ cup water

Directions for Cooking:
1. In a large mixing bowl, whisk eggs with cinnamon, vanilla, brown sugar and milk.
2. Add bread pieces and blueberries. Mix until well coated.

3. Spray baking dish with cooking spray and pour prepared mixture in.
4. Pour ¾ cup water into instant pot. Place trivet in the pot. Place baking dish on top of the trivet.
5. Seal pot with lid and select Pressure Cook mode. Set timer for 25 minutes.
6. Serve and enjoy.

Nutrition information per serving:
Calories: 212; Carbohydrates: 35.7g; Protein: 8.8g; Fat: 4.2g; Sugar: 16.2g; Sodium: 270mg

Healthy Green Beans

(Servings: 10|Cooking Time: 8 minutes)

Ingredients:
- 14 oz. can green beans, undrained
- ½ cup butter
- 4 bacon slices, chopped
- Pepper
- Salt

Directions for Cooking:
1. Add all ingredients into instant pot and stir well.
2. Seal pot with lid and select manual high pressure for 8 minutes.
3. Allow pressure to release naturally, then open lid.
4. Stir well and serve.

Nutrition information per serving:
Calories: 151; Carbohydrates: 5.7g; Protein: 4.3g; Fat: 12.4g; Sugar: 2.8g; Sodium: 788mg

Chocó Cherry Oatmeal

(Servings: 4|Cooking Time: 15 minutes)

Ingredients:
- 2 cups steel cuts oats
- ¼ cup chocolate chips
- 2 cups cherries
- ½ tsp. cinnamon
- 4 tbsp. honey
- 2 cups water
- 2 cups milk
- Pinch of salt

Directions for Cooking:
1. Spray inside instant pot with cooking spray.
2. Add all ingredients to the instant pot and stir well.
3. Seal pot with lid and cook on manual high pressure for 15 minutes.
4. Allow pressure to release naturally, then open lid.
5. Stir well and serve.

Nutrition information per serving:
Calories: 307; Carbohydrates: 54.7g; Protein: 8.2g; Fat: 7.5g; Sugar: 38.4g; Sodium: 116mg

Strawberry Oatmeal

(Servings: 4|Cooking Time: 5 minutes)

Ingredients:
- ¼ cup sugar
- 1 cup strawberries, chopped
- 3 cups water
- 2 tsp. vanilla
- 2 tbsp. butter
- 1 cup steel cut oats
- ¼ tsp. salt

Directions for Cooking:
1. Add all ingredients except strawberries to the instant pot and stir well.

2. Seal pot with lid and cook on manual high pressure for 5 minutes.
3. Allow pressure to release naturally, then open lid.
4. Stir in strawberries and serve.

Nutrition information per serving:
Calories: 193; Carbohydrates: 29.4g; Protein: 3g; Fat: 7.2g; Sugar: 14.7g; Sodium: 195mg

Delicious Egg Bake

(Servings: 2|Cooking Time: 9 minutes)

Ingredients:
- 8 eggs
- 2 cups hash brown potatoes, thawed
- 5 bacon pieces, diced
- 1 cup cheddar cheese, shredded
- ½ cup milk
- ¼ tsp. salt

Directions for Cooking:
1. Set instant pot on Sauté mode.
2. Add bacon to the instant pot and sauté for 1-2 minutes or until lightly brown.
3. Add hash brown potatoes over the top of bacon. Sprinkle ½ cup cheese on top.
4. In a bowl, whisk together eggs, milk and salt. Pour over the bacon and potatoes.
5. Sprinkle with remaining cheese.
6. Seal instant pot with lid and close the valve.
7. Select manual high for 7 minutes.
8. Once the timer goes off, remove the lid; there is no pressure to release.
9. Season with pepper and salt. Serve.

Nutrition information per serving:
Calories: 484; Carbohydrates: 29.9g; Protein: 22.4g; Fat: 30.5g; Sugar: 3.4g; Sodium: 785mg

Apple Cinnamon Oatmeal

(Servings: 4|Cooking Time: 5 minutes)

Ingredients:
- 1 cup steel cut oats
- 3 tbsp. butter
- 2 tbsp. brown sugar
- 1 cup apple, peeled and diced
- 2 ½ cups water
- 1/8 tsp. cinnamon
- 2 tbsp. raisins

Directions for Cooking:
1. Add butter into instant pot and set on Sauté mode.
2. Once butter is melted, turn off Sauté mode.
3. Add water, raisins, cinnamon, apples, brown sugar and oats. Stir well.
4. Seal instant pot with lid and close steam valve. Set the instant pot on manual high pressure for 5 minutes.
5. Quick release pressure then open the lid.
6. Stir well and serve.

Nutrition information per serving:
Calories: 214; Carbohydrates: 29.6g; Protein:3.1 g; Fat: 5.7g; Sugar: 13.1g; Sodium: 69mg

Healthy Banana Oatmeal

(Servings: 3|Cooking Time: 5 minutes)

Ingredients:
- 1 cup old-fashioned oatmeal
- 1 tbsp. brown sugar
- 2 tsp. cinnamon
- 2 bananas

- 1 cup water
- 1 cup milk

Directions for Cooking:

1. Spray instant pot bottom using cooking spray.
2. Add oatmeal, water and milk. Stir well.
3. Slice one banana and add it into instant pot.
4. Add brown sugar and cinnamon. Stir well to combine.

5. Seal instant pot with lid and select manual high pressure for 5 minutes.
6. Allow pressure to release naturally for 10 minutes, then release using quick release method.
7. Stir oatmeal and scoop into the serving bowls. Top with sliced banana and serve.

Nutrition information per serving:
Calorie: 256; Carbohydrates: 49.2g; Protein: 8.6 g; Fat: 1.6g; Sugar: 17.2g; Sodium: 42mg

Crust-less Breakfast Quiche

(Servings: 6|Cooking Time: 30 minutes)

Ingredients:

- 8 eggs
- 1 ½ cup mozzarella cheese, shredded
- 2 green onions, chopped
- 1 cup tomatoes, chopped
- 1 red pepper, chopped
- ½ cup flour
- ½ cup milk
- ¼ tsp. pepper
- ¼ tsp. salt

Directions for Cooking:

1. Pour 1 cup water into instant pot. Place trivet into instant pot.
2. In a large bowl, whisk eggs, flour, milk, pepper and salt.

3. Add vegetables and cheese. Stir until combined.
4. Pour egg mixture into a dish that will fit inside your instant pot. Cover dish with foil and place on the trivet.
5. Seal instant pot with lid and select manual high pressure for 30 minutes.
6. Allow pressure to release naturally for 10 minutes, then release using quick release method.
7. Serve and enjoy.

Nutrition information per serving:
Calorie: 166; Carbohydrates: 12.8g; Protein: 11.7g; Fat: 7.7g; Sugar: 3.3g; Sodium: 234mg

Creamy Rice Pudding

(Servings: 6|Cooking Time: 10 minutes)

Ingredients:

- 2 cups milk
- 1 cup rice, rinsed and drained
- ¼ cup maple syrup
- ¾ cup heavy cream
- 1 ¼ cups water
- 1/8 tsp. sea salt

Directions for Cooking:

1. Add all ingredients except for heavy cream into instant pot and mix well.

2. Seal instant pot with lid and select Porridge mode.
3. Allow pressure to release naturally for 10 minutes, then release using quick release method.
4. Stir in heavy cream and serve.

Nutrition information per serving:
Calorie: 478; Carbohydrates: 75.8g; Protein: 10.4g; Fat: 14.9g; Sugar: 23.1g; Sodium: 174mg

Mushroom Cheese Omelet

(Servings: 4|Cooking Time: 10 minutes)

Ingredients:

- 5 eggs, lightly beaten
- 2 tbsp. butter
- 1 onion, chopped
- 2 tbsp. chives, minced
- 1 ½ cups mushrooms, sliced
- ½ cup coconut milk
- ½ tbsp. cheddar cheese
- 1 bell pepper, chopped

Directions for Cooking:

1. Add butter into instant pot and set on Sauté mode.
2. In a bowl, whisk eggs until well combined. Add remaining ingredients and mix well.
3. Pour egg mixture into instant pot and cook for 2 minutes.
4. Seal pot with lid and select manual high pressure for 8 minutes.
5. Quick release pressure then open the lid.
6. Serve hot and enjoy.

Nutrition information per serving:
Calorie: 229; Carbohydrates: 7.8g; Protein: 9.4g; Fat: 18.9g; Sugar: 4.6g; Sodium: 131mg

Delicious Mashed Potatoes

(Servings: 4|Cooking Time: 3 minutes)

Ingredients:

- 3 potatoes, peeled and cubed
- 2 tbsp. parsley, chopped
- ¼ cup parmesan cheese, grated
- ½ cup milk
- 3 tbsp. butter
- 1 cup water
- 1/8 tsp. ground black pepper
- 1 tsp. Himalayan salt

Directions for Cooking:

1. Add potatoes, salt and 1 cup water into instant pot. Stir well.
2. Seal pot with lid and select manual high pressure for 3 minutes.
3. Quick release pressure then open the lid.
4. Drain potatoes well and place in a large bowl.
5. Add butter into the potatoes. Mash potatoes until smooth and creamy.
6. Add milk and pepper, and stir well to combine.
7. Garnish with parmesan cheese and parsley.
8. Serve and enjoy.

Nutrition information per serving:
Calorie: 263; Carbohydrates: 27.8g; Protein: 9.8g; Fat: 13.4g; Sugar: 3.2g; Sodium: 468mg

Pumpkin Oatmeal

(Servings: 4|Cooking Time: 10 minutes)

Ingredients:

- 1 cup steel cut oats
- 2 tbsp. maple syrup
- ¼ cup pumpkin
- ¼ tsp. cinnamon
- 1 tbsp. brown sugar
- 1 tsp. vanilla
- 1 ¼ cups water
- 14 oz. can coconut milk
- ½ tsp. salt

Directions for Cooking:

1. Add oats, vanilla, water, coconut milk and salt into instant pot. Stir well.

2. Seal pot with lid and select manual high pressure for 10 minutes.
3. Quick release pressure then open the lid.
4. Stir in cinnamon, brown sugar, maple syrup and pumpkin.

5. Serve and enjoy.

Nutrition information per serving:
Calorie: 187; Carbohydrates: 25.9g; Protein: 4.5g; Fat: 7.2g; Sugar: 10.6g; Sodium: 303mg

Peach Flax Oatmeal

(Servings: 4|Cooking Time: 3 minutes)

Ingredients:

- 2 cups rolled oats
- 4 cups water
- 2 tbsp. flax meal
- 1 tsp. vanilla extract
- 1 medium peach, chopped

Directions for Cooking:

1. Add oats, water, chopped peaches, and vanilla to the instant pot. Stir well.

2. Seal pot with lid and select manual high pressure for 3 minutes.
3. Allow release pressure naturally, then the open lid.
4. Stir well and pour into the serving bowls.
5. Top with flax meal and serve.

Nutrition information per serving:
Calorie: 188; Carbohydrates: 32.3g; Protein: 6.5g; Fat: 4g; Sugar: 4g; Sodium: 10mg

Tasty Herbed Potatoes

(Servings: 4|Cooking Time: 20 minutes)

Ingredients:

- 1 ½ lbs. baby potatoes
- 1 rosemary spring
- 5 tbsp. olive oil
- 1 cup water
- 3 garlic cloves
- Pepper
- Salt

Directions for Cooking:

1. Add oil in instant pot and set on Sauté mode.

2. Add potatoes, rosemary and garlic. Sauté for 10 minutes.
3. Add water and stir well. Seal pot with lid and cook on manual high pressure for 10 minutes.
4. Quick release pressure then open the lid carefully.
5. Season with pepper and salt. Serve and enjoy.

Nutrition information per serving:
Calories: 252; Carbohydrates: 21.9g; Protein: 4.5g; Fat: 17.7g; Sugar: 0g; Sodium: 58mg

Mac and Cheese

(Servings: 4|Cooking Time: 7 minutes)

Ingredients:

- 2 cups noodles, gluten-free
- 1 cup heavy cream
- 1 cup chicken stock
- 4 tbsp. butter
- 2 cups cheddar cheese, shredded
- Pepper

- Salt

Directions for Cooking:

1. Add cream, noodles and stock into instant pot.
2. Seal pot with lid and cook for 7 minutes.
3. Quick release pressure then open the lid carefully.

4. Add butter and cheese, and stir until melted.
5. Season with pepper and salt. Serve and enjoy.

Nutrition information per serving:
Calories: 546; Carbohydrates: 21.9g; Protein: 18.6g; Fat: 43.1g; Sugar: 0.8g; Sodium: 678mg

Creamy Potato Mash

(Servings: 6|Cooking Time: 8 minutes)

Ingredients:
- 3 lbs. potatoes, clean and diced
- 4 tbsp. half and half
- 2 tbsp. butter
- 1 cup chicken stock
- ¼ tsp. pepper
- 3/4 tsp. salt

Directions for Cooking:
1. Place steamer rack in the instant pot then pour in chicken stock.
2. Add potatoes and seal pot with lid. Cook on manual high pressure for 8 minutes.
3. Quick release pressure then open the lid carefully.
4. Transfer potatoes in large bowl and mash with masher.
5. Add half and half, butter, pepper and salt. Stir to combine.
6. Serve and enjoy.

Nutrition information per serving:
Calories: 205; Carbohydrates: 36.2g; Protein: 4.3g; Fat: 5.3g; Sugar: 2.8g; Sodium: 463mg

Roasted Potatoes

(Servings: 4|Cooking Time: 12 minutes)

Ingredients:
- 1 ½ lbs. russet potatoes, cut into wedges
- 1 cup chicken stock
- ½ tsp. onion powder
- 4 tbsp. olive oil
- ¼ tsp. paprika
- 1 tsp. garlic powder
- ¼ tsp. pepper
- 1 tsp. sea salt

Directions for Cooking:
1. Add oil into instant pot and select Sauté.
2. Add potatoes and sauté for 5-6 minutes.
3. Add remaining ingredients to the pot and stir well.
4. Seal pot with lid and cook on manual high pressure for 6 minutes.
5. Quick release pressure then open the lid carefully.
6. Stir well and serve.

Nutrition information per serving:
Calories: 244; Carbohydrates: 27.8g; Protein: 3.2g; Fat: 14.3g; Sugar: 2.4g; Sodium: 670mg

Brussels sprouts with Nut

(Servings: 4|Cooking Time: 3 minutes)

Ingredients:
- 1 lb. Brussels sprouts
- 4 tbsp. pine nuts
- 1 cup water
- ½ tbsp. olive oil
- Pepper
- Salt

Directions for Cooking:
1. Pour water into instant pot.
2. Add Brussels sprouts into steamer basket and place basket in the pot.

3. Seal pot with lid and cook on manual high pressure for 3 minutes.
4. Release pressure using quick release method. Open lid carefully.

5. Season with pepper and salt. Drizzle with olive oil, sprinkle with pine nuts and serve.

Nutrition information per serving:
Calories: 122; Carbohydrates: 11.5g; Protein: 5.1g; Fat: 8g; Sugar: 2.8g; Sodium: 69mg

Cinnamon Banana Buckwheat Porridge

(Servings: 2|Cooking Time: 5 minutes)

Ingredients:
- ½ cup buckwheat groats, rinse
- 2 tbsp. raisins
- ½ banana, sliced
- 1 ½ cups almond milk
- ¼ tsp. vanilla
- ½ tsp. cinnamon

Directions for Cooking:

1. Add all ingredients into instant pot and stir well to combine.
2. Seal pot with lid and cook on manual high pressure for 5 minutes.
3. Allow pressure to release naturally, then open lid.
4. Stir and serve.

Nutrition information per serving:
Calories: 571; Carbohydrates: 45.6g; Protein: 8.5g; Fat: 44g; Sugar: 15.8g; Sodium: 32mg

Creamy Butter Polenta

(Servings: 3|Cooking Time: 5 minutes)

Ingredients:
- ½ cup dry polenta, gluten-free
- 1 cup almond milk
- ½ tbsp. butter
- 1 cup water
- ¼ tsp. salt

Directions for Cooking:
1. Add almond milk, water and salt into instant pot. Stir well. Set instant pot on Sauté mode.
2. When almond milk mixture begins to boil, add polenta slowly and stir well to combine.

3. Seal pot with lid and cook on manual high pressure for 5 minutes.
4. Allow pressure to release naturally. Open lid carefully.
5. Set pot on Sauté mode and cook until all liquid absorbed.
6. Stir and serve.

Nutrition information per serving:
Calories: 293; Carbohydrates: 24.7g; Protein: 3.8g; Fat: 21.2g; Sugar: 2.9g; Sodium: 223mg

Sweet Cranberry Apple Oatmeal

(Servings: 6|Cooking Time: 40 minutes)

Ingredients:
- 2 cups steel cut oats
- 1 tsp. vanilla
- 1 tsp. fresh lemon juice
- 2 tbsp. coconut oil

- 1 ¼ cup cranberries
- 4 medium apples, diced
- 3 cups water
- 4 tbsp. maple syrup

- ½ tsp. nutmeg
- 1 tsp. cinnamon
- 2 cups almond milk
- ½ tsp. salt

Directions for Cooking:
1. Grease instant pot with coconut oil.
2. Add all ingredients into instant pot except vanilla, maple syrup and salt. Stir well and soak overnight.
3. Add maple syrup and salt. Stir well.
4. Seal pot with lid and select Porridge mode.
5. Quick release pressure then open the lid carefully.
6. Stir in vanilla and serve.

Nutrition information per serving:
Calories: 455; Carbohydrates: 55g; Protein: 5.9g; Fat: 25.8g; Sugar: 27.3g; Sodium: 214mg

Lemon Parsley Quinoa

(Servings: 4|Cooking Time: 1 minute)

Ingredients:
- 2 cups quinoa, rinse
- 1 fresh lemon juice
- 3 cups water
- 2 tbsp. fresh parsley, chopped
- ¼ tsp. salt

Directions for Cooking:
1. Add all ingredients except lemon juice and parsley into instant pot. Stir well.
2. Seal pot with lid and cook on manual high pressure for 1 minute.
3. Allow pressure to release naturally. Open lid carefully.
4. Fluff quinoa with a fork. Add lemon juice and parsley. Stir well.
5. Serve warm and enjoy.

Nutrition information per serving:
Calories: 317; Carbohydrates: 54.9g; Protein: 12.2g; Fat: 5.3g; Sugar: 0.3g; Sodium: 161mg

Coconut Cinnamon Oatmeal

(Servings: 6|Cooking Time: 4 minutes)

Ingredients:
- 2 cups steel cut oats
- ¼ tsp. vanilla
- 4 cups unsweetened coconut milk
- 2 tbsp. coconut sugar
- ½ tsp. ground cinnamon
- ¼ salt

Directions for Cooking:
1. Add all ingredients into instant pot and stir well.
2. Seal pot with lid and cook on manual high pressure for 4 minutes.
3. Allow pressure to release naturally. Open lid carefully.
4. Stir well and serve.

Nutrition information per serving:
Calories: 504; Carbohydrates: 33.8g; Protein: 7.6g; Fat: 39.9g; Sugar: 5.6g; Sodium: 47mg

Creamy Garlic Potato Mash

(Servings: 4|Cooking Time: 4 minutes)

Ingredients:

- 4 russet potatoes, peeled and diced
- 5 garlic cloves, chopped
- 1 cup vegetable stock
- 4 tbsp. parsley, chopped
- ½ cup coconut milk
- Pepper
- Salt

Directions for Cooking:

1. Add garlic, potatoes and stock into instant pot.
2. Seal pot with lid and cook on manual high pressure for 4 minutes.
3. Quick release pressure then open the lid carefully.
4. Transfer potatoes into a large bowl and add coconut milk.
5. Mash potatoes using potato masher until smooth.
6. Add parsley and salt. Mix well.
7. Serve and enjoy.

Nutrition information per serving:

Calories: 226; Carbohydrates: 37.1g; Protein: 4.6g; Fat: 7.9g; Sugar: 4g; Sodium: 239mg

Coconut Almond Breakfast Risotto

(Servings: 4|Cooking Time: 5 minutes)

Ingredients:

- 1 cup Arborio rice
- 1 tsp. vanilla
- 1/3 cup coconut sugar
- 1 cup coconut milk
- 2 tbsp. almonds, sliced and toasted
- 2 tbsp. coconut flakes, sliced and toasted
- 2 cups almond milk

Directions for Cooking:

1. Add coconut milk and almond milk in instant pot and set on saute mode.
2. When milk mixture begins to boil then add rice and stir well.
3. Seal pot with lid and cook on manual high pressure for 5 minutes.
4. Allow pressure to release naturally, then open lid.
5. Add remaining ingredients and stir well to combine.
6. Serve and enjoy.

Nutrition information per serving:

Calories: 366; Carbohydrates: 44.8g; Protein: 5.8g; Fat: 18.6g; Sugar: 2.4g; Sodium: 106mg

Sweet Almond Breakfast Quinoa

(Servings: 6|Cooking Time: 1 minute)

Ingredients:

- 1 ½ cups quinoa, uncooked and rinsed
- ½ tsp. vanilla
- ¼ tsp. ground cinnamon
- 2 tbsp. sliced almonds
- 2 tbsp. maple syrup
- 2 ¼ cups water

Directions for Cooking:

1. Add water, quinoa, vanilla, maple syrup, cinnamon and salt in instant pot.
1. Seal pot with lid and cook on manual high pressure for 1 minute.
2. Quick release pressure then open the lid carefully.
3. Stir well. Top with sliced almonds and serve.

Nutrition information per serving:

Calories: 187; Carbohydrates: 32.3g; Protein: 6.4g; Fat: 3.6g; Sugar: 4.1g; Sodium: 6mg

Apple Blueberry Oatmeal

(Servings: 3|Cooking Time: 20 minutes)

Ingredients:

- 2 medium apples, peeled and diced
- ½ cup blueberries
- 1 ½ cups water
- ½ cups plain yogurt
- 2 tbsp. maple syrup
- ¼ tsp. ground nutmeg
- ¼ tsp. ground cinnamon
- 2 tbsp. butter
- 1 tsp. vanilla
- 1 cup almond milk
- 1 cup quick oats
- ¼ tsp. salt

Directions for Cooking:

1. Spray instant pot from inside with cooking spray.
2. Add blueberries, apples, water, yogurt, oats, nutmeg and cinnamon into instant pot. Stir well and soak overnight.
3. Add salt and maple syrup. Cook on Porridge mode for 20 minutes.
4. Quick release pressure then open the lid.
5. Add almond milk and vanilla. Stir well.
6. Serve and enjoy.

Nutrition information per serving:
Calories: 516; Carbohydrates: 59.2g; Protein: 8.4g; Fat: 29.5g; Sugar: 31.9g; Sodium: 297mg

Healthy Carrot Raisins

(Servings: 4|Cooking Time: 3 minutes)

Ingredients:

- 1 lb. carrots, peeled and sliced
- 3 tbsp. raisins
- 1 tbsp. maple syrup
- 1 tbsp. butter
- 1 cup water
- ½ tsp. pepper

Directions for Cooking:

1. Add water, carrots and raisins into instant pot.
2. Seal pot with lid and cook on manual high pressure for 3 minutes.
3. Quick release pressure then open the lid carefully.
4. Drain carrot well and transfer into a bowl.
5. Add butter and maple syrup, and toss well until butter is melted.
6. Season with black pepper.
7. Serve and enjoy.

Nutrition information per serving:
Calories: 106; Carbohydrates: 20.1g; Protein: 1.2g; Fat: 2.9g; Sugar: 12.6g; Sodium: 102mg

Almond Pecan Banana Oatmeal

(Servings: 4|Cooking Time: 10 minutes)

Ingredients:

- 2 ripe bananas, mashed
- 2 cups quick oats
- 1 tsp. vanilla
- 3 1/3 cups water
- 1 tsp. cinnamon
- ¼ tsp. nutmeg
- ¼ cup pecans, chopped
- 4 tbsp. maple syrup
- ¼ cup sliced almonds
- Pinch of salt

Directions for Cooking:

1. Add mashed bananas, oats, cinnamon, nutmeg, vanilla, water and salt into instant pot. Stir well.
2. Seal pot with lid and select Porridge mode. Set timer for 10 minutes.
3. Allow pressure to release naturally, then open lid.
4. Add chopped pecans, almonds and maple syrup. Stir well.
5. Serve and enjoy.

Nutrition information per serving:
Calories: 509; Carbohydrates: 60.5g; Protein: 10.3g; Fat: 27.9g; Sugar: 21g; Sodium: 50mg

Chapter 3 Instant Pot Beans & Grains

Bacon Pinto Beans

(Servings: 6|Cooking Time: 70 minutes)

Ingredients:

- 16 oz. dry pinto beans, rinsed
- ¼ cup cilantro, chopped
- 4 cups water
- 2 ½ tbsp. taco seasoning
- 2 garlic cloves, minced
- 1 medium onion, diced
- 1 jalapeno pepper
- 4 bacon slices, chopped
- Salt

Directions for Cooking:

1. Add all ingredients except cilantro into instant pot and stir well.
2. Seal pot with lid and cook on manual high pressure for 70 minutes.
3. Allow pressure to release naturally for 20 minutes, then release using quick release method.
4. Discard jalapeno pepper.
5. Add cilantro and stir well. Season beans with pepper and salt.
6. Serve and enjoy.

Nutrition information per serving:
Calories: 335; Carbohydrates: 52.2g; Protein: 21.2g; Fat: 6.3g; Sugar: 3.1g; Sodium: 598mg

Hearty Mustard Baked Beans

(Servings: 8|Cooking Time: 8 minutes)

Ingredients:

- 15 oz. can northern beans, rinsed and drained
- 15 oz. can pinto beans, rinsed and drained
- 15 oz. can kidney beans, rinsed and drained
- 1 tsp. chili powder
- 1 tbsp. yellow mustard
- 1/3 cup brown sugar
- ¾ cup water
- ½ cup ketchup
- 1 onion, diced

Directions for Cooking:

1. Add all ingredients into instant pot and stir well.
2. Seal pot with lid and cook on manual high pressure for 8 minutes.
3. Allow pressure to release naturally for 15 minutes, then release using quick release method.
4. Stir well and serve.

Nutrition information per serving:

Calories: 183; Carbohydrates: 36.1g; Protein: 9.1g; Fat: 0.8g; Sugar: 11.3g; Sodium: 644mg

Sweet & Salty Baked Beans

(Servings: 6|Cooking Time: 60 minutes)

Ingredients:

- 8 oz. dried navy beans, soaked in water overnight and drained
- ¼ tsp. white pepper
- 1 tsp. dried mustard
- 2 tsp. Worcestershire sauce
- 1 tbsp. tomato paste
- ¼ cup brown sugar
- ¼ cup ketchup
- ¼ cup molasses
- 1 ½ cups water
- 3 garlic cloves, minced
- 1 onion, sliced
- 4 bacon slices, cooked and chopped
- 1 tbsp. olive oil
- 1 ½ tsp. kosher salt

Directions for Cooking:

1. Add olive oil into instant pot and set on Sauté mode.
2. Add onion and garlic. Sauté until onion is softened.
3. Add remaining ingredients and stir well.
4. Seal pot with lid and cook on manual high pressure for 50 minutes.
5. Allow pressure to release naturally for 10 minutes, then release using quick release method.
6. Set pot on Sauté mode and cook until sauce thickens.
7. Stir and serve.

Nutrition information per serving:

Calories: 304; Carbohydrates: 45.1g; Protein: 13.9g; Fat: 8.4g; Sugar: 18.7g; Sodium: 1018mg

Mexican Black Beans

(Servings: 12|Cooking Time: 25 minutes)

Ingredients:

- 6 cups water
- 1 tbsp. cumin
- 1 jalapeno pepper, diced
- 4 garlic cloves, minced
- 1 onion, diced
- 1 lb. black beans, dried and rinsed
- 1 tsp. salt

Directions for Cooking:

1. Add all ingredients into instant pot and stir well to combine.
2. Seal pot with lid and cook on manual high pressure for 25 minutes.
3. Allow pressure to release naturally for 20 minutes, then release using quick release method.
4. Drain excess liquid and serve.

Nutrition information per serving:

Calories: 136; Carbohydrates: 25.1g; Protein: 8.4g; Fat: 0.7g; Sugar: 1.3g; Sodium: 201mg

Flavorful Italian Black Beans

(Servings: 12|Cooking Time: 45 minutes)

Ingredients:

- 1 lb. dried black beans, rinsed and drained
- ¼ cup coconut milk
- 4 cups water
- 2 vegetable bouillons
- ¼ tsp. cayenne pepper
- ¼ tsp. allspice
- 1 tsp. Italian seasoning
- 1 tsp. thyme
- ¼ bell pepper, diced
- 2 garlic cloves, minced
- 1 onion, chopped
- 1 tbsp. olive oil
- ½ tsp. salt

Directions for Cooking:

1. Add olive oil into instant pot and set on Sauté mode.
2. Add garlic, onion, vegetable bouillon, cayenne pepper, allspice, Italian seasoning, thyme and bell pepper. Sauté until onion is softened.
3. Add black beans, coconut milk, and water. Stir well.
4. Seal pot with lid and cook on manual high pressure for 45 minutes.
5. Allow pressure to release naturally for 20 minutes, then release using quick release method.
6. Stir well and serve.

Nutrition information per serving:

Calories: 157; Carbohydrates: 25.2g; Protein: 8.4g; Fat: 3.1g; Sugar: 1.5g; Sodium: 103mg

Flavorful White Beans

(Servings: 6|Cooking Time: 30 minutes)

Ingredients:

- 1 lb. great northern beans, rinsed and drained
- 6 cup vegetable broth
- 1 bay leaf
- 2 tsp. garlic powder
- 1 tbsp. onion powder
- 1 tsp. salt

Directions for Cooking:

1. Add all ingredients to the instant pot and stir well.
2. Seal pot with lid and select Bean/Chili mode.
3. Allow pressure to release naturally for 20 minutes, then release using quick release method.
4. Stir well and serve over rice.

Nutrition information per serving:
Calories: 302; Carbohydrates: 49.7g; Protein: 21.7g; Fat: 2.3g; Sugar: 3.1g; Sodium: 1162mg

Sweet Maple Baked Beans

(Servings: 12|Cooking Time: 40 minutes)

Ingredients:

- 1 lb. dried navy beans, soaked overnight, rinsed, and drained
- 1 cup vegetable stock
- 1 tsp. apple cider vinegar
- 1/3 cup maple syrup
- 1 onion, minced
- 2 tsp. seasoned salt
- 1 tsp. dried mustard
- 8 oz. tomato sauce
- 2 cups tomato juice
- 2 cups apple juice

Directions for Cooking:

1. Add all ingredients into instant pot and stir well.
2. Seal pot with lid and cook on manual high pressure for 40 minutes.
3. Allow pressure to release naturally, then open lid.
4. Stir well and serve.

Nutrition information per serving:
Calories: 186; Carbohydrates: 37.4g; Protein: 9.2g; Fat: 1g; Sugar: 13.5g; Sodium: 526mg

Tasty Pinto Beans

(Servings: 8|Cooking Time: 25 minutes)

Ingredients:

- 1 lb. dried pinto beans, soaked overnight, rinsed and drained
- 2 liters water
- 2 tbsp. chili powder
- 2 tbsp. onion powder
- 3 tbsp. garlic powder
- 1 tsp. oregano
- 1 tsp. salt

Directions for Cooking:

1. Add all ingredients into instant pot and stir well.
2. Seal pot with lid and cook on manual high pressure for 25 minutes.
3. Allow pressure to release naturally, then open lid.
4. Stir well and serve.

Nutrition information per serving:
Calories: 220; Carbohydrates: 40.3g; Protein: 13.1g; Fat: 1.1g; Sugar: 2.7g; Sodium: 326mg

Flavors Chipotle Black Beans

(Servings: 4|Cooking Time: 35 minutes)

Ingredients:

- 1 cup dried black beans
- 1 tsp. chipotle powder
- 1 tsp. paprika
- 2 tsp. cumin powder
- 3 cups vegetable broth
- 2 garlic cloves, minced
- ½ onion, diced

Directions for Cooking:

1. Set instant pot on Sauté mode.
2. Add onion and garlic to the pot and sauté until onion is softened.
3. Add broth, all spices, and beans to the pot and stir well.
4. Seal pot with lid and select Bean/Chili mode and set timer for 35 minutes.
5. Allow pressure to release naturally for 15 minutes, then release using quick release method.
6. Stir well and serve.

Nutrition information per serving:
Calories: 207; Carbohydrates: 33.5g; Protein: 14.6g; Fat: 2g; Sugar: 2.2g; Sodium: 578mg

Beans with Tomatillos

(Servings: 6|Cooking Time: 40 minutes)

Ingredients:

- 1 ½ cups dried great northern beans, soaked overnight, rinsed and drained
- 2 tsp. dried oregano
- 1 ½ cups water
- 1 ½ tsp. ground cumin
- ½ jalapeno pepper, chopped
- 1 cup onion, chopped
- 1 cup poblano, chopped
- 2 cups tomatillos, chopped
- Pepper
- Salt

Directions for Cooking:

1. Add ground cumin, jalapeno pepper, onion, poblano and tomatillos into the food processor. Process until vegetables are well diced.
2. Pour blended mixture into instant pot and set on Sauté mode. Cook for 4 minutes.
3. Add remaining ingredients and stir well to combine.
4. Seal pot with lid and cook on manual high pressure for 35 minutes.
5. Allow pressure to release naturally, then open lid.
6. Stir well and serve.

Nutrition information per serving:
Calories: 226; Carbohydrates: 44.2g; Protein: 13.5g; Fat: 1.2g; Sugar: 1.9g; Sodium: 40mg

Delicious Beans with Bacon

(Servings: 8|Cooking Time: 38 minutes)

Ingredients:

- 1 lb. dried pinto beans
- 2 tbsp. hot sauce
- ½ tsp. thyme
- 1 tsp. garlic powder
- 7 cups vegetable broth
- 2 lbs. bacon, cooked and chopped
- ½ tsp. black pepper
- 1 tsp. sea salt

Directions for Cooking:

1. Add all ingredients into instant pot and stir well to combine.
2. Seal pot with lid and cook on manual high pressure for 38 minutes.

3. Allow pressure to release naturally for 20 minutes, then release using quick release method.
4. Stir well and serve over rice.

Nutrition information per serving:
Calories: 846; Carbohydrates: 38.3g; Protein: 58.5g; Fat: 49.3g; Sugar: 2g; Sodium: 3623mg

Wheat Berry Pilaf

(Servings: 6|Cooking Time: 30 minutes)

Ingredients:
- 3 cups water
- 1 ½ cups wheat berries, rinsed and drained
- 2 garlic cloves, minced
- 1 ½ tsp. turmeric
- ½ tsp. ground coriander
- 1 ½ tsp. ground cumin
- ½ cup onion, minced
- 1 tbsp. olive oil
- Salt

Directions for Cooking:
1. Add oil into instant pot and set on Sauté mode.
2. Add onion and garlic, and sauté until onion softened.
3. Stir in turmeric, coriander and cumin, and sauté for 1-2 minutes.
4. Add wheat berries and sauté for 1-2 minutes.
5. Add water and stir well.
6. Seal pot with lid and cook on manual high pressure for 30 minutes.
7. Allow pressure to release naturally, then open lid.
8. Stir and serve.

Nutrition information per serving:
Calories: 83; Carbohydrates: 13.3g; Protein: 2.3g; Fat: 2.9g; Sugar: 0.5g; Sodium: 37mg

Healthy Vegetable Quinoa

(Servings: 4|Cooking Time: 20 minutes)

Ingredients:
- 1 ½ cup quinoa, rinsed and drained
- ¼ cup cilantro, chopped
- 1 ½ cups water
- ¼ cup coconut milk
- 1 tsp. garam masala
- ½ tsp. chili powder
- ½ tsp. black pepper
- ¼ tsp. turmeric
- 1 carrot, chopped
- 1 cup green beans, chopped
- 1 potato, cubed
- 1 tomato, chopped
- 1 onion, chopped
- 2 tsp. ginger paste
- 1 garlic clove, minced
- 1 bay leaf
- 2-star anise
- 3 cloves
- 1 tsp. cumin seeds
- 2 tbsp. olive oil
- Salt

Directions for Cooking:
1. Add oil into instant pot and set on Sauté mode.
2. Add cumin seeds, cloves and star anise. Sauté for 30 seconds.
3. Add ginger paste, garlic, tomatoes, onions and all dry spices. Stir well.
4. Add all vegetables, milk and salt. Stir for 30 seconds.
5. Add quinoa and water. Stir well.
6. Seal pot with lid and cook on manual high pressure for 4 minutes.

7. Allow pressure to release naturally for 10 minutes, then release using quick release method.
8. Stir well and serve.

Nutrition information per serving:
Calories: 403; Carbohydrates: 58.3g; Protein: 11.6g; Fat: 14.8g; Sugar: 3.9g; Sodium: 71mg

Quinoa with Sausage

(Servings: 4|Cooking Time: 6 minutes)

Ingredients:
- 2 cups quinoa, rinsed and drained
- 5 oz. mushrooms, halved
- 2 cups broccoli, chopped
- 2 bell peppers, chopped
- 2 cups vegetable stock
- ½ tsp. turmeric
- 1 tsp. paprika
- 2 tbsp. olive oil
- 1 onion, diced
- 1 lb. sausage meat

Directions for Cooking:
1. Add oil into instant pot and set on Sauté mode.
2. Add onion and sausage meat. Sauté until sausage is lightly browned and cooked.
3. Add turmeric and paprika. Stir well.
4. Add remaining ingredients and stir well.
5. Seal pot with lid and cook on manual high pressure for 1 minute.
6. Allow pressure to release naturally for 10 minutes, then release using quick release method.
7. Fluff quinoa with fork and serve.

Nutrition information per serving:
Calories: 816; Carbohydrates: 66.8g; Protein: 37.4g; Fat: 45.3g; Sugar: 6.1g; Sodium: 1054mg

Chicken Salsa Brown Rice

(Servings: 4|Cooking Time: 25 minutes)

Ingredients:
- 1 cup chicken stock
- 1 cup salsa
- ½ tsp. sea salt
- ½ tsp. cumin
- 1 tsp. chili powder
- 1 cup brown rice
- 1 ½ cups can black beans, rinsed and drained
- 2 chicken breasts, cut into chunks
- 2 garlic cloves, minced
- 1 small onion, diced
- 1 tbsp. coconut oil

Directions for Cooking:
1. Add oil into instant pot and set on Sauté mode.
2. Add onion and sauté until softened. Add garlic and cook for a minute. Stir constantly.
3. Add seasonings, beans, brown rice and chicken. Stir well.
4. Pour in stock and salsa. stir well.
5. Seal pot with lid and cook on manual high pressure for 18 minutes.
6. Allow pressure to release naturally, then open lid.
7. Stir well and serve.

Nutrition information per serving:
Calories: 462; Carbohydrates: 60.3g; Protein: 31.5g; Fat: 10.9g; Sugar: 3.7g; Sodium: 1248mg

Indian Bulgur Pilaf

(Servings: 4|Cooking Time: 10 minutes)

Ingredients:

- 1 cup bulgur
- 1 tbsp. fresh lemon juice
- 1 tbsp. olive oil
- 2 cups water
- 2 cups mix vegetables
- 3 garlic cloves, chopped
- 1 green chili pepper, chopped
- 2 tomato, chopped
- 1 onion, chopped
- 1 tsp. salt
- 10 black peppercorns
- 1 tsp. coriander powder
- ½ tsp. chili powder
- ½ tsp. turmeric
- 1 tsp. cumin seeds

Directions for Cooking:

1. Add oil into instant pot and set on Sauté mode.
2. Add cumin seeds, green chilies and black peppercorns to the pot, and sauté for 30 seconds.
3. Add onion and sauté for 2-3 minutes or until lightly browned.
4. Add spices, tomato and salt. Sauté for 2 minutes.
5. Add mix vegetables and stir well.
6. Add bulgur and water. Stir.
7. Seal pot with lid and cook on manual high pressure for 5 minutes.
8. Allow pressure to release naturally for 10 minutes, then release using quick release method.
9. Stir and serve.

Nutrition information per serving:
Calories: 211; Carbohydrates: 41.2g; Protein: 5.3g; Fat: 4.3g; Sugar: 4.9g; Sodium: 625mg

Indian Kidney Beans

(Servings: 6|Cooking Time: 62 minutes)

Ingredients:

- 2 cups red kidney beans, soaked overnight
- 1 onion, chopped
- 2 tbsp. vegetable oil
- 1 tsp. coriander powder
- 1 tsp. turmeric powder
- ¼ tsp. chili powder
- 5 tomatoes puree
- 5 garlic cloves, minced
- 1 tbsp. ginger, grated
- 1 tsp. cumin seeds
- 1 tsp. salt

Directions for Cooking:

1. Add beans into instant pot. Pour enough water into the pot to cover beans.
2. Seal pot with lid and select manual high pressure for 15 minutes.
3. Quick release pressure then open the lid carefully.
4. Remove beans from the instant pot and set aside.
5. Add garlic, ginger and onion into the blender, and blend until smooth paste.
6. Add 1 tbsp. oil into instant pot and select Sauté.
7. Add cumin seeds and let them crackle.
8. Add garlic mixture and sauté for 10 minutes.
9. Add tomato puree and stir well. Cook for 5 minutes.
10. Add remaining oil and all spices. Stir for 2 minutes.
11. Now add cooked beans and water. Stir well.

12. Seal pot again. Select Bean/Chili mode and set the timer for 30 minutes.
13. Serve and enjoy.

Nutrition information per serving:
Calories: 274; Carbohydrates: 43.2g; Protein: 14.7g; Fat: 5.4g; Sugar: 3.2g; Sodium: 403mg

Chili Lime Black Beans

(Servings: 6|Cooking Time: 40 minutes)

Ingredients:
- 2 cups dried black beans, rinsed and drained
- 1 tsp. paprika
- 1 tbsp. red chili powder
- 4 garlic cloves, minced
- 2 tsp. vegetable oil
- 1 onion, chopped
- 3 cups water
- 1 lime juice
- 2 tsp. salt

Directions for Cooking:
1. Add oil into instant pot and select Sauté mode.
2. Add garlic and onion. Sauté for a minute.
3. Add beans, paprika, chili powder, water and salt. Stir well.
4. Seal pot with lid and select manual. Set timer for 40 minutes.
5. Allow pressure to release naturally, then open lid.
6. Add lime juice and stir well.
7. Serve and enjoy.

Nutrition information per serving:
Calories: 251; Carbohydrates: 44.2g; Protein: 14.5g; Fat: 2.7g; Sugar: 2.4g; Sodium: 796mg

Black Garbanzo Beans

(Servings: 6|Cooking Time: 30 minutes)

Ingredients:
- 1 cup dried black garbanzo beans
- ½ tsp. cayenne pepper
- 1 tsp. garam masala
- ½ tsp. turmeric
- 2 tsp. ginger, minced
- ½ tsp. cumin seeds
- 2 bay leaves
- 4 cups water
- 1 tsp. salt
- 1 lemon juice
- 1 tbsp. olive oil

Directions for Cooking:
1. Add chickpeas, bay leaves, water and salt into instant pot. Stir well.
2. Seal pot with lid and select manual high pressure for 30 minutes.
3. Allow pressure to release naturally, then open lid.
4. Drain water and place cooked chickpeas in a bowl.
5. Add oil into instant pot and select Sauté.
6. Add cumin seeds in hot oil and let them crackle.
7. Add ginger and sauté for 30 seconds.
8. Add cooked chickpeas and remaining ingredients and stir well.
9. Serve and enjoy.

Nutrition information per serving:
Calories: 66; Carbohydrates: 7.9g; Protein: 2.2g; Fat: 2.9g; Sugar: 0.5g; Sodium: 542mg

White Bean Curry

(Servings: 6|Cooking Time: 90 minutes)

Ingredients:

- 2 cups dry white beans
- 1 tbsp. curry powder
- 2 garlic cloves, minced
- ½ onion, diced
- 1 sweet potato, peeled and sliced
- 10 cups water
- 1 tsp. coriander powder
- 1 tsp. red pepper flakes
- 2 cups brown rice
- 1 tbsp. salt

Directions for Cooking:

1. Add all ingredients into instant pot and stir well.
2. Seal pot with lid. Select Stew mode and set timer for 1 hour 30 minutes.
3. Allow pressure to release naturally, then open lid.
4. Stir well and serve.

Nutrition information per serving:

Calories: 480; Carbohydrates: 94.7g; Protein: 21.2g; Fat: 2.5g; Sugar: 3.1g; Sodium: 1196mg

Perfect Salsa Pinto Beans

(Servings: 6|Cooking Time: 42 minutes)

Ingredients:

- 20 oz. package ham pinto beans, rinsed
- ¼ cup cilantro, chopped
- ½ cup salsa verde
- 1 packet taco seasoning
- 1 garlic clove, chopped
- 1 jalapeno, diced
- 1 onion, diced
- 5 cups chicken broth
- Pepper
- Salt

Directions for Cooking:

1. Add all ingredients into instant pot and stir well.
2. Seal pot with lid and cook on manual high pressure for 42 minutes.
3. Allow pressure to release naturally, then open lid.
4. Stir and serve.

Nutrition information per serving:

Calories: 367; Carbohydrates: 57.2g; Protein: 23.3g; Fat: 2.6g; Sugar: 4.4g; Sodium: 948mg

Easy Refried Beans

(Servings: 4|Cooking Time: 30 minutes)

Ingredients:

- 1 lb. dried pinto beans
- 2 bacon slices, chopped
- 1 tbsp. salt
- Water

Directions for Cooking:

1. Add all ingredients into instant pot and stir well.
2. Seal pot with lid and cook on manual high pressure for 30 minutes.
3. Quick release pressure then open the lid.
4. Remove bacon pieces from beans and mash until smooth.
5. Serve and enjoy.

Nutrition information per serving:

Calories: 445; Carbohydrates: 71.1g; Protein: 27.8g; Fat: 5.4g; Sugar: 2.4g; Sodium: 1197mg

Garlic Beans

(Servings: 4|Cooking Time: 20 minutes)

Ingredients:

- 1 lb. pinto beans, soaked overnight
- ½ tsp. dried sage
- 4 cups vegetable stock
- ½ tsp. dried oregano
- ½ tsp. garlic powder
- 14 oz. tomatoes, chopped
- 2 tbsp. olive oil
- 1 onion, chopped
- Pepper
- Salt

Directions for Cooking:

1. Add 1 tbsp. of oil in instant pot and select Sauté mode.
2. Add onion and sauté for 5 minutes.
3. Add soaked pinto beans, stock and remaining oil in instant pot. Stir well.
4. Seal pot with a lid then select Bean/Chili mode.
5. Release the pressure using quick release method, then open lid carefully.
6. Add tomatoes, sage, oregano, garlic powder, pepper and salt. Stir well to combine.
7. Select Sauté mode and set timer for 15 minutes.
8. Serve and enjoy.

Nutrition information per serving:
Calories: 494; Carbohydrates: 79.8g; Protein: 25.6g; Fat: 10.7g; Sugar: 8.3g; Sodium: 778mg

Flavors Refried Beans

(Servings: 4|Cooking Time: 30 minutes)

Ingredients:

- 1 cup dried pinto beans, rinsed
- ½ tsp. cumin, ground
- 1 tsp. oregano
- 2 cups water
- ½ onion, chopped
- 2 cups vegetable stock
- ½ jalapeno, minced
- 2 garlic cloves, minced
- ½ tbsp. olive oil
- ¼ tsp. pepper
- ½ tsp. salt

Directions for Cooking:

1. Add olive oil to instant pot and select Sauté mode.
2. Add onion, jalapeno and garlic. Cook until softened.
3. Add all remaining ingredients and stir well.
4. Seal pot with lid and select manual for 30 minutes.
5. Allow pressure to release naturally, then open lid.
6. Transfer bean mixture into the bowl and mash until smooth.
7. Season with pepper and salt.
8. Serve and enjoy.

Nutrition information per serving:
Calories: 196; Carbohydrates: 33g; Protein: 10.7g; Fat: 3g; Sugar: 2.2g; Sodium: 481mg

Smoked Baked Beans

(Servings: 4|Cooking Time: 30 minutes)

Ingredients:

- 1 lb. dry kidney beans, soaked overnight and drained
- ¼ cup molasses
- 1 onion, chopped

- 1/8 tsp. liquid smoke
- 4 tsp. dry mustard powder
- ¼ cup brown rice
- Salt

Directions for Cooking:

1. Add all ingredients into instant pot and stir well.

2. Seal pot with lid and cook on the manual setting for 30 minutes.
3. Quick release pressure then open the lid.
4. Stir well and serve.

Nutrition information per serving:

Calories: 511; Carbohydrates: 97.6g; Protein: 27.6g; Fat: 2.5g; Sugar: 15.2g; Sodium: 62mg

Simple Black Eyed Peas

(Servings: 10|Cooking Time: 30 minutes)

Ingredients:

- 1 lb. dried black-eyed peas
- 6 ½ cup chicken stock
- 5 oz. ham, diced

Directions for Cooking:

1. Add all ingredients into instant pot and stir well.
2. Seal pot with lid and select manual high pressure for 30 minutes.

3. Allow pressure to release naturally, then open lid.
4. Season with pepper and salt.
5. Serve and enjoy.

Nutrition information per serving:

Calories: 140; Carbohydrates: 29.2g; Protein: 13.8g; Fat: 1.6g; Sugar: 1.7g; Sodium: 700mg

Healthy Bean Chili

(Servings: 4|Cooking Time: 35 minutes)

Ingredients:

- 1 lb. dry cranberry beans
- 1 tsp. garlic, minced
- 1 tsp. chili powder
- 1 ½ tsp. ground cumin
- 2 tbsp. tomato paste
- ½ tsp. chipotle powder
- ½ tsp. liquid smoke
- 1 tsp. dried oregano
- 14.5 oz. can tomatoes, diced
- 5 cups water
- ¼ cup millet
- ½ cup bulgur

Directions for Cooking:

1. Add beans and 3 cups water into instant pot.
2. Seal pot with lid and cook on manual high pressure for 25 minutes.
3. Allow pressure to release naturally, then open lid.
4. Add remaining ingredients and stir well.
5. Seal pot with lid and cook on manual high pressure for 10 minutes.
6. Allow pressure to release naturally, then open lid.
7. Stir and serve.

Nutrition information per serving:

Calories: 523; Carbohydrates: 98.4g; Protein: 31.2g; Fat: 2.5g; Sugar: 4.6g; Sodium: 254mg

Beans with Yams & Lentils

(Servings: 8|Cooking Time: 30 minutes)

Ingredients:

- 1 cup navy beans, soaked
- 1 tbsp. rosemary
- 1 cup yams, diced
- 1 cup brown lentils
- 1 ½ cups brown rice
- 4 cups water
- 1 tbsp. garlic, minced
- ½ cup onion, chopped
- 1 tbsp. thyme

Directions for Cooking:

1. Spray instant pot with cooking spray.
2. Set instant pot on Sauté mode. Add garlic and onion into the pot. Sauté for 4 minutes.
3. Add remaining ingredients to pot and stir well.
4. Seal pot with lid and cook on manual high pressure for 23 minutes.
5. Allow pressure to release naturally, then open lid.
6. Stir and serve.

Nutrition information per serving:
Calories: 326; Carbohydrates: 63.3g; Protein: 14.9g; Fat: 2g; Sugar: 1.4g; Sodium: 10mg

Simple Brown Rice Pilaf

(Servings: 6|Cooking Time: 27 minutes)

Ingredients:

- 1 ½ cups brown rice, rinsed and drained
- ½ cup onion, diced
- 2 tbsp. butter
- 2 tbsp. parsley, chopped
- 1 3/4 cups chicken broth
- 2 garlic cloves, minced
- ½ tsp. salt

Directions for Cooking:

1. Add butter into instant pot and select Sauté mode.
2. Add onion and garlic. Sauté for 5 minutes.
3. Add rice and stir well.
4. Add broth and salt. Stir well.
5. Seal pot with lid and select manual. Set timer for 22 minutes.
6. Allow pressure to release naturally, then open lid.
7. Garnish with parsley and serve.

Nutrition information per serving:
Calories: 223; Carbohydrates: 37.8g; Protein: 5.2g; Fat: 5.5g; Sugar: 0.6g; Sodium: 447mg

Mushroom Rice Pilaf

(Servings: 8|Cooking Time: 24 minutes)

Ingredients:

- 2 cups brown rice
- 2 garlic cloves, minced
- 2 cups mushrooms, sliced
- 1 onion, diced
- 1 2/3 cup olive oil
- ¼ cup parsley, chopped
- 2 ½ tsp. better then bouillon vegetable base
- 2 ½ cups water
- Pepper
- Salt

Directions for Cooking:

1. Add olive oil into instant pot and select Sauté mode.

2. Add onion and mushrooms to the pot. Sauté for 4 minutes.
3. Add garlic and sauté for 30 seconds.
4. Add remaining ingredients and stir well.
5. Seal pot with lid and select manual high pressure for 20 minutes.
6. Allow pressure to release naturally, then open lid.
7. Stir well and serve.

Nutrition information per serving:
Calories: 554; Carbohydrates: 39.1g; Protein: 4.7g; Fat: 43.5g; Sugar: 0.9g; Sodium: 239mg

Brown Rice Peas Risotto

(Servings: 4|Cooking Time: 22 minutes)

Ingredients:

- 1 ½ cups brown rice
- 1 cup peas
- 2 ½ cups vegetable stock
- 3 garlic cloves, minced
- ½ cup onion, diced
- 1 tbsp. soy sauce
- 1 cup mushrooms, sliced
- 2 cup squash, cubed
- 2 tsp. olive oil
- Pepper
- Salt

Directions for Cooking:

1. Add olive oil into instant pot and select Sauté mode.
2. Add onion and garlic into the pot and sauté for a minute.
3. Add remaining ingredients into the pot and stir well.
4. Seal pot with lid and cook on manual high pressure for 22 minutes.
5. Allow pressure to release naturally, then open lid.
6. Stir and serve.

Nutrition information per serving:
Calories: 334; Carbohydrates: 64.9g; Protein: 9.1g; Fat: 5.1g; Sugar: 4.5g; Sodium: 457mg

Coconut Pineapple Quinoa

(Servings: 6|Cooking Time: 8 minutes)

Ingredients:

- 1 cup quinoa, rinsed and drained
- 2 cups pineapple, diced
- 8 oz. snap peas
- 1 can coconut milk
- 1 tsp. onion, minced
- ¼ cup honey
- ¼ cup coconut aminos
- ½ tsp. sea salt

Directions for Cooking:

1. Add all ingredients into instant pot and stir well.
2. Seal pot with lid and select manual high pressure for 8 minutes.
3. Allow pressure to release naturally, then open lid.
4. Stir and serve.

Nutrition information per serving:
Calories: 250; Carbohydrates: 43.7g; Protein: 7.5g; Fat: 5.8g; Sugar: 20.3g; Sodium: 165mg

Spanish Black beans Quinoa

(Servings: 4|Cooking Time: 10 minutes)

Ingredients:

- 1 lb. beef ground meat, cooked and seasoned with taco seasoning
- 1 large onion, diced
- 1 bell pepper, diced

- 1 cup quinoa, rinsed and drained
- ¼ cup juice from pickled jalapenos
- 1 ¼ cups vegetable broth
- 1 cup black beans, rinsed and drained

Directions for Cooking:

1. Add all ingredients into instant pot.
2. Seal pot with lid and select manual. Set timer for 10 minutes.

3. Quick release pressure then open the lid.
4. Serve and enjoy.

Nutrition information per serving:

Calories: 577; Carbohydrates: 63.6g; Protein: 51.8g; Fat: 12.4g; Sugar: 4.3g; Sodium: 342mg

Butter Almond Quinoa Pilaf

(Servings: 4|Cooking Time: 6 minutes)

Ingredients:

- 1 ½ cups quinoa, rinsed and drained
- 2 tbsp. fresh parsley, chopped
- ½ cup onion, chopped
- 1 tbsp. butter
- ½ cup sliced almonds
- ¼ cup water
- 14 oz. vegetable stock
- 1 celery stalk, chopped
- ½ tsp. salt

Directions for Cooking:

1. Add butter into instant pot and select Sauté mode.

2. Add onion and celery. Sauté for 5 minutes.
3. Add water, broth, quinoa and salt into the pot. Stir well.
4. Seal pot with lid and cook on manual high pressure for 1 minute.
5. Quick release pressure then open the lid.
6. Add parsley and almonds. Stir well.
7. Serve and enjoy.

Nutrition information per serving:

Calories: 342; Carbohydrates: 45.9g; Protein: 12.2g; Fat: 12.8g; Sugar: 1.9g; Sodium: 370mg

Creamy Cheese Polenta

(Servings: 6|Cooking Time: 8 minutes)

Ingredients:

- 1 cup cornmeal
- 4 ½ cups water
- 2 tbsp. butter
- 3 oz. cheddar cheese, shredded
- 1 tsp. sea salt

Directions for Cooking:

1. Pour 1 cup water into instant pot then insert trivet.
2. Add remaining ingredients except for cheese into the heat-safe bowl.

3. Place bowl on top of the trivet.
4. Seal pot with lid and cook on manual high pressure for 8 minutes.
5. Allow pressure to release naturally, then open lid.
6. Add cheese and stir until melted.
7. Serve and enjoy.

Nutrition information per serving:

Calories: 165; Carbohydrates: 15.8g; Protein: 5.2g; Fat: 9.3g; Sugar: 0.2g; Sodium: 440mg

Basil Cheese Polenta

(Servings: 6|Cooking Time: 20 minutes)

Ingredients:

- ¼ cup basil, chopped
- ¼ cup parsley, chopped
- ½ cup heavy cream
- 2 tbsp. butter
- 1 cup Romano cheese, grated
- 1 cup polenta
- 1 cup parmesan cheese, grated
- 4 cups vegetable stock
- ¼ tsp. black pepper
- 1 tsp. kosher salt

Directions for Cooking:

1. Add all ingredients except cheeses and herbs into instant pot and stir well.
2. Seal pot with lid and cook on manual high pressure for 20 minutes.
3. Allow pressure to release naturally, then open lid.
4. Add herbs and cheeses. Stir well to combine.
5. Serve and enjoy.

Nutrition information per serving:
Calories: 336; Carbohydrates: 22.1g; Protein: 15.6g; Fat: 20.5g; Sugar: 1.6g; Sodium: 1621mg

Polenta with Grape Tomatoes

(Servings: 4|Cooking Time: 17 minutes)

Ingredients:

- 1 cup polenta
- 4 cups water
- 1 tsp. salt
- 1 tbsp. butter
- For roasted tomatoes:
- 2 thyme sprigs
- 2 tsp. olive oil
- 2 cups grape tomatoes
- ½ tsp. salt

Directions for Cooking:

1. Add polenta, water, butter and salt into instant pot. Stir well.
a. Seal pot with lid and cook on Porridge mode for 7 minutes.
2. Allow pressure to release naturally, then open lid.
3. Toss together Grape tomatoes, olive oil, thyme and salt. Place on baking sheet and broil for 10 minutes.
4. Mix together polenta and tomatoes.
5. Serve warm and enjoy.

Nutrition information per serving:
Calories: 200; Carbohydrates: 33.9g; Protein: 3.7g; Fat: 5.7g; Sugar: 2.8g; Sodium: 906mg

Simple Pearl Barley

(Servings: 4|Cooking Time: 25 minutes)

Ingredients:

- 1 ½ cups pearl barley, rinsed and drained
- 3 cups vegetable stock
- 1 tsp. salt

Directions for Cooking:

1. Add all ingredients into instant pot and stir well.

2. Seal pot with lid and cook on manual high pressure for 25 minutes.
3. Allow pressure to release naturally, then open lid.

4. Stir and serve.

Nutrition information per serving:
Calories: 272; Carbohydrates: 59.8g; Protein: 7.4g; Fat: 2.4g; Sugar: 2.1g; Sodium: 1128mg

Lemon Dill Couscous
(Servings: 6|Cooking Time: 7 minutes)

Ingredients:
- 1 cup couscous
- 1 tbsp. olive oil
- 1 tsp. dried dill
- 2 cups vegetable stock
- 8 oz. snap peas, trimmed
- 1 fresh lemon juice
- ¼ tsp. pepper
- ½ tsp. salt

Directions for Cooking:
1. Add olive oil into instant pot and set on Sauté mode.
2. Add couscous into the pot and stir for 1 minute. Pour broth into the pot and stir well.
3. Seal pot with lid and cook on manual high pressure for 5 minutes.
4. Quick release pressure then open the lid.
5. Stir in snap peas, pepper and salt. Stir well.
6. Seal pot with lid again and cook on manual high pressure for 1 minute.
7. Release pressure using quick release method.
8. Add lemon juice and stir well.
9. Serve and enjoy.

Nutrition information per serving:
Calories: 165; Carbohydrates: 28.8g; Protein: 5.8g; Fat: 3.4g; Sugar: 3g; Sodium: 441mg

Butter Brown Rice
(Servings: 6|Cooking Time: 23 minutes)

Ingredients:
- 2 cups brown rice
- 1 ¼ cups vegetable stock
- ½ cup butter
- 1 ¼ cups onion soup

Directions for Cooking:
1. Add all ingredients to instant pot. Mix well.
2. Seal pot with lid and select manual high pressure for 23 minutes.
3. Allow pressure to release naturally, then open lid.
4. Serve and enjoy.

Nutrition information per serving:
Calories: 391; Carbohydrates: 52.1g; Protein: 6.5g; Fat: 18.2g; Sugar: 1.8g; Sodium: 702mg

Vegetable Pesto Quinoa
(Servings: 6|Cooking Time: 15 minutes)

Ingredients:
- 1 ½ cups quinoa
- ¼ cup sliced almonds
- ½ cup feta cheese, crumbled
- 1/3 cup pesto
- ½ cup can olives
- 2 tomato, chopped
- 1 ½ cups vegetable stock
- 4 cups spinach
- 1 bell pepper, chopped
- 3 celery stalk, chopped

- ¼ tsp. salt

Directions for Cooking:

1. Add all ingredients except tomatoes, pesto, olives, sliced almonds and feta cheese into instant pot. Stir well.
2. Seal pot with lid and select manual high pressure for 1 minute.

3. Allow pressure to release naturally for 10 minutes, then release using quick release method.
4. Fluff the quinoa with a fork.
5. Add pesto, olives and tomatoes. Stir well.
6. Top with sliced almonds and feta cheese.
7. Serve and enjoy.

Nutrition information per serving:
Calories: 303; Carbohydrates: 33.8g; Protein: 11.1g; Fat: 14.7g; Sugar: 3.6g; Sodium: 565mg

Garlic Lima Beans

(Servings: 6|Cooking Time: 50 minutes)

Ingredients:

- 1 lb. dry baby lima beans
- 1 bay leaf
- 1 tsp. black pepper
- 4 cups water
- 3 cups vegetable stock
- 1 tbsp. garlic, minced
- 1 onion, chopped
- 4 cups cooked ham, shredded

Directions for Cooking:

1. Add all ingredients into instant pot and stir well.

2. Seal pot with lid and cook on manual high pressure for 25 minutes.
3. Allow pressure to release naturally for 10 minutes, then release using quick release method.
4. Remove bay leaf from beans.
5. Stir well and serve.

Nutrition information per serving:
Calories: 247; Carbohydrates: 22.1g; Protein: 20.4g; Fat: 9.4g; Sugar: 2.9g; Sodium: 1546mg

Hearty White Beans with Tomato

(Servings: 6|Cooking Time: 40 minutes)

Ingredients:

- 2 cups vegetable broth
- 1 tbsp. olive oil
- 6 oz. tomato paste
- 28 oz. can plum tomatoes
- 2 ¼ cups dry cannellini beans
- 1 bay leaf
- 2 garlic cloves, minced
- 1 onion, chopped
- 4 bacon slices, cooked and chopped
- ½ tsp. kosher salt

Directions for Cooking:

1. Add olive oil into instant pot and set on Sauté mode.

2. Add garlic and onion to the pot. Sauté until softened.
3. Add broth, tomato paste, tomatoes, beans, bay leaf, bacon and salt. Stir well.
4. Seal pot with lid and cook on manual high pressure for 40 minutes.
5. Allow pressure to release naturally, then open lid.
6. Mash the tomatoes lightly with a fork. Season with pepper and salt.
7. Serve and enjoy.

Nutrition information per serving:
Calories: 390; Carbohydrates: 53.5g; Protein: 26.2g; Fat: 8.8g; Sugar: 9.2g; Sodium: 1157mg

Garlic Garbanzo Beans

(Servings: 6|Cooking Time: 35 minutes)

Ingredients:

- 1 cup dry garbanzo beans, rinsed and drained
- ½ tsp. chicken bouillon
- 2 bay leaves
- 4 garlic cloves
- 4 cups water

Directions for Cooking:

1. Add all ingredients into instant pot and stir well.
2. Seal pot with lid and cook on manual high pressure for 35 minutes.
3. Allow pressure to release naturally for 15 minutes, then release using quick release method.
4. Drain beans and serve.

Nutrition information per serving:

Calories: 124; Carbohydrates: 20.9g; Protein: 6.6g; Fat: 2g; Sugar: 3.6g; Sodium: 15mg

Classic Wild Rice

(Servings: 6|Cooking Time: 35 minutes)

Ingredients:

- 2 cups wild rice
- 5 cups chicken broth
- 2 tsp. salt

Directions for Cooking:

1. Add all ingredients into instant pot and stir well.
2. Seal pot with lid and cook on manual high pressure for 35 minutes.
3. Quick release pressure then open the lid carefully.
4. Fluff rice with a fork and serve.

Nutrition information per serving:

Calories: 222; Carbohydrates: 40.7g; Protein: 11.9g; Fat: 1.7g; Sugar: 1.9g; Sodium: 1415mg

Butter Sugar Lima Beans

(Servings: 6|Cooking Time: 8 minutes)

Ingredients:

- 16 oz. lima beans
- ¼ cup light brown sugar
- ½ onion, chopped
- 2 tbsp. butter
- 4 bacon slices, cooked and chopped
- ½ cup water
- Pepper
- Salt

Directions for Cooking:

1. Add butter into instant pot and set on Sauté mode.
2. Add onion and sauté until softened.
3. Add lima beans, water, bacon and brown sugar. Stir well.
4. Seal pot with lid and cook on manual high pressure for 8 minutes.
5. Quick release pressure then open the lid carefully.
6. Season with pepper and salt.
7. Stir and serve.

Nutrition information per serving:

Calories: 215; Carbohydrates: 22.2g; Protein: 10g; Fat: 9.8g; Sugar: 7.4g; Sodium: 356mg

Garlic Smoky Beans

(Servings: 4|Cooking Time: 45 minutes)

Ingredients:

- 1 lb. dry pinto beans, soaked overnight and rinsed
- 1 tbsp. liquid smoke
- 1 onion, chopped
- 4 garlic cloves, minced
- Water
- Salt

Directions for Cooking:

1. Add all ingredients into instant pot and stir well.
2. Seal pot with lid and cook on manual high pressure for 45 minutes.
3. Allow pressure to release naturally, then open lid.
4. Remove ¼ cup liquid and 1 cup beans from the pot.
5. Blend the remaining beans until smooth.
6. Return reserved beans and liquid into the pot and stir well.
7. Serve and enjoy.

Nutrition information per serving:

Calories: 409; Carbohydrates: 74.5g; Protein: 24.8g; Fat: 1.4g; Sugar: 3.6g; Sodium: 54mg

Wild Rice Pilaf

(Servings: 8|Cooking Time: 25 minutes)

Ingredients:

- 2 cups wild rice, rinsed and drained
- ¼ cup fresh parsley, chopped
- 2 ½ tsp. better then bouillon vegetable base
- 2 ½ cups water
- 2 garlic cloves, minced
- 2 cups mushrooms, sliced
- 1 onion, diced
- 1 2/3 tbsp. olive oil
- Pepper
- Salt

Directions for Cooking:

1. Add oil into instant pot and set on Sauté mode.
2. Add mushrooms and onion to the pot and sauté for 4 minutes.
3. Add garlic and sauté for 30 seconds.
4. Add rice and stir for 2-3 minutes.
5. Add better then bouillon vegetable base and water and stir well.
6. Seal pot with lid and cook on manual high pressure for 20 minutes.
7. Allow pressure to release naturally, then open lid.
8. Fluff rice with fork.
9. Season with pepper and salt.
10. Serve and enjoy.

Nutrition information per serving:

Calories: 179; Carbohydrates: 32.2g; Protein: 6.7g; Fat: 3.4g; Sugar: 1.9g; Sodium: 27mg

Farro Wild Rice Pilaf

(Servings: 6|Cooking Time: 35 minutes)

Ingredients:

- ½ cup hazelnut, toasted and chopped
- ¾ cup dried cherries
- 1 tsp. sea salt
- 1 tbsp. fresh herbs
- 6 cups chicken stock
- 1 ½ cups whole grain farro
- ¾ cup wild rice
- 1 tsp. garlic, minced

- ½ small onion, chopped
- 1 tbsp. olive oil

Directions for Cooking:

1. Add olive oil into the pot and set on Sauté mode.
2. Add garlic and onion. Sauté until onion softens.
3. Add farro and wild rice. Stir well.
4. Add stock, pepper, fresh herbs and salt. Stir well.
5. Seal pot with lid and cook on manual high pressure for 25 minutes.
6. Meanwhile, boil cherries in boiling water for 10 minutes. Drain well.
7. Once instant pot beeps, allow to release pressure naturally for 5 minutes, then release using quick release method.
8. Drain excess liquid from the instant pot using a mesh sieve.
9. Add chopped hazelnuts and cherries. Toss well to combine.
10. Garnish with fresh herbs and serve.

Nutrition information per serving:
Calories: 237; Carbohydrates: 39.6g; Protein: 5.4g; Fat: 6.9g; Sugar: 13.7g; Sodium: 1082mg

Shallot Butter Barley

(Servings: 6|Cooking Time: 40 minutes)

Ingredients:

- 3 cups chicken stock
- ¼ cup fresh parsley, chopped
- 2 tbsp. butter
- ½ cup shallots, minced
- 2 cups barley, rinsed and drained

Directions for Cooking:

1. Add butter into instant pot and set on Sauté mode.
2. Add shallots and sauté for 5-6 minutes.
3. Add barley and cook for 8-10 minutes.
4. Add remaining ingredients and stir well.
5. Seal pot with lid and cook on manual high pressure for 20 minutes.
6. Quick release pressure then open the lid carefully.
7. Fluff barley and serve.

Nutrition information per serving:
Calories: 266; Carbohydrates: 47.8g; Protein: 8.4g; Fat: 5.6g; Sugar: 0.9g; Sodium: 419mg

Chapter 4 Instant Pot Chicken Recipes

Ranch Bacon Chicken

(Servings: 4|Cooking Time: 15 minutes)

Ingredients:

- 1 cup cheddar cheese, shredded
- ½ cup water
- 8 oz. cream cheese
- 1 packet ranch seasoning
- 2 lbs. chicken breast, boneless
- 6 bacon slices, cooked and chopped

Directions for Cooking:

1. Add cream cheese and chicken into instant pot.
2. Sprinkle ranch seasoning on top of chicken. Add water.
3. Seal pot with lid and cook on manual high pressure for 15 minutes.
4. Quick release pressure then open the lid.
5. Remove chicken from pot and shred using a fork.
6. Return shredded chicken to the pot. Add bacon and cheese. Stir well.
7. Serve and enjoy.

Nutrition information per serving:

Calories: 724; Carbohydrates: 2.3g; Protein: 70g; Fat: 46.7g; Sugar: 0.3g; Sodium: 1118mg

Sweet & Savory Adobo Chicken

(Servings: 2|Cooking Time: 25 minutes)

Ingredients:

- 3 chicken thighs, boneless
- 1 tbsp. scallion, chopped
- 1 tbsp. cilantro, chopped
- ½ cup water
- ½ cup chicken stock
- ½ tsp. red chili flakes
- 2 tbsp. sugar
- 2 tbsp. white vinegar
- 5 tbsp. soy sauce
- 2 garlic cloves, minced
- ½ onion, sliced
- Pepper
- Salt

Directions for Cooking:

1. Season chicken with pepper and salt. Place chicken into instant pot.
2. Add sliced onion on top of chicken.

3. In a small bowl, mix together soy sauce, stock, chili flakes, sugar, water and vinegar. Add to the instant pot.
4. Seal pot with lid and select Poultry mode. Set timer for 10 minutes.
5. Quick release pressure then open the lid.
6. Remove chicken from pot and set on Sauté mode. Cook sauce on Sauté mode until sauce thickens, about 15 minutes.

7. Return chicken to the pot and stir well.
8. Serve and enjoy.

Nutrition information per serving:
Calories: 505; Carbohydrates: 19.2g; Protein: 66.6g; Fat: 16.5g; Sugar: 14.2g; Sodium: 3296mg

Simple Shredded Chicken

(Servings: 6|Cooking Time: 30 minutes)

Ingredients:
- 2 chicken breasts, boneless and skinless
- 14.5 oz. chicken broth
- ¼ tsp. pepper
- ½ tsp. salt

Directions for Cooking:
1. Add all ingredients into instant pot.
2. Seal pot with lid and cook on manual high pressure for 30 minutes.

3. Allow pressure to release naturally, then open lid.
4. Remove chicken from pot and shred using a fork.
5. Serve and enjoy.

Nutrition information per serving:
Calories: 104; Carbohydrates: 0.3g; Protein: 15.5g; Fat: 4g; Sugar: 0.2g; Sodium: 454mg

Perfect Mississippi Chicken

(Servings: 6|Cooking Time: 8 minutes)

Ingredients:
- 6 pepperoncini
- 2 tbsp. brown gravy mix
- 2 tbsp. ranch mix
- 1 cup pepperoncini juice
- 1 cup chicken stock
- 3 lbs. chicken thighs, boneless

Directions for Cooking:
1. Add all ingredients into instant pot and stir well.
2. Seal pot with lid and cook on manual high pressure for 8 minutes.

3. Allow pressure to release naturally for 10 minutes, then release using quick release method.
4. Remove chicken from pot and shred using a fork.
5. Return shredded chicken to the pot and stir well.
6. Serve and enjoy.

Nutrition information per serving:
Calories: 440; Carbohydrates: 17.1g; Protein: 65.9g; Fat: 17.1g; Sugar: 0.1g; Sodium: 1009mg

Orange Chicken

(Servings: 6|Cooking Time: 15 minutes)

Ingredients:

- 4 chicken breasts, boneless and cut into chunks
- 2 tsp. cornstarch
- ¾ cup orange marmalade
- 2 tbsp. soy sauce
- ¾ cup BBQ sauce

Directions for Cooking:

1. Add chicken, soy sauce, and BBQ sauce into instant pot and stir well.
2. Seal pot with lid and cook on manual high pressure for 4 minutes.
3. Quick release pressure then open the lid.
4. Remove ¼ cup sauce mixture from instant pot and mix with cornstarch in a bowl.
5. Pour cornstarch mixture into instant pot and stir well.
6. Add marmalade and stir well.
7. Set pot on Sauté mode and sauté chicken until sauce thickens, about 5-6 minutes.
8. Stir well and serve.

Nutrition information per serving:
Calories: 336; Carbohydrates: 39.1g; Protein: 28.6 g; Fat: 7.3g; Sugar: 32.2g; Sodium: 756mg

Tasty Tamarind Chicken

(Servings: 4|Cooking Time: 15 minutes)

Ingredients:

- 2 lbs. chicken breasts, skinless, boneless, and cut into pieces
- 1 tbsp. arrowroot powder
- ½ cup tamarind paste
- ½ tsp. salt
- 2 tbsp. brown sugar
- 1 tbsp. ketchup
- 1 tbsp. vinegar
- 2 tbsp. ginger, grated
- 2 garlic cloves, minced
- 3 tbsp. olive oil
- ½ tsp. salt

Directions for Cooking:

1. Add oil into instant pot and set on Sauté mode.
2. Add ginger and garlic. Sauté for 30 seconds.
3. Add chicken and sauté for 3-4 minutes or until chicken is lightly browned.
4. In a small bowl, combine together tamarind paste, brown sugar, ketchup, vinegar and salt, and pour into instant pot. Stir well.
5. Seal pot with lid and cook on manual high pressure for 8 minutes.
6. Quick release pressure then open the lid.
7. Remove ¼ cup sauce mixture from instant pot and combine with arrowroot powder in a small bowl. Pour into the pot and stir everything well.
8. Serve and enjoy.

Nutrition information per serving:
Calories: 599; Carbohydrates: 27.6g; Protein: 66.5g; Fat: 27.6g; Sugar: 14g; Sodium: 825mg

Flavors Chicken Thighs

(Servings: 6|Cooking Time: 15 minutes)

Ingredients:

- 6 chicken thighs, remove skin
- 1 cup water
- 2 tbsp. olive oil
- 1 tsp. smoked paprika
- 1 tsp. garlic powder
- Pepper
- Salt

Directions for Cooking:

1. Season chicken with paprika, garlic powder, pepper and salt.
2. Add oil into instant pot and set on Sauté mode.
3. Add chicken into the pot and sauté until lightly browned.
4. Remove chicken from pot.
5. Add water to the pot and stir well.
6. Place trivet into the pot. Place chicken on top of the trivet.
7. Seal pot with lid and cook on manual high pressure for 10 minutes.
8. Allow pressure to release naturally, then open lid.
9. Serve and enjoy.

Nutrition information per serving:
Calories: 320; Carbohydrates: 0.6g; Protein: 42.4g; Fat: 15.5g; Sugar: 0.2g; Sodium: 154mg

Italian Creamy Chicken

(Servings: 8|Cooking Time: 10 minutes)

Ingredients:
- 2 lbs. chicken breasts, skinless and boneless
- 8 oz. cream cheese
- ¼ cup butter
- 14 oz. can cream of chicken soup
- 0.5 oz. dry Italian dressing mix
- 1 cup chicken stock

Directions for Cooking:
1. Add stock to the instant pot.
2. Add cream of chicken soup, Italian dressing mix, and butter into the pot. Stir well.
3. Seal pot with lid and cook on manual high pressure for 10 minutes.
4. Quick release pressure then open the lid.
5. Add cream cheese and stir until cheese is melted.
6. Serve and enjoy.

Nutrition information per serving:
Calories: 416; Carbohydrates: 5.5g; Protein: 36.3g; Fat: 27g; Sugar: 0.4g; Sodium: 738mg

Chicken Pasta

(Servings: 4|Cooking Time: 8 minutes)

Ingredients:
- 8 oz. penne pasta, dry
- 1 lb. chicken breasts, boneless and skinless, cut into bite-size pieces
- 3 tbsp. fajita seasoning, divided into half
- 7 oz. can tomatoes
- 4 garlic cloves, minced
- 1 onion, diced
- 1 cup chicken stock
- 2 bell peppers, seeded and diced
- 2 tbsp. olive oil

Directions for Cooking:
1. Add olive oil in instant pot and set on Sauté mode.
2. Add chicken and half of fajita seasoning. Stir well and sauté until chicken is white.
3. Add garlic, bell pepper, onions, and remaining fajitas seasoning. Stir well and sauté for 2 minutes.
4. Add tomatoes, stock, and pasta in the pot. Stir well.
5. Seal pot with lid and cook on manual high pressure for 6 minutes.
6. Quick release pressure then open the lid.
7. Serve and enjoy.

Nutrition information per serving:

Calories: 510; Carbohydrates: 46.5g; Protein: 40.9g; Fat: 17g; Sugar: 6.1g; Sodium: 806mg

Potato Mustard Chicken

(Servings: 4|Cooking Time: 15 minutes)

Ingredients:

- 2 lbs. chicken thighs, boneless and skinless
- 3/4 cup chicken stock
- 4 tbsp. lemon juice
- 2 tbsp. Italian seasoning
- 3 tbsp. Dijon mustard
- 2 lbs. potatoes, quartered
- 2 tbsp. olive oil
- Pepper
- Salt

Directions for Cooking:

1. Add olive oil into instant pot and set on Sauté mode.
2. Season chicken with pepper and salt. Place into instant pot.
3. In a small bowl, mix together lemon juice, stock and Dijon mustard. Stir well and pour over the chicken.
4. Add potatoes and Italian seasoning to the pot.
5. Seal pot with lid and cook on manual high pressure for 15 minutes.
6. Quick release pressure then open the lid carefully.
7. Serve and enjoy.

Nutrition information per serving:
Calories: 682; Carbohydrates: 37.5g; Protein: 70.2g; Fat: 26.8g; Sugar: 3.8g; Sodium: 529mg

Chicken & Rice

(Servings: 2|Cooking Time: 7 minutes)

Ingredients:

- 2 chicken thighs, skinless and boneless
- 1 garlic clove, minced
- ½ small onion, diced
- 3/4 cup long grain rice, rinsed
- 2 tsp. olive oil
- 1 cup chicken broth
- 1 tbsp. jerk seasoning

Directions for Cooking:

1. Add oil into instant pot and set on Sauté mode.
2. Add onion and sauté for a few minutes or until onion softens.
3. Add garlic and sauté for 10 seconds. Stir well.
4. Add jerk seasoning and stir well to combine.
5. Add rice and chicken broth, and stir well. Add chicken.
6. Seal instant pot with lid and select pressure cook mode and set the timer for 7 minutes.
7. Allow pressure to release naturally for 5 minutes. Release using quick release method, then open lid.
8. Stir well and serve.

Nutrition information per serving:
Calories: 599; Carbohydrates: 58.1g; Protein: 49.9g; Fat: 16.7g; Sugar: 1.2g; Sodium: 512mg

Herb Chicken Piccata

(Servings: 4|Cooking Time: 10 minutes)

Ingredients:

- 1 ½ lbs. chicken breasts, skinless and boneless
- 4 oz. capers, drained
- 3/4 cup chicken stock
- 1 garlic clove, minced
- 1 tbsp. olive oil
- 1 tsp. dried basil
- 1 tsp. dried oregano
- ¼ cup lemon juice
- Pepper
- Salt

Directions for Cooking:

1. Add olive oil into instant pot and select Sauté mode.
2. Season chicken with pepper and salt. Place chicken into the pot and sauté until lightly brown on all sides.
3. Remove chicken from pot and place on a plate.
4. Add garlic and sauté for a minute.
5. Add broth, basil, oregano and lemon juice. Stir well.
6. Return chicken into the pot and top with capers.
7. Seal pot with lid and select manual high pressure for 10 minutes.
8. Quick release pressure then open the lid.
9. Serve and enjoy.

Nutrition information per serving:
Calories: 368; Carbohydrates: 2.4g; Protein: 50.2g; Fat: 16.6g; Sugar: 0.6g; Sodium: 1172mg

Sweet Mango Pineapple Chicken

(Servings: 4|Cooking Time: 10 minutes)

Ingredients:

- 3 chicken breasts, skinless and boneless
- 14 oz. pineapple mango salsa
- 1 tsp. red pepper flakes
- 1 cup pineapple, cubed
- 1 mango, peel and cube
- Pepper
- Salt

Directions for Cooking:

1. Set instant pot on Sauté mode.
2. Season chicken with pepper and salt.
3. Place chicken into instant pot and sauté until brown.
4. Add remaining ingredients into the pot and stir well.
5. Seal pot with lid and cook on manual high pressure for 10 minutes.
6. Quick release pressure then open the lid.
7. Serve and enjoy.

Nutrition information per serving:
Calories: 332; Carbohydrates: 32g; Protein: 32.6g; Fat: 8.6g; Sugar: 25.8g; Sodium: 134mg

Simple Shredded Salsa Chicken

(Servings: 4|Cooking Time: 5 minutes)

Ingredients:

- 1 lb. chicken breast, skinless and boneless
- 3/4 tsp. cumin
- 1 cup salsa
- ¼ tsp. oregano
- ¼ tsp. pepper
- ½ tsp. salt

Directions for Cooking:

1. Season chicken with oregano, cumin, black pepper and salt.
2. Place chicken in the pot. Pour salsa over the top of chicken.
3. Seal pot with lid. Select Poultry mode and cook for 5 minutes.
4. Release the pressure using quick release method, then open lid.
5. Transfer chicken to serving plate.
6. Shred the chicken using a fork and serve.

Nutrition information per serving:

Calories: 149; Carbohydrates: 4.4g; Protein: 25.1g; Fat: 3g; Sugar: 2g; Sodium: 739mg

Sweet Orange Chicken

(Servings: 4|Cooking Time: 17 minutes)

Ingredients:

- 1 lb. Chicken breast, skinless and boneless cut into cubed
- ¼ cup chicken stock
- 2 tbsp. Flour
- 1 tbsp. coconut oil
- 3 drops orange essential oil
- 1 tbsp. ketchup
- 2 tbsp. brown sugar

Directions for Cooking:

1. Add chicken and flour in a zip-lock bag. Shake to coat well.
2. Add coconut oil in instant pot and select Sauté mode.
3. Add chicken to pot and cook for 2 minutes. Turn off the pot.
4. Now add chicken stock, orange essential oil, ketchup and brown sugar in a pot. Mix well.
5. Seal pot with lid and cook on manual high pressure for 15 minutes.
6. Release pressure using quick release method.
7. Stir well and serve.

Nutrition information per serving:

Calories: 194; Carbohydrates: 8.4g; Protein: 24.6g; Fat: 6.3g; Sugar: 5.3g; Sodium: 149mg

Cheesy Salsa Lemon Chicken

(Servings: 3|Cooking Time: 8 minutes)

Ingredients:

- 3 chicken breast, boneless and skinless
- 1 tbsp. olive oil
- ½ tsp. red chili powder
- ¼ cup fresh lemon juice
- 1 cup salsa
- ½ cup goat cheese, crumbled
- ½ tsp. ground cumin

Directions for Cooking:

1. Add olive oil into instant pot and set on Sauté mode.
2. Place chicken in the pot and sauté until lightly brown on both sides. Transfer chicken to a plate.

3. Add cumin, chili powder, salsa and lemon juice to the pot. Stir well and return the chicken to the pot.
4. Seal pot with lid and select manual high pressure for 8 minutes.
5. Quick release pressure then open the lid.
6. Sprinkle with crumbled cheese and serve.

Nutrition information per serving:
Calories: 345; Carbohydrates: 6g; Protein: 43.7g; Fat: 15.8g; Sugar: 2.7g; Sodium: 651mg

Whole Chicken

(Servings: 6|Cooking Time: 25 minutes)

Ingredients:

- 4 lbs. whole chicken
- ¼ tsp. poultry seasoning
- ¼ tsp. dried thyme
- 1 tsp. paprika
- 1 ½ cup chicken stock
- 1 tbsp. coconut oil
- ¼ tsp. pepper
- ½ tsp. salt

Directions for Cooking:

1. Add coconut oil to instant pot and set on Sauté mode.
2. Place chicken in a pot and cook until lightly brown from all sides.
3. In a small bowl, mix together pepper, poultry seasoning, dried thyme, paprika and salt.
4. Once the chicken is brown, add seasoning and chicken stock.
5. Seal pot with lid and cook on manual high pressure for 25 minutes.
6. Allow pressure to release naturally, then open lid.
7. Transfer chicken onto a serving dish. Drizzle pot juices over the chicken and serve.

Nutrition information per serving:
Calories: 598; Carbohydrates: 0.5g; Protein: 87.7g; Fat: 24.9g; Sugar: 0.2g; Sodium: 645mg

Flavors Chicken Taco

(Servings: 6|Cooking Time: 15 minutes)

Ingredients:

- 1 ½ lbs. chicken breasts, boneless
- ½ tbsp. cumin
- ¼ tsp. chipotle powder
- 2 tsp. garlic cloves, minced
- ½ ancho chile, dried and soaked
- 1 ½ tomato puree
- ½ cup onion, diced
- ½ tsp. sea salt
- 6 corn tortillas

Directions for Cooking:

1. Add soaked ancho chile, cumin, garlic, chipotle powder, salt and ½ cup water in a blender. Blend until pureed.
2. Add tomato puree, onions, chicken and puree mixture into instant pot. Stir well.
3. Seal pot with lid and cook on manual high pressure for 15 minutes.
4. Quick release pressure then open the lid.
5. Spoon taco filling into the corn tortillas and serve.

Nutrition information per serving:
Calories: 299; Carbohydrates: 17.7g; Protein: 35.5g; Fat: 9.3g; Sugar: 3.7g; Sodium: 283mg

Delicious Parmesan Chicken

(Servings: 6|Cooking Time: 15 minutes)

Ingredients:

- 1 ½ lbs. chicken tenders
- ½ cup olive oil
- ¼ tsp. garlic powder
- ½ cup parmesan cheese, grated
- 2 cups mozzarella cheese, shredded
- 24 oz. tomato sauce
- 2 tbsp. butter, salted

Directions for Cooking:

1. Add olive oil into instant pot and set on Sauté mode.
2. Add chicken into the pot and sauté until lightly brown.
3. Add garlic powder, tomato sauce, butter and parmesan cheese.
4. Seal pot with lid and cook on manual high pressure for 15 minutes.
5. Quick release pressure then open the lid.
6. Sprinkle cheese on top of chicken and cover pot with lid until cheese is melted.
7. Serve and enjoy.

Nutrition information per serving:
Calories: 498; Carbohydrates: 6.5g; Protein: 41.1g; Fat: 33.9g; Sugar: 4.9g; Sodium: 976mg

Tangerine Chicken

(Servings: 2|Cooking Time: 15 minutes)

Ingredients:

- 1 lb. chicken thighs
- 2 tbsp. white wine
- ½ cup tangerine juice
- 2 tbsp. lemon juice
- 1/8 tsp. thyme, dried
- ½ tsp. fresh rosemary, chopped
- 1 tsp. garlic, minced
- Pepper
- Salt

Directions for Cooking:

1. Place chicken into instant pot.
2. In a bowl, mix together tangerine juice, garlic, white wine, lemon juice, thyme, rosemary, pepper and salt.
3. Pour bowl mixture over the chicken thighs.
4. Seal pot with lid and cook on manual high pressure for 15 minutes.
5. Allow pressure to release naturally. Open lid carefully.
6. Serve and enjoy.

Nutrition information per serving:
Calories: 473; Carbohydrates: 17g; Protein: 66.3g; Fat: 17g; Sugar: 6g; Sodium: 280mg

Chicken Tacos

(Servings: 8|Cooking Time: 15 minutes)

Ingredients:

- 2 lbs. chicken breasts
- 2 tbsp. cumin
- ½ cup chicken stock
- 1 tbsp. olive oil
- 1 onion, chopped
- 14 oz. tomato paste
- 1 tsp. hot sauce
- ½ tsp. red pepper, crushed
- ½ tsp. cilantro
- 1 tbsp. coriander
- Pepper
- Salt

Directions for Cooking:

1. Add oil in instant pot and set on Sauté mode.

2. Add onion to the pot and sauté for 3 minutes.
3. Add chicken to the pot and sauté until brown.
4. Add remaining ingredients and stir well.
5. Seal pot with lid and select Poultry mode.
6. Quick release pressure then open the lid carefully.
7. Remove chicken from pot and shred using a fork.
8. Return shredded chicken to the pot and stir well.
9. Serve and enjoy.

Nutrition information per serving:
Calories: 285; Carbohydrates: 12g; Protein: 35.5g; Fat: 10.8g; Sugar: 7.1g; Sodium: 232mg

Herb Chicken Wings

(Servings: 4|Cooking Time: 10 minutes)

Ingredients:
- 12 chicken wings
- 1 tbsp. chicken seasoning
- 6 tbsp. chicken broth
- 3 tbsp. extra virgin olive oil
- 1 tbsp. basil
- 1 tbsp. oregano
- 3 tbsp. tarragon
- 1 tbsp. garlic puree
- 1 cup water
- Pepper
- Salt

Directions for Cooking:

1. Add all ingredients into the large bowl and mix well.
2. Pour water into instant pot then insert trivet.
3. Place marinated chicken on top of the trivet.
4. Seal pot with lid and cook on manual high pressure for 10 minutes.
5. Quick release pressure then open the lid carefully.
6. Serve and enjoy.

Nutrition information per serving:
Calories: 141; Carbohydrates: 2.9g; Protein: 3.3g; Fat: 13.5g; Sugar: 0.1g; Sodium: 151mg

Leek Mushroom Chicken

(Servings: 6|Cooking Time: 8 minutes)

Ingredients:
- 6 chicken breasts, skinless and boneless
- ½ cup chicken broth
- 3 lbs. leeks, sliced
- 4 tbsp. butter
- ½ cup unsweetened almond milk
- 2 tbsp. arrowroot
- 1 ¼ lbs. mushrooms, sliced
- ¼ tsp. pepper
- ½ tsp. pink Himalayan salt

Directions for Cooking:
1. Season chicken with pepper and salt.
2. Add butter into the pot and set on Sauté mode.
3. Add chicken to the pot and brown on both the sides.
4. Remove chicken from pot and place on a plate.
5. Add chicken broth, mushrooms, leeks and chicken to the pot. Stir well.
6. Seal pot with lid and cook on manual high pressure for 8 minutes.
7. Allow pressure to release naturally for 5 minutes, then release using quick release method. Open lid.

8. Transfer chicken to a plate.
9. Stir almond milk and arrowroot into the pot and select Sauté mode. Cook for 2 minutes.
10. Serve and enjoy.

Nutrition information per serving:
Calories: 512; Carbohydrates: 35.9g; Protein: 49.3g; Fat: 19.9g; Sugar: 10.5g; Sodium: 310mg

Spicy Chicken

(Servings: 8|Cooking Time: 12 minutes)

Ingredients:

- 2 lbs. chicken breasts
- ½ onion, chopped
- 1 tbsp. olive oil
- ½ cup hot sauce
- ½ red bell pepper, chopped

Directions for Cooking:

1. Add oil into instant pot and set on Sauté mode.
2. Add onion and bell peppers to the pot and sauté for 4 minutes.
3. Add chicken and hot sauce; stir well.
4. Seal pot with lid and cook on manual high pressure for 12 minutes.
5. Quick release pressure then open the lid carefully.
6. Remove chicken from pot and shred the chicken using a fork.
7. Return shredded chicken to the instant pot and stir well.
8. Serve and enjoy.

Nutrition information per serving:
Calories: 237; Carbohydrates: 1.5g; Protein: 33g; Fat: 10.2g; Sugar: 0.9g; Sodium: 479mg

Mexican Chili Lime Chicken

(Servings: 6|Cooking Time: 12 minutes)

Ingredients:

- 2 lbs. chicken breasts
- 2 tsp. garlic powder
- 4 oz. jalapenos, diced
- 10 oz. tomatoes, diced
- ½ cup green bell pepper
- ½ cup red bell pepper
- 1 fresh lime juice
- 2/3 cup chicken broth
- ½ tsp. chili powder
- 2 tsp. cumin
- ½ cup onion, diced
- 1 tbsp. olive oil
- ¼ tsp. salt

Directions for Cooking:

1. Add oil into instant pot and set on Sauté mode.
2. Add onion, bell peppers and salt into the pot; sauté for 3 minutes.
3. Add remaining ingredients into the pot and stir well.
4. Seal pot with lid and cook on manual high pressure for 12 minutes.
5. Quick release pressure then open the lid carefully.
6. Remove chicken from pot and shred the chicken using a fork.
7. Return shredded chicken to the pot and stir well.
8. Serve and enjoy.

Nutrition information per serving:
Calories: 341; Carbohydrates: 6.4g; Protein: 45.5g; Fat: 14.1g; Sugar: 3.3g; Sodium: 319mg

Spicy Chicken

(Servings: 6|Cooking Time: 12 minutes)

Ingredients:

- 2 lbs. chicken breasts
- 2/3 cup onion, chopped
- ½ cup celery, diced
- ½ cup chicken broth
- ½ cup buffalo wing sauce

Directions for Cooking:

1. Add all ingredients into instant pot and stir well.
2. Seal pot with lid and cook on manual high pressure for 12 minutes.
3. Quick release pressure then open the lid carefully.
4. Remove chicken from pot and shred the chicken using a fork.
5. Return chicken to the pot and stir well.
6. Serve and enjoy.

Nutrition information per serving:

Calories: 297; Carbohydrates: 1.6g; Protein: 44.3g; Fat: 11.3g; Sugar: 0.7g; Sodium: 233mg

Chicken Wraps

(Servings: 4|Cooking Time: 10 minutes)

Ingredients:

- 1 lb. ground chicken
- ½ cup water chestnuts, drain and slice
- 1/8 tsp. allspice
- ½ tsp. ground ginger
- 5 tsp. garlic, minced
- 2 tbsp. balsamic vinegar
- ¼ cup chicken broth
- ¼ cup coconut amino
- 3/4 cup onion, diced

Directions for Cooking:

1. Add all ingredients into instant pot and stir well.
2. Seal pot with lid. Select manual and set timer for 10 minutes.
3. Quick release pressure then open the lid.
4. Add meat into lettuce leaves and serve.

Nutrition information per serving:

Calories: 293; Carbohydrates: 16g; Protein: 34.2 g; Fat: 8.9g; Sugar: 2.9g; Sodium: 164mg

Chicken Coconut Curry

(Servings: 8|Cooking Time: 25 minutes)

Ingredients:

- 4 lbs. chicken thighs
- 1 Tsp garlic powder
- 1 Tsp kosher salt
- 1 tbsp. coconut sugar
- 4 cups potatoes, peeled and diced
- 1 cup water
- 2 cups coconut milk
- 2 tbsp. olive oil
- 2 tbsp. curry powder
- 1 Tsp onion powder

Directions for Cooking:

1. In a large bowl, combine together chicken, oil, 1 tbsp. curry powder, onion powder, garlic powder and salt. Set aside for 1 hour.
2. Add marinated chicken into instant pot.
3. Set the instant pot on Sauté mode and brown the chicken.
4. Add coconut sugar, potatoes, remaining curry powder and coconut milk into the pot; stir well.

5. Seal pot with lid and cook on manual high pressure for 25 minutes.
6. Quick release pressure then open the lid.
7. Stir well and serve.

Nutrition information per serving:
Calorie: 670; Carbohydrates: 18.9g; Protein: 68.7 g; Fat: 34.9g; Sugar: 3.1g; Sodium: 506mg

Zucchini Chicken Curry

(Servings: 4|Cooking Time: 21 minutes)

Ingredients:

- 1 ¼ lbs. chicken thighs, skinless, boneless and cut into pieces
- 1 tbsp. coconut palm sugar
- 2 tbsp. green curry paste
- 1 medium onion, sliced
- 3 small zucchini, diced
- 1 tbsp. olive oil
- ¼ cup fresh cilantro, chopped
- 1 large sweet potato, peeled and diced
- 14 oz. can coconut milk
- 1 tsp. sea salt

Directions for Cooking:

1. Add oil into instant pot and set on Sauté mode.
2. Add zucchini to pot and sauté for 6 minutes. Remove from pot and set aside.
3. Add onion and sauté for 5 minutes.
4. Stir in coconut sugar, curry paste and salt. Cook for a few minutes.
5. Add coconut milk and stir well.
6. Add sweet potatoes and chicken; stir well.
7. Seal pot with lid and cook on manual high pressure for 10 minutes.
8. Quick release pressure then open the lid.
9. Stir in cilantro and zucchini.
10. Serve and enjoy.

Nutrition information per serving:
Calorie: 670; Carbohydrates: 18.9g; Protein: 68.7g; Fat: 34.9g; Sugar: 3.1g; Sodium: 506mg

Lemon Olive Chicken

(Servings: 4|Cooking Time: 10 minutes)

Ingredients:

- 4 chicken breasts, skinless and boneless
- 1 cup chicken broth
- ½ lemon juice
- ½ cup butter
- ½ tsp. cumin
- ½ cup onion, sliced
- 6 oz. can green olives, pitted
- ¼ tsp. black pepper
- 1 tsp. sea salt

Directions for Cooking:

1. Season chicken with pepper and salt.
2. Set the instant pot on Sauté mode. Place season chicken into the pot and brown.
3. Add all remaining ingredients and seal pot with lid. Cook on manual high pressure for 10 minutes.
4. Quick release pressure then open the lid.
5. Serve and enjoy.

Nutrition information per serving:
Calorie: 570; Carbohydrates: 4.7g; Protein: 44.5g; Fat: 40g; Sugar: 0.9g; Sodium: 1829mg

Chapter 5 Instant Pot Seafood & Fish Recipes

Delicious Jambalaya

(Servings: 6|Cooking Time: 10 minutes)

Ingredients:

- 1 ½ cup rice
- ¼ cup scallions, sliced
- 12 oz. shrimp, cooked
- 1 3/4 cup chicken stock
- 14.5 oz. can tomatoes, diced
- ½ tsp. thyme
- 2 tsp. Cajun seasoning
- 3 garlic cloves, minced
- 2 celery ribs, chopped
- 1 green pepper, chopped
- 1 lb. chicken thighs, cut into pieces
- 12 oz. andouille sausage, sliced
- 2 tsp. olive oil
- ½ tsp. salt

Directions for Cooking:

1. Add oil into instant pot and set on Sauté mode.
2. Add sausage to the pot and sauté for 5 minutes.
3. Remove sausage from pot and set aside. Add chicken to pot and sauté until brown, about 3 minutes.
4. Add onion, rice, garlic, celery and green pepper to the pot. Stir well and cook for 2 minutes.
5. Add stock, tomatoes, thyme, Cajun seasoning and salt. Stir to mix.
6. Seal pot with lid and cook on manual high pressure for 8 minutes.
7. Allow pressure to release naturally for 5 minutes, then release using quick release method. Remove lid.
8. Set pot on Sauté mode. Add sausage and cooked shrimp. Sauté for 5 minutes.
9. Garnish with scallions and serve.

Nutrition information per serving:
Calories: 614; Carbohydrates: 45.9g; Protein: 50.2g; Fat: 24.1g; Sugar: 3.8g; Sodium: 1475mg

Tasty Shrimp Boil

(Servings: 6|Cooking Time: 1 minute)

Ingredients:

- 2 lbs. frozen shrimp, deveined
- 12 oz. sausage, sliced
- 6 frozen half corn on the cobs
- 2 tbsp. garlic, crushed
- 1 onion, chopped
- 1 tsp. red pepper flakes
- 1 tbsp. old bay seasoning
- 1 cup chicken stock
- ½ tsp. salt

Directions for Cooking:

1. Add all ingredients into instant pot and stir well.
2. Seal pot with lid and cook on manual high pressure for 1 minute.
3. Quick release pressure then open the lid.
4. Stir well and serve.

Nutrition information per serving:
Calories: 457; Carbohydrates: 23.3g; Protein: 45.4g; Fat: 20g; Sugar: 6g; Sodium: 1294mg

Shrimp Pasta

(Servings: 8|Cooking Time: 4 minutes)

Ingredients:

- 1 lb. spaghetti noodles, break in half
- 1 lb. shrimp, cooked
- 3 ½ cups vegetable stock
- ¼ cup fresh parsley, chopped
- For sauce:
- 1 ½ tbsp. fresh lime juice
- 1 tbsp. hot sauce
- 1 tbsp. honey
- ½ cup sweet chili sauce
- 3/4 cup mayonnaise

1. Add spaghetti noodles into instant pot then pour stock over noodles to cover.
2. Seal pot with lid and cook on manual high pressure for 4 minutes.
3. Quick release pressure then open the lid.
4. In a small bowl, mix together all sauce ingredients and pour over cooked noodles.
5. Add cooked shrimp and stir well.
6. Garnish with parsley and serve.

Nutrition information per serving:
Calories: 357; Carbohydrates: 45.8g; Protein: 19.6g; Fat: 9.9g; Sugar: 9.9g; Sodium: 568mg

Directions for Cooking:

Garlic Honey Shrimp

(Servings: 4|Cooking Time: 8 minutes)

Ingredients:

- 1 lb. shrimp, peeled and deveined
- 2 tsp. olive oil

For sauce:

- 1 tbsp. ginger, minced
- 1 tbsp. garlic, minced
- ¼ cup honey
- ¼ cup soy sauce

Directions for Cooking:

1. In a mixing bowl, mix all sauce ingredients together.
2. Add shrimp into the bowl and toss well to coat.
3. Add oil into instant pot and set on Sauté mode.

4. Add shrimp with sauce mixture into instant pot and sauté for 3 minutes.
5. Seal pot with lid and cook on manual high pressure for 5 minutes.
6. Quick release pressure then open the lid.
7. Stir well and serve.

Nutrition information per serving:
Calories: 235; Carbohydrates: 22g; Protein: 27.1g; Fat: 4.4g; Sugar: 17.7g; Sodium: 1177mg

Simple Fish Tacos

(Servings: 2|Cooking Time: 8 minutes)

Ingredients:
- 2 tilapia fillets
- ¼ cup fresh cilantro, chopped
- 1 fresh lime juice
- 2 tbsp. paprika
- 1 tsp. olive oil
- Pinch of salt

Directions for Cooking:
1. Place fish fillets in the middle of parchment paper.
2. Drizzle fish fillet with oil and lime juice. Season with paprika, chopped cilantro and salt.
3. Fold parchment paper around the fish fillet to make a packet.
4. Pour 1 ½ cups water into instant pot, then insert trivet.
5. Place parchment paper packet on top of the trivet.
6. Seal pot with lid and cook on manual high pressure for 8 minutes.
7. Quick release pressure then open the lid.
8. Serve and enjoy.

Nutrition information per serving:
Calories: 186; Carbohydrates: 5.8g; Protein: 33.2g; Fat: 5.2g; Sugar: 1.1g; Sodium: 141mg

Balsamic Salmon

(Servings: 2|Cooking Time: 3 minutes)

Ingredients:
- 2 salmon fillets
- 1 cup water
- 2 tbsp. balsamic vinegar
- 2 tbsp. honey
- Pepper
- Salt

Directions for Cooking:
1. Season salmon fish fillets with pepper and salt.
2. In a small bowl, mix together vinegar and honey. Brush on top of fish fillets.
3. Pour water into instant pot then insert trivet.
4. Place seasoned fish fillets skin side down on top of the trivet.
5. Seal pot with lid and cook on manual high pressure for 3 minutes.
6. Release pressure using quick release method then open lid.
7. Remove fish fillets and garnish with parsley.
8. Serve and enjoy.

Nutrition information per serving:
Calories: 303; Carbohydrates: 17.5g; Protein: 34.6g; Fat: 11g; Sugar: 17.3g; Sodium: 34.6mg

Shrimp Gumbo

(Servings: 4|Cooking Time: 25 minutes)

Ingredients:

- 1 lb. shrimp, peeled and deveined
- 1 bay leaf
- 2/3 cup chicken stock
- 14.5 oz. can tomatoes, drained and diced
- 2 tbsp. creole seasoning
- 1 onion, diced
- 2 celery ribs, diced
- 1 bell pepper, diced
- 12 oz. andouille sausage, sliced
- 2 tbsp. olive oil
- Pepper
- Salt

Directions for Cooking:

1. Add oil into instant pot and set on Sauté mode.
2. Add sausage into the pot and sauté until brown, about 2-3 minutes.
3. Remove sausage from pot and place on a plate.
4. Add pepper, seasoning, onion and celery to the pot. Sauté for 1-2 minutes.
5. Return sausage to the pot with stock, bay leaf and tomatoes. Stir well.
6. Seal pot with lid and cook on manual high pressure for 5 minutes.
7. Allow pressure to release naturally for 5 minutes, then release using quick release method.
8. Set pot on Sauté mode. Add shrimp and sauté for 3-4 minutes. Season with pepper and salt.
9. Serve and enjoy.

Nutrition information per serving:
Calories: 531; Carbohydrates: 15.6g; Protein: 43.7g; Fat: 32.4g; Sugar: 7g; Sodium: 3310mg

Quick Garlic Mussels

(Servings: 4|Cooking Time: 6 minutes)

Ingredients:

- 2 lbs. mussels, cleaned
- ½ cup white wine
- ½ cup chicken broth
- 3 garlic cloves, minced
- 2 shallots, chopped
- 2 tbsp. butter

Directions for Cooking:

1. Add butter to the instant pot and set on Sauté mode.
2. Add onion to the pot and sauté until softened
3. Add garlic and sauté for 1 minute.
4. Add remaining ingredients and stir well.
5. Seal pot with lid and cook on manual high pressure for 5 minutes.
6. Allow pressure to release naturally, then open lid.
7. Stir well and serve.

Nutrition information per serving:
Calories: 279; Carbohydrates: 10g; Protein: 27.8g; Fat: 11g; Sugar: 0.3g; Sodium: 787mg

Shrimp Risotto

(Servings: 6|Cooking Time: 16 minutes)

Ingredients:

- 1 ½ cups Arborio rice
- ¼ cup parmesan cheese, grated
- 3/4 lb. shrimp, cooked
- 1 cup asparagus, chopped

- 1 tbsp. butter
- 3 ½ cups chicken stock
- ½ cup white wine
- 1 cup cremini mushrooms, sliced
- 1 small onion, diced
- 2 tsp. olive oil
- ½ tsp. pepper
- Salt

Directions for Cooking:

1. Add oil into instant pot and set on Sauté mode.
2. Add onion to the pot and sauté for 2-3 minutes.
3. Add mushrooms and cook for 4-5 minutes.

4. Add rice and sauté until lightly brown.
5. Add stock and wine; stir well.
6. Seal pot with lid and cook on manual high pressure for 6 minutes,
7. Quick release pressure then open the lid.
8. Set pot on Sauté mode. Add asparagus and butter; sauté for 1 minute.
9. Add shrimp and cook until shrimp are pink, about 1 minute.
10. Add cheese and stir until melted.
11. Serve and enjoy.

Nutrition information per serving:
Calories: 329; Carbohydrates: 42.2g; Protein: 19.4g; Fat: 6.6g; Sugar: 1.7g; Sodium: 731mg

Basil Tomato Tilapia

(Servings: 4|Cooking Time: 4 minutes)

Ingredients:

- 4 tilapia fillets
- 2 tbsp. olive oil
- ¼ cup basil, chopped
- 2 garlic cloves, minced
- 3 tomatoes, chopped
- ½ cup water
- 1/8 tsp. pepper
- ¼ tsp. salt

Directions for Cooking:

1. Pour water into instant pot.
2. Add fish fillets into instant pot steamer basket and season with pepper and salt.

3. Seal pot with lid and cook on manual high pressure for 2 minutes.
4. Quick release pressure then open the lid.
5. In a bowl, mix together tomatoes, oil, garlic, vinegar, pepper and salt.
6. Place cooked fish fillets on serving dish and top with tomato mixture.
7. Serve and enjoy.

Nutrition information per serving:
Calories: 219; Carbohydrates: 4.2g; Protein: 33g; Fat: 9.2g; Sugar: 2.5g; Sodium: 212mg

Shrimp Herb Risotto

(Servings: 4|Cooking Time: 17 minutes)

Ingredients:

- 1 lb. shrimp, peeled, deveined, and chopped
- ½ cup parmesan cheese, grated
- 1 cup clam juice
- 3 cups chicken stock
- ¼ cup dry sherry
- 1 ½ cups Arborio rice
- 1 tbsp. sweet paprika

- 1 tbsp. oregano, minced
- 1 red pepper, chopped
- 1 onion, chopped
- 2 tbsp. butter
- ½ tsp. pepper
- ½ tsp. salt

Directions for Cooking:

1. Add butter into instant pot and set on Sauté mode.
2. Add onion and pepper and sauté until onion is softened.
3. Add paprika, oregano, pepper, and salt. Stir for minute.
4. Add rice and stir for a minute. Add sherry, clam juice and stock. Stir well.
5. Seal pot with lid and cook on manual high pressure for 10 minutes.
6. Quick release pressure then open the lid.
7. Set pot on Sauté mode. Add shrimp and cook for 2 minutes.
8. Add cheese and stir until melted.
9. Serve and enjoy.

Nutrition information per serving:
Calories: 583; Carbohydrates: 72.2g; Protein: 38.5g; Fat: 13.6g; Sugar: 5.4g; Sodium: 1707mg

Tuna Cheese Noodles

(Servings: 6|Cooking Time: 4 minutes)

Ingredients:
- 3 cups water
- 4 oz. cheddar cheese, shredded
- 28 oz. can cream of mushroom soup
- 1 cup frozen peas
- 16 oz. egg noodles
- 1 can tuna, drained

Directions for Cooking:
1. Add noodles and water into instant pot.
2. Add cream of mushroom soup, peas, and tuna on top of noodles.
3. Seal pot with lid and cook on manual high pressure for 4 hours.
4. Quick release pressure then open the lid.
5. Add cheese and stir well.
6. Serve and enjoy.

Nutrition information per serving:
Calories: 325; Carbohydrates: 33.8g; Protein: 19g; Fat: 12.5g; Sugar: 4.5g; Sodium: 665mg

Healthy Fish Fillet

(Servings: 2|Cooking Time: 28 minutes)

Ingredients:
- 2 fish fillets, skinned and deboned
- 1 bell pepper, cut into strips
- ½ onion, sliced
- 1 carrot, sliced
- 1 zucchini, sliced
- ¼ tsp. basil
- 4 tbsp. olive oil
- ¼ tsp. seasoned salt
- 1 ½ cups water

Directions for Cooking:
1. Add all vegetables into the center of large piece of parchment paper.
2. Drizzle 2 tablespoons of oil over veggies.
3. Place fish fillets on top of veggies.
4. Drizzle remaining oil on top of fish fillets. Season fish fillets with basil and seasoned salt.
5. Fold parchment paper around the veggies and fish fillets to make a parchment paper pocket.
6. Pour water into instant pot then insert trivet.
7. Place fish fillet pocket on top of the trivet.
8. Seal pot with lid and cook on manual high pressure for 28 minutes.
9. Quick release pressure then open the lid.
10. Serve and enjoy.

Nutrition information per serving:
Calories: 509; Carbohydrates: 28.8g; Protein: 15.7g; Fat: 39.5g; Sugar: 7.4g; Sodium: 708mg

Mediterranean Fish Fillet

(Servings: 6|Cooking Time: 15 minutes)

Ingredients:

- 1 ½ lbs. cod
- 28 oz. can tomatoes, diced
- 1 tsp. oregano
- 1 onion, sliced
- 1 lemon, sliced
- 3 tbsp. butter
- ½ tsp. pepper
- 1 tsp. salt

Directions for Cooking:

1. Add butter into the pot and set on Sauté mode.
2. Add remaining ingredients except for cod and cook for 8-10 minutes.
3. Arrange cod fillets on top of sauce mixture in the instant pot.
4. Seal pot with lid and cook on manual high pressure for 5 minutes.
5. Quick release pressure then open the lid.
6. Serve and enjoy.

Nutrition information per serving:

Calories: 207; Carbohydrates: 8.7g; Protein: 27.4g; Fat: 6.8g; Sugar: 5.3g; Sodium: 799mg

Coconut Shrimp Curry

(Servings: 2|Cooking Time: 1 minute)

Ingredients:

- 1 lb. frozen shrimp
- 2 tbsp. fresh cilantro, chopped
- 2 tbsp. coconut milk
- ½ tsp. garam masala
- ½ cup water
- 1/8 tsp. cayenne
- 3/4 cup onion masala
- ½ tsp. salt

Directions for Cooking:

1. Add all ingredients into instant pot except coconut milk and cilantro.
2. Stir well and seal pot with lid and select high pressure for 1 minute.
3. Quick release pressure then open the lid.
4. Stir in coconut milk and garnish with cilantro.
5. Serve and enjoy.

Nutrition information per serving:

Calories: 276; Carbohydrates: 3g; Protein: 46.7g; Fat: 7.7g; Sugar: 0.5g; Sodium: 928mg

Easy Sweet & Sour Fish

(Servings: 3|Cooking Time: 20 minutes)

Ingredients:

- 1 lb. fish chunks
- ½ tbsp. sugar
- 1 tbsp. olive oil
- 1 tbsp. vinegar
- 1 tbsp. soy sauce
- Pepper
- Salt

Directions for Cooking:

1. Add oil into instant pot and set on Sauté mode.
2. Add fish chunks and sauté for 3 minutes.
3. Add remaining ingredients and stir well to combine.
4. Seal pot with lid and select manual high pressure for 6 minutes.
5. Allow pressure to release naturally, then open lid.
6. Stir well and serve.

Nutrition information per serving:

Calories: 245; Carbohydrates: 2.5g; Protein: 36g; Fat: 9.2g; Sugar: 2.1g; Sodium: 921mg

Shrimp with Asparagus

(Servings: 4|Cooking Time: 2 minutes)

Ingredients:
- 1 lb. shrimp, peeled and deveined
- ½ tbsp. Cajun seasoning
- 1 cup water
- 1 tsp. olive oil
- 16 asparagus spear

Directions for Cooking:
1. Pour water into instant pot then place the steam rack inside.
2. Place asparagus on a steam rack in a single layer.
3. Place shrimp on the top of asparagus. Sprinkle Cajun seasoning and olive oil over the shrimp.
4. Seal pot with lid and select Steam mode. Cook on low pressure for 2 minutes.
5. Quick release pressure then open the lid.
6. Serve and enjoy.

Nutrition information per serving:
Calories: 164; Carbohydrates: 5.4g; Protein: 28g; Fat: 3.2g; Sugar: 1.8g; Sodium: 297mg

Coconut Garlic Shrimp

(Servings: 4|Cooking Time: 4 minutes)

Ingredients:
- 1 lb. shrimp, deveined
- ½ tsp. cayenne pepper
- 1 tsp. garam masala
- 1 tbsp. ginger, minced
- ½ tsp. turmeric
- 1 tbsp. garlic, minced
- 6.5 oz. unsweetened coconut milk
- 1 tsp. salt

Directions for Cooking:
1. Add all ingredients into the microwave safe bowl. Stir well and cover the bowl with foil.
2. Pour 1 cup water into instant pot, then insert trivet.
3. Place bowl on top of trivet. Seal pot with lid and cook on low pressure for 4 minutes.
4. Quick release pressure then open the lid.
5. Serve and enjoy.

Nutrition information per serving:
Calories: 250; Carbohydrates: 6.2g; Protein: 27.2g; Fat: 13.1g; Sugar: 1.6g; Sodium: 867mg

Quick Shrimp

(Servings: 6|Cooking Time: 1 minute)

Ingredients:
- 28 oz. frozen shrimp, deveined
- ½ cup apple cider vinegar
- ½ cup chicken stock

Directions for Cooking:
1. Add all ingredients into instant pot and stir well.
2. Seal pot with lid and cook on manual high pressure for 1 minute.
3. Quick release pressure then open the lid.
4. Serve and enjoy.

Nutrition information per serving:
Calories: 146; Carbohydrates: 1.4g; Protein: 27.1g; Fat: 2.4g; Sugar: 0.1g; Sodium: 264mg

Shrimp Grits

(Servings: 6|Cooking Time: 7 minutes)

Ingredients:

- 1 lb. shrimp, thawed
- ¼ tsp. red pepper flakes
- 1 tsp. smoked paprika
- 2 tbsp. cilantro, chopped
- ½ cup cheddar cheese, shredded
- ½ cup quick grits
- 1 tbsp. butter
- 1 ½ cups chicken broth
- 1 tbsp. coconut oil
- ½ tsp. kosher salt

Directions for Cooking:

1. Add oil into the pot and select Sauté mode.
2. Add shrimp into the pot and cook until they turn pink. Season with red pepper flakes and salt.
3. Remove shrimp from the pot and set aside.
4. Add remaining ingredients into the pot and mix well.
5. Seal pot with lid and select manual high pressure for 7 minutes.
6. Allow pressure to release naturally, then open lid.
7. Add cheese and stir until melted.
8. Top with shrimp and serve.

Nutrition information per serving:

Calories: 222; Carbohydrates: 12.1g; Protein: 21.9g; Fat: 9.2g; Sugar: 0.3g; Sodium: 641mg

Chili Lemon Fish Fillets

(Servings: 4|Cooking Time: 5 minutes)

Ingredients:

- 4 salmon fillets
- 2 tbsp. chili pepper
- 1 lemon juice
- 1 cup water
- Pepper
- Salt

Directions for Cooking:

1. Season salmon fillet with chili pepper, lemon juice, pepper and salt.
2. Place steam rack into the bottom of the instant pot.
3. Pour 1 cup water into the pot and place salmon fillets over the steam rack.
4. Seal pot with lid and select manual high pressure for 5 minutes.
5. Quick release pressure then open the lid.
6. Serve and enjoy.

Nutrition information per serving:

Calories: 242; Carbohydrates: 1.1g; Protein: 34.7g; Fat: 11.2g; Sugar: 0.7g; Sodium: 122mg

Tender Turkey Breast

(Servings: 8|Cooking Time: 30 minutes)

Ingredients:

- 6 lbs. turkey breast
- 1 tsp. thyme
- 1 ½ cups chicken broth
- 1 onion, peeled and quartered
- 1 celery rib, cut into 1-inch pieces
- Pepper
- Salt

Directions for Cooking:

1. Pour chicken broth into instant pot.

2. Add celery, onion and thyme into the chicken broth.
3. Season turkey breast with pepper and salt.
4. Insert trivet into instant pot, then place seasoned turkey breast on trivet.
5. Seal pot with lid and select manual. Set timer for 30 minutes.
6. Allow pressure to release naturally, then open lid.
7. Transfer turkey breast to serving dish.
8. Slice and serve.

Nutrition information per serving:
Calories: 367; Carbohydrates: 15.9g; Protein: 59.1g; Fat: 5.9g; Sugar: 12.7g; Sodium: 3616mg

Creamy Turkey Breast

(Servings: 6|Cooking Time: 25 minutes)

Ingredients:
- 4 lbs. turkey breast, boneless
- 1 ½ cups chicken broth
- 2 tbsp. onion soup mix
- 1 cup celery, diced

Directions for Cooking:
1. Pour chicken broth into instant pot.
2. Add celery into the broth. Place trivet into instant pot.
3. Place turkey breast on trivet then sprinkle onion soup mix over the turkey breast.
4. Seal pot with lid and cook on manual high pressure for 25 minutes.
5. Allow pressure to release naturally, then open lid.
6. Serve and enjoy.

Nutrition information per serving:
Calories: 332; Carbohydrates: 14.8g; Protein: 53g; Fat: 5.4g; Sugar: 11.7g; Sodium: 3554mg

Salmon Chowder

(Servings: 4|Cooking Time: 8 minutes)

Ingredients:
- 1 lb. frozen salmon
- 1 cup can corn
- 1 potato, cubed
- 2 cups half and half
- 4 cups vegetable broth
- 2 garlic cloves, minced
- 2 tbsp. butter
- 2 celery stalk, chopped
- 1 small onion, chopped

Directions for Cooking:
1. Add butter into instant pot and select Sauté mode.
2. Add onion and garlic into the pot, and sauté for 3 minutes.
3. Add remaining ingredients, except for half and a half, and stir well.
4. Seal pot with lid and cook on manual high pressure for 5 minutes.
5. Allow pressure to release naturally, then open lid.
6. Add half and half; stir well.
7. Serve and enjoy.

Nutrition information per serving:
Calories: 559; Carbohydrates: 23.6g; Protein: 36.4g; Fat: 35g; Sugar: 3.3g; Sodium: 1056mg

Shellfish with Sausage

(Servings: 6|Cooking Time: 5 minutes)

Ingredients:

- ½ cup parsley, chopped
- 1 lb. frozen shrimp
- 1 ½ cups sausage, sliced
- 3 ears corn, cut in thirds
- 1 lemon, wedges
- 2 cups chicken broth
- 1 tbsp. old bay seasoning
- 6 small potatoes, diced
- 4 garlic cloves, minced
- 1 large onion, chopped

Directions for Cooking:

1. Add all ingredients into instant pot.
2. Seal pot with lid and cook on manual high pressure for 5 minutes.
3. Quick release pressure then open the lid.
4. Serve and enjoy.

Nutrition information per serving:

Calories: 331; Carbohydrates: 50.6g; Protein: 24.6g; Fat: 4.3g; Sugar: 6.1g; Sodium: 812mg

Steamed Fish Filets

(Servings: 4|Cooking Time: 2 minutes)

Ingredients:

- 1 lb. fish fillets, cut in half
- 1 ½ cup chicken stock
- ½ cup green chutney

Directions for Cooking:

1. Place fish fillets on the center of aluminum foil.
2. Pour green chutney over fish filets and wrap foil around fish.
3. Pour stock into instant pot then insert trivet. Place fish wrap on trivet.
4. Seal pot with lid and cook on low pressure for 2 minutes.
5. Allow pressure to release naturally, then open lid.
6. Serve and enjoy.

Nutrition information per serving:

Calories: 267; Carbohydrates: 19.5g; Protein: 16.9g; Fat: 14.2g; Sugar: 0.3g; Sodium: 890mg

Orange Ginger Fish Fillets

(Servings: 4|Cooking Time: 7 minutes)

Ingredients:

- 4 white fish fillets
- 1 orange juice
- 1 tbsp. olive oil
- 1 cup chicken stock
- 1 tbsp. ginger, chopped
- Pepper
- Salt

Directions for Cooking:

1. Add fish fillets into steamer basket.
2. Add remaining ingredients into instant pot; stir well.
3. Place steamer basket into instant pot.
4. Seal pot with lid and cook on manual high pressure for 7 minutes.
5. Allow pressure to release naturally, then open lid.
6. Serve and enjoy.

Nutrition information per serving:

Calories: 312; Carbohydrates: 3.4g; Protein: 38.1 g; Fat: 15.3g; Sugar: 2g; Sodium: 330mg

Shrimp with Beans

(Servings: 4|Cooking Time: 5 minutes)

Ingredients:

- 1 lb. frozen shrimp
- 1 ½ cups chicken broth
- 2 tbsp. garlic, minced
- 14.5 oz. can black beans, rinsed and drained
- 1 cup rice
- ¼ cup butter
- Salt and Pepper

Directions for Cooking:

1. Add butter into instant pot and select Sauté mode.
2. Add rice into the pot and sauté until brown.
3. Add remaining ingredients into the pot and stir well.
4. Seal pot with lid and cook on manual high pressure for 5 minutes.
5. Allow pressure to release naturally, then open lid.
6. Stir well and serve.

Nutrition information per serving:
Calorie: 507; Carbohydrates: 57.9g; Protein: 34.2 g; Fat: 14.8g; Sugar: 1.2g; Sodium: 960mg

Cajun Fish Fillet

(Servings: 6|Cooking Time: 2 minutes)

Ingredients:

- 1 ½ lbs. mahi-mahi fillets
- 1 tbsp. Cajun seasoning
- 2 tbsp. olive oil
- ½ tbsp. garlic powder

Directions for Cooking:

1. Pour 1 cup water into instant pot then place trivet into the pot.
2. Place fish filets on trivet; sprinkle with Cajun seasoning and garlic powder.
3. Seal pot with lid and cook on manual high pressure for 1 minute.
4. Quick release pressure then open the lid.
5. Heat oil in pan over medium heat.
6. Place fish fillets in the hot pan and cook for 2 minutes.
7. Serve and enjoy.

Nutrition information per serving:
Calorie: 143; Carbohydrates: 0.5g; Protein: 21.6g; Fat: 5.7g; Sugar: 0.2g; Sodium: 170mg

Easy and Quick Salmon

(Servings: 2|Cooking Time: 4 minutes)

Ingredients:

- 2 salmon fillets
- 1 cup water
- 2 tbsp. olive oil
- Pepper
- Sea salt

Directions for Cooking:

1. Pour water into instant pot and insert trivet. Place salmon on trivet.
2. Seal pot with lid and cook on low for 2 minutes.
3. Quick release pressure then open the lid.
4. Heat oil in pan over medium heat.
5. Season salmon with pepper and salt. Place skin side down in the pan and cook for 2 minutes.
6. Serve and enjoy.

Nutrition information per serving:
Calorie: 356; Carbohydrates: 0g; Protein: 34.5g; Fat: 25g; Sugar: 0g; Sodium: 82mg

Alaskan Lemon Fish Filet

(Servings: 3|Cooking Time: 5 minutes)

Ingredients:

- 3 wild Alaskan salmon fillets
- 1 cup chicken stock
- 2 lemons, sliced
- Pepper
- Salt

Directions for Cooking:

1. Pour stock into instant pot then insert steamer rack.
2. Place salmon fillets on steamer rack and season with pepper and salt.
3. Place lemon slices on salmon fillets.
4. Seal pot with lid and cook on the manual setting for 5 minutes.
5. Quick release pressure then open the lid carefully.
6. Serve and enjoy.

Nutrition information per serving:
Calorie: 259; Carbohydrates: 5.4g; Protein: 30.6g; Fat: 14.3g; Sugar: 2.7g; Sodium: 476mg

Asian Salmon

(Servings: 2|Cooking Time: 2 minutes)

Ingredients:

- 2 salmon fillets
- 2 tbsp. maple syrup
- 3 tbsp. coconut aminos
- 1 tbsp. brown sugar
- 1 tbsp. coconut oil
- 1 tsp. sesame seeds
- ¼ tsp. ginger
- 1 tsp. paprika

Directions for Cooking:

1. Add coconut oil into instant pot and select Sauté mode.
2. Add brown sugar into the pot and stir until melted.
3. Add maple syrup, coconut aminos, ginger and paprika; stir well.
4. Place salmon fillets skin side down into the pot. Season with pepper and salt.
5. Seal pot with lid and cook on low for 2 minutes.
6. Allow pressure to release naturally, then open lid.
7. Garnish with sesame seeds and serve.

Nutrition information per serving:
Calorie: 398; Carbohydrates: 23.4g; Protein: 35g; Fat: 18.7g; Sugar: 16.4g; Sodium: 108mg

Garlic Cajun Fish Fillet

(Servings: 8|Cooking Time: 3 minutes)

Ingredients:

- 1 ½ lbs. fish filets
- ½ tbsp. garlic powder
- 1 tbsp. Cajun seasoning
- 2 tbsp. coconut oil
- 1 cup water

Directions for Cooking:

1. Pour water into instant pot then insert trivet.
2. Place fish filets on trivet. Season with Cajun seasoning and garlic powder.
3. Seal pot with lid and cook on manual high pressure for 1 minute.
4. Quick release pressure then open the lid.
5. Heat oil in pan over medium heat. Place fish fillets in the hot pan and cook for 2 minutes.
6. Serve and enjoy.

Nutrition information per serving:
Calorie: 228; Carbohydrates: 13.9g; Protein: 12.6g; Fat: 13.9g; Sugar: 0.1g; Sodium: 471mg

Flavorful Salmon Casserole

(Servings: 3|Cooking Time: 8 minutes)

Ingredients:

- 14.5 oz. can cream of celery soup
- 2 cups frozen vegetables
- 1 tsp. garlic, minced
- ¼ cup olive oil
- 2 frozen salmon pieces
- 2 cups milk
- 2 cups chicken broth
- Pepper
- Salt

Directions for Cooking:

1. Add all ingredients into instant pot and stir well.
2. Seal pot with lid and cook on manual high pressure for 8 minutes.
3. Quick release pressure then open the lid.
4. Stir well and serve.

Nutrition information per serving:

Calorie: 547; Carbohydrates: 34.5g; Protein: 26.6g; Fat: 34g; Sugar: 13.4g; Sodium: 1700mg

Ginger White Fish Fillets

(Servings: 4|Cooking Time: 7 minutes)

Ingredients:

- 4 white fish fillets
- 1 tbsp. ginger, chopped
- 1 orange juice
- 1 tbsp. olive oil
- 1 cup chicken stock
- 3 spring onions
- Pepper
- Salt

Directions for Cooking:

1. Add fish fillets into steamer basket.
2. Add remaining ingredients into instant pot. Stir well.
3. Place steamer basket into instant pot.
4. Seal pot with lid and cook on manual high pressure for 7 minutes.
5. Allow pressure to release naturally, then open lid.
6. Place fish fillets on serving the dish and pour pot sauce over fillets.
7. Serve and enjoy.

Nutrition information per serving:

Calories: 315; Carbohydrates: 4.2g; Protein: 38.3g; Fat: 15.4g; Sugar: 2.3g; Sodium: 332mg

Veggies Shrimp Risotto

(Servings: 6|Cooking Time: 5 minutes)

Ingredients:

- 1 cup jasmine rice
- ¼ cup parmesan cheese, shredded
- 1 lb. frozen shrimp
- 2 tbsp. butter
- 1 cup water
- ¼ cup frozen vegetables
- 1 tbsp. lemon juice
- Pepper
- Salt

Directions for Cooking:

1. Add butter into the pot and set on Sauté mode.
2. Add rice, lemon juice, water, pepper and salt. Stir well.
3. Add remaining ingredients into the pot and stir well.

4. Seal pot with lid and cook on manual high pressure for 5 minutes.
5. Quick release pressure then open the lid.
6. Stir well and serve.

Nutrition information per serving:
Calories: 134; Carbohydrates: 7.7g; Protein: 17.5g; Fat: 6.1g; Sugar: 0.3g; Sodium: 229mg

Chicken Prawn jambalaya

(Servings: 6|Cooking Time: 2 minutes)

Ingredients:
- 1 lb. sausage, cooked and sliced
- 1 tbsp. Worcestershire sauce
- 1 tbsp. creole seasoning
- 2 cups bell pepper, diced
- 2 cups onion, diced
- 1 lb. shrimp
- 1 lb. chicken breasts, diced
- 2 tbsp. olive oil
- 1 cup tomatoes, crushed
- 3 ½ cups chicken stock
- 1 ½ cups rice
- 2 tbsp. garlic, minced

Directions for Cooking:
1. Add all ingredients except shrimp and sausage into instant pot. Stir well.
2. Seal pot with lid and select rice setting.
3. Quick release pressure then open the lid.
4. Add shrimp and sausage. Stir well.
5. Seal pot with lid and cook on manual high pressure for 2 minutes.
6. Quick release pressure then open the lid.
7. Stir well and serve.

Nutrition information per serving:
Calories: 744; Carbohydrates: 47.7g; Protein: 58.7g; Fat: 33.8g; Sugar: 5.4g; Sodium: 835mg

Delicious Carrot Shrimp Rice

(Servings: 3|Cooking Time: 7 minutes)

Ingredients:
- 1 egg
- 1/8 tsp. cayenne pepper
- 2 cups water
- 1 small onion, chopped
- 6 oz. frozen shrimp, peeled
- 1 cup rice, rinsed and drained
- 3/4 cup frozen carrots and peas
- 2 garlic cloves, minced
- ¼ tsp. ground ginger
- 2 tbsp. soy sauce
- 1 ½ tbsp. olive oil
- Pepper
- Salt

Directions for Cooking:
1. Add 1 tbsp. olive oil in instant pot and set on Sauté mode.
2. Add egg into the pot; scramble.
3. Remove scrambled egg from the pot and set aside.
4. Add remaining oil with garlic and onion. Sauté for 2 minutes.
5. Add carrots, peas, shrimp, rice, water, ginger, soy sauce, pepper and salt. Mix well.
6. Seal pot with lid and cook on manual high pressure for 5 minutes.
7. Quick release pressure then open the lid.
8. Add scrambled egg and mix well.
9. Serve and enjoy.

Nutrition information per serving:
Calories: 404; Carbohydrates: 57.8g; Protein: 20.1g; Fat: 10.1g; Sugar: 3.1g; Sodium: 794mg

Dill Salmon

(Servings: 4 | Cooking Time: 5 minutes)

Ingredients:

- 4 salmon fillets
- 3/4 cup water
- ¼ cup lemon juice
- 1 tbsp. butter
- 1 bunch fresh dill weed
- ¼ tsp. black pepper
- ¼ tsp. salt

Directions for Cooking:

1. Pour water and lemon juice into instant pot then insert steamer rack.
2. Place salmon fillets on steamer rack and sprinkle with dill.
3. Seal pot with lid and cook on manual high pressure for 5 minutes.
4. Quick release pressure then open the lid.
5. Serve hot with butter, pepper and salt.

Nutrition information per serving:
Calories: 265; Carbohydrates: 0.4g; Protein: 34.7g; Fat: 14g; Sugar: 0.3g; Sodium: 251mg

Poached Salmon

(Servings: 4 | Cooking Time: 4 minutes)

Ingredients:

- 16 oz. salmon fillet
- ¼ cup fresh dill
- ½ tsp. fennel seeds
- 3 black peppercorns
- 1 lemon zest
- 4 scallions, chopped
- 2 cups chicken broth
- ½ cup dry white wine
- 1 bay leaf
- 1 tsp. white wine vinegar
- Pepper
- Salt

Directions for Cooking:

1. Place a steamer basket into instant pot.
2. Season salmon fillet with pepper and salt. Place in steamer basket.
3. Cover fish with vinegar, wine and broth, then add remaining ingredients.
4. Seal pot with lid and cook on manual high pressure for 4 minutes.
5. Quick release pressure then open the lid carefully.
6. Serve and enjoy.

Nutrition information per serving:
Calories: 207; Carbohydrates: 4.2g; Protein: 25.4g; Fat: 7.9g; Sugar: 0.9g; Sodium: 481mg

Rice Fish Pilaf

(Servings: 2 | Cooking Time: 5 minutes)

Ingredients:

- 2 salmon fillet
- 1 tbsp. butter
- ½ cup jasmine rice
- 1 cup chicken broth
- ¼ cup dried vegetable soup mix
- ¼ tsp. sea salt

Directions for Cooking:

1. Add all ingredients except salmon into instant pot and stir well.
2. Place steamer rack above the rice mixture, then arrange salmon fillets on steamer rack.
3. Season salmon with pepper and salt.
4. Seal pot with lid and cook on manual high pressure for 5 minutes.
5. Quick release pressure then open the lid.

6. Serve and enjoy.

Nutrition information per serving:

Calories: 339; Carbohydrates: 15.1g; Protein: 38.8g; Fat: 18.4g; Sugar: 2.2g; Sodium: 1142mg

Salmon with Orange Sauce

(Servings: 4|Cooking Time: 3 minutes)

Ingredients:

- 1 lb. salmon fillets
- 2 tsp. ginger, minced
- 1 tbsp. soy sauce
- 2 tbsp. marmalade
- 1 tsp. garlic, minced
- 1 tsp. ground pepper
- 1 tsp. salt

Directions for Cooking:

1. Place salmon into the zip-lock bag.
2. Combine together all remaining ingredients into the bowl. Pour over salmon and allow to marinate for 30 minutes.
3. Pour 2 cups water into instant pot then insert steamer rack.
4. Place marinated salmon fillet on steamer rack.
5. Seal pot with lid and cook on low for 3 minutes.
6. Allow pressure to release naturally, then open lid.
7. Serve and enjoy.

Nutrition information per serving:

Calories: 182; Carbohydrates: 8.1g; Protein: 22.5g; Fat: 7.1g; Sugar: 6.1g; Sodium: 863mg

Fish Fillet with Chili Lime Sauce

(Servings: 2|Cooking Time: 5 minutes)

Ingredients:

- 2 salmon fillets
- 1 cup water
- Black pepper
- Sea salt
- For sauce:
- ½ tsp. cumin
- 1 tbsp. olive oil
- 1 tbsp. honey
- 1 garlic cloves, minced
- 1 lime juice
- 1 jalapeno pepper, seeds removed and diced
- ½ tsp. paprika
- 1 tbsp. parsley, chopped
- 1 tbsp. hot water

Directions for Cooking:

1. In a small bowl, combine all sauce ingredients and set aside.
2. Pour water into instant pot then insert steamer rack.
3. Season salmon with pepper and salt. Place on top of steamer rack.
4. Seal pot with lid and cook on manual high pressure for 5 minutes.
5. Quick release pressure then open the lid carefully.
6. Place salmon on serving dish and drizzle with chili lime sauce.
7. Serve and enjoy.

Nutrition information per serving:

Calories: 336; Carbohydrates: 10.2g; Protein: 35g; Fat: 18.3g; Sugar: 9g; Sodium: 85mg

Wild Alaskan Salmon

(Servings: 3|Cooking Time: 5 minutes)

Ingredients:

- 3 wild Alaskan sockeye salmon fillets
- 2 lemons, sliced
- 1 cup water
- Pepper
- Salt

Directions for Cooking:

1. Pour water into instant pot then insert steamer rack.
2. Place salmon fillets on top of steamer rack and season with pepper and salt.
3. Place lemon slices on salmon fillets.
4. Seal pot with lid and cook on manual high pressure for 5 minutes.
5. Quick release pressure then open the lid carefully.
6. Serve and enjoy.

Nutrition information per serving:

Calories: 182; Carbohydrates: 4.7g; Protein: 25.5g; Fat: 7.7g; Sugar: 1.1g; Sodium: 100mg

White Fish with Sauce

(Servings: 4|Cooking Time: 7 minutes)

Ingredients:

- 4 white fish fillets
- 1-inch ginger, chopped
- 1 orange juice and zest
- 1 cup fish stock
- 3 spring onions
- Olive oil
- Salt and Pepper

Directions for Cooking:

1. Rub olive oil all over the fish fillets then season with pepper and salt.
2. Pour fish stock into instant pot.
3. Add orange zest, orange juice, ginger and spring onions. Stir well.
4. Place steamer basket into the pot then place fish fillets into the steamer basket.
5. Seal pot with lid and cook on manual high pressure for 7 minutes.
6. Quick release pressure then open the lid carefully.
7. Sere and enjoy.

Nutrition information per serving:

Calories: 278; Carbohydrates: 0.9g; Protein: 39.2g; Fat: 12.1g; Sugar: 0.3g; Sodium: 232mg

Wild Alaskan Cod with Tomato

(Servings: 1|Cooking Time: 5 minutes)

Ingredients:

- 1 large wild Alaskan cod, cut into pieces
- 1 cup cherry tomatoes
- 2 tbsp. butter
- 1 cup water
- Salt and Pepper

Directions for Cooking:

1. Take one oven-safe dish which fits into instant pot. Place cherry tomatoes into the dish then place cod pieces on top of cherry tomatoes.
2. Season with pepper and salt. Top with butter. Pour water into instant pot then insert trivet.
3. Place oven-safe dish on top of the trivet.
4. Seal pot with lid and cook on manual high pressure for 5 minutes.
5. Quick release pressure then open the lid carefully.
6. Serve and enjoy.

Nutrition information per serving:

Calories: 446; Carbohydrates: 25.1g; Protein: 15.8g; Fat: 32.4g; Sugar: 6.8g; Sodium: 627mg

Flavors Sea Bass Curry

(Servings: 4|Cooking Time: 3 minutes)

Ingredients:

- 1 lb. sea bass, cut into 1-inch cubes
- 2 garlic cloves, minced
- 2 tsp. sriracha
- 1 tsp. honey
- 1 tsp. coconut aminos
- 1 tsp. fish sauce
- ¼ cup fresh cilantro, chopped
- ½ tsp. white pepper
- 1 tsp. ground ginger
- 1 tsp. ground turmeric
- 1 tbsp. red curry paste
- 1 lime juice
- 14.5 oz. coconut milk
- ½ tsp. sea salt

Directions for Cooking:

1. Place bass cubes into instant pot.
2. Mix together all remaining ingredients and pour over the bass.
3. Seal pot with lid and cook on manual high pressure for 3 minutes.
4. Quick release pressure then open the lid carefully.
5. Stir well and serve.

Nutrition information per serving:
Calories: 446; Carbohydrates: 25.1g; Protein: 15.8g; Fat: 32.4g; Sugar: 6.8g; Sodium: 627mg

Shrimp Cheese & Tomatoes

(Servings: 6|Cooking Time: 1 minute)

Ingredients:

- 1 lb. frozen shrimp
- 14.5 oz. can tomatoes
- 2 tbsp. butter
- 1 tsp. oregano
- 1 tsp. salt
- ¼ cup parsley, chopped
- ½ cup black olives, sliced
- 1 ½ cups onion, chopped
- ½ tsp. red pepper flakes
- 1 tbsp. garlic
- 1 cup feta cheese, crumbled

Directions for Cooking:

1. Add butter into instant pot and set on Sauté mode.
2. Add garlic and red pepper flakes. Stir well.
3. Add oregano, tomatoes, onion and salt. Stir well.
4. Add frozen shrimp and stir well.
5. Seal pot with lid and cook on low pressure for 1 minute.
6. Quick release pressure then open the lid.
7. Stir in parsley, olives and feta cheese.
8. Serve and enjoy.

Nutrition information per serving:
Calories: 223; Carbohydrates: 9.4g; Protein: 20.3g; Fat: 11.8g; Sugar: 4.6g; Sodium: 1054mg

Shrimp Alfredo

(Servings: 4|Cooking Time: 12 minutes)

Ingredients:

- 2 tsp. flour
- 1 cup parmesan cheese, grated
- 2 cups chicken broth
- 1 tbsp. olive oil
- ¼ cup onion, diced
- 1 box pasta
- 1 bag frozen shrimp, cooked
- 1 cup half and half
- Pepper
- Salt

Dircctions for Cooking:

1. Add olive oil into the pot and select Sauté mode.
2. Add onion into the pot and sauté for 5 minutes.
3. Add broth, shrimp and pasta. Stir well.
4. Seal pot with lid and cook on manual high pressure for 7 minutes.
5. Quick release pressure then open the lid.
6. Set instant pot on Sauté mode.
7. Stir in cheese, flour and half and half. Cook until thickened.
8. Season with pepper and salt.
9. Stir well and serve.

Nutrition information per serving:
Calories: 352; Carbohydrates: 13.7g; Protein: 21.9g; Fat: 21.2g; Sugar: 3.2g; Sodium: 1184mg

Shrimp Boil

(Servings: 6|Cooking Time: 4 minutes)

Ingredients:

- ½ lb. shrimp
- 12 oz. smoked sausage, cooked
- 4 ears of corn
- 16 oz. can beer
- ½ lb. tiny potatoes, cut into chunks
- 8 garlic cloves, crushed
- 2 onion, cut into chunks
- 1 tsp. red pepper flakes
- 1 tbsp. old bay seasoning
- ½ tsp. salt

Directions for Cooking:

1. Add all ingredients into instant pot and stir well.
2. Seal pot with lid and cook on manual high pressure for 4 minutes.
3. Quick release pressure then open the lid.
4. Stir well and serve.

Nutrition information per serving:
Calories: 430; Carbohydrates: 40.4g; Protein: 24.3g; Fat: 19.5g; Sugar: 14.7g; Sodium: 1076mg

Yummy Shrimp Mac 'n' Cheese

(Servings: 2|Cooking Time: 7 minutes)

Ingredients:

- 15 shrimp
- 1 tbsp. butter
- 3/4 cup cheese, shredded
- 3/4 tbsp. all-purpose flour
- 1 tbsp. Cajun spice
- 1 ¼ cups pasta
- ¼ green pepper, chopped
- ¼ red pepper, chopped
- 2/3 cup milk

Directions for Cooking:

1. Add butter into instant pot and set on Sauté mode.

2. Add peppers and sauté for 2 minutes.
3. Add pasta and water and stir well.
4. Seal pot with lid and select manual high pressure for 3 minutes.
5. Quick release pressure then open the lid.
6. Add flour and Cajun spices. Mix well.
7. Set instant pot on Sauté mode. Add shrimp and sauté for 2 minutes.
8. Stir in milk, cheese and Cajun spice.
9. Serve and enjoy.

Nutrition information per serving:
Calories: 711; Carbohydrates: 63.1g; Protein: 56.4g; Fat: 25.7g; Sugar: 5g; Sodium: 823mg

Easy Shrimp Scampi

(Servings: 6|Cooking Time: 1 minute)

Ingredients:
- 2 lbs. shrimp, cleaned and thawed
- 1 tsp. garlic
- 2 tbsp. butter
- 1 tbsp. olive oil
- 1 tbsp. lemon juice
- ½ cup chicken broth
- ½ cup water
- 1 tsp. salt

Directions for Cooking:
1. Add all ingredients into instant pot and stir well.
2. Seal pot with lid and cook on manual high pressure for 1 minute.
3. Allow pressure to release naturally, then open lid.
4. Stir well and serve.

Nutrition information per serving:
Calories: 711; Carbohydrates: 63.1g; Protein: 56.4g; Fat: 25.7g; Sugar: 5g; Sodium: 823mg

Shrimp Paella

(Servings: 4|Cooking Time: 5 minutes)

Ingredients:
- 1 lb. frozen shrimp
- 1 lemon juice
- 1/8 tsp. red pepper, crushed
- ¼ cup parsley, chopped
- ¼ cup butter
- 4 garlic cloves, minced
- 1 ½ cups chicken broth
- 1/8 tsp. saffron
- 1 cup jasmine rice
- 1 tsp. sea salt

Directions for Cooking:
1. Add all ingredients into instant pot and stir well.
2. Seal pot with lid and cook on manual high pressure for 5 minutes.
3. Quick release pressure then open the lid.
4. Stir well and serve.

Nutrition information per serving:
Calories: 246; Carbohydrates: 11.9g; Protein: 26.3g; Fat: 14.2g; Sugar: 0.8g; Sodium: 1012mg

Quick Seasoned Shrimp

(Servings: 6|Cooking Time: 1 minute)

Ingredients:

- 28 oz. frozen shrimp, deveined
- ½ cup apple cider vinegar
- 1 tsp. Creole seasoning
- ½ cup water

Directions for Cooking:

1. Add all ingredients into instant pot and stir well.
2. Seal pot with lid and cook on manual high pressure for 1 minute.
3. Quick release pressure then open the lid.
4. Stir well and serve.

Nutrition information per serving:

Calories: 145; Carbohydrates: 1.4g; Protein: 27g; Fat: 2.4g; Sugar: 0.1g; Sodium: 381mg

Spicy Coconut Shrimp

(Servings: 4|Cooking Time: 4 minutes)

Ingredients:

- 1 lb. shrimp, deveined
- ½ tsp. turmeric
- 1 tbsp. garlic, minced
- 1 tbsp. ginger, minced
- ½ can coconut milk, unsweetened
- 1 tsp. garam masala
- 1 cup water
- ½ tsp. cayenne pepper
- 1 tsp. salt

Directions for Cooking:

1. Add all ingredients into the oven-safe bowl. Mix well and cover the bowl with foil.
2. Pour water into instant pot then insert trivet.
3. Place bowl on top of the trivet. Seal pot with lid and cook on low pressure for 4 minutes.
4. Quick release pressure then open the lid.
5. Stir well and serve.

Nutrition information per serving:

Calories: 231; Carbohydrates: 4.9g; Protein: 26.8g; Fat: 11.4g; Sugar: 1.3g; Sodium: 872mg

Seafood Pulao

(Servings: 4|Cooking Time: 5 minutes)

Ingredients:

- 1 ½ cups rice
- 1 red pepper, sliced
- 3 carrots, shredded
- 1 onion, chopped
- 1 package frozen seafood blend
- 1 lemon, sliced
- 3 cups water
- 2 tbsp. butter
- ½ cup dried cranberries
- Pepper
- Salt

Directions for Cooking:

1. Add butter into instant pot and select Sauté mode.
2. Add pepper, carrots and onion into the pot. Sauté for 5 minutes.
3. Add remaining ingredients and stir well.
4. Seal pot with lid and select Rice setting.
5. Quick release pressure then open the lid.
6. Serve and enjoy.

Nutrition information per serving:

Calories: 380; Carbohydrates: 68g; Protein: 10.2g; Fat: 6.6g; Sugar: 5.9g; Sodium: 210mg

Crab Legs

(Servings: 4|Cooking Time: 2 minutes)

Ingredients:

- 2 lbs. frozen crab legs
- 3/4 cup water
- 1 lemon juice
- 4 tbsp. butter, melted

Directions for Cooking:

1. Pour water into instant pot.
2. Place crab leg into the steamer basket and insert steamer basket.
3. Seal pot with lid and cook on manual high pressure for 2 minutes.
4. Quick release pressure then open the lid.
5. Pour melted butter over crab leg and serve.

Nutrition information per serving:

Calories: 145; Carbohydrates: 145g; Protein: 0.2g; Fat: 11.9g; Sugar: 0.3g; Sodium: 555mg

Ginger Garlic Scallops

(Servings: 3|Cooking Time: 2 minutes)

Ingredients:

- 1 lb. jumbo sea scallops, thawed
- 3 tbsp. maple syrup
- ½ cup coconut aminos
- ½ tsp. ground ginger
- ½ tsp. garlic powder
- 1 tbsp. olive oil
- ½ tsp. sea salt

Directions for Cooking:

1. Add oil into instant pot and set on Sauté mode.
2. Add scallops into instant pot and sear for a minute on each side.
3. In a small bowl, whisk together all remaining ingredients and pour over scallops.
4. Seal pot with lid and select the Steam setting. Set the timer for 2 minutes.
5. Quick release pressure then open the lid.
6. Serve and enjoy.

Nutrition information per serving:

Calories: 198; Carbohydrates: 23.3g; Protein: 11.4g; Fat: 6.4g; Sugar: 12g; Sodium: 596mg

Pasta with Clam Sauce

(Servings: 4|Cooking Time: 5 minutes)

Ingredients:

- 8 oz. linguine
- 1 ½ cups water
- 3 garlic cloves, minced
- 4 tbsp. olive oil
- 1 tbsp. basil
- 1 tbsp. oregano
- ¼ cup white wine
- 2 cans clams with juice, minced
- 4 tbsp. butter
- ½ tsp. black pepper
- 1 ½ tsp. salt

Directions for Cooking:

1. Add butter into instant pot and set on Sauté mode.
2. Add remaining ingredients into the pot and stir well.
3. Seal pot with lid and select manual. Set timer for 5 minutes.
4. Allow pressure to release naturally, then open lid.
5. Stir well and serve.

Nutrition information per serving:
Calories: 405; Carbohydrates: 33.1g; Protein: 6.9g; Fat: 27g; Sugar: 0.2g; Sodium: 973mg

Simple Frozen Shrimp

(Servings: 4|Cooking Time: 5 minutes)

Ingredients:

- ½ cup water
- 1 lb. shrimp, frozen

Directions for Cooking:

1. Add water and shrimp into instant pot. Stir well.
2. Seal pot with lid and cook on manual high pressure for 1 minute.
3. Quick release pressure then open the lid.
4. Drain shrimp well and serve.

Nutrition information per serving:
Calories: 135; Carbohydrates: 1.7g; Protein: 25.8g; Fat: 1.9g; Sugar: 0g; Sodium: 278mg

Chapter 6 Instant Pot Lamb, Beef & Pork Recipes

Balsamic Beef Roast

(Servings: 6|Cooking Time: 30 minutes)

Ingredients:
- 3 lbs. beef roast, boneless and cut into pieces
- 1 tbsp. soy sauce
- 1 tbsp. Worcestershire sauce
- ½ cup balsamic vinegar
- 1 cup chicken stock
- 4 garlic cloves, chopped
- ½ tsp. red pepper flakes
- 1 tbsp. honey

Directions for Cooking:
1. Place beef roast into instant pot.
2. In a bowl, mix together all remaining ingredients and pour over beef roast.
3. Seal pot with lid and cook on manual high pressure for 30 minutes.
4. Allow pressure to release naturally, then open lid.
5. Stir well and serve.

Nutrition information per serving:
Calories: 445; Carbohydrates: 4.6g; Protein: 69.2g; Fat: 14.3g; Sugar: 3.7g; Sodium: 456mg

Delicious Country Style Ribs

(Servings: 4|Cooking Time: 45 minutes)

Ingredients:
- 3 lbs. country style pork ribs
- Dry Rub:
- 1 tsp. cumin
- 1 tsp. pepper
- 1 tsp. onion powder
- 1 tsp. garlic powder
- 3/4 cup chicken stock
- ¼ tsp. cayenne pepper
- 1 tsp. paprika
- 1 tbsp. brown sugar
- 1 tsp. salt

Directions for Cooking:
1. In a small bowl, mix together all rub ingredients and rub over meat.

2. Pour stock into instant pot then place ribs inside.
3. Seal pot with lid and cook on manual high pressure for 45 minutes.
4. Allow pressure to release naturally, then open lid.

5. Stir well and serve.
Nutrition information per serving:
Calories: 652; Carbohydrates: 4.3g; Protein: 66.8g; Fat: 39.5g; Sugar: 2.8g; Sodium: 938mg

Potato Beef Chili

(Servings: 8|Cooking Time: 35 minutes)

Ingredients:
- 2 lbs. ground beef
- 3 medium sweet potatoes, peeled and cubed
- 2 carrots, chopped
- 2 cups chicken stock
- 30 oz. tomato sauce
- ½ tsp. thyme
- 1 tsp. oregano
- 2 tbsp. chili powder
- 1 small onion, chopped
- 2 garlic cloves, minced
- 1 tsp. olive oil
- 1 ½ tsp. pepper
- 2 tsp. sea salt

Directions for Cooking:

1. Add olive oil into instant pot and set on Sauté mode.
2. Place ground beef into the pot and cook until brown.
3. Add remaining ingredients into the pot and stir well.
4. Seal pot with lid and select Meat/Stew mode. Set timer for 35 minutes.
5. Allow pressure to release naturally, then open lid.
6. Stir and serve.
Nutrition information per serving:
Calories: 276; Carbohydrates: 13.2g; Protein: 36.8g; Fat: 8.4g; Sugar: 6.7g; Sodium: 1330mg

Tender Ribs

(Servings: 4|Cooking Time: 35 minutes)

Ingredients:
- 2 ½ lbs. country-style spare ribs, boneless
- 14.5 oz. can chicken stock
- 1 tbsp. liquid smoke
- 1 tbsp. sea salt

Directions for Cooking:
1. Season spare ribs with sea salt and set aside.
2. Add liquid smoke and broth to instant pot.

3. Place spare ribs into the pot. Seal pot with lid and select Meat mode. Set timer for 35 minutes.
4. Quick release pressure then open the lid.
5. Serve and enjoy.
Nutrition information per serving:
Calories: 716; Carbohydrates: 10.9g; Protein: 68.5g; Fat: 44.8g; Sugar: 8.1g; Sodium: 2373mg

Italian Beef

(Servings: 8|Cooking Time: 60 minutes)

Ingredients:

- 5 lbs. chuck roast
- 16 oz. pepperoncini peppers, sliced
- 1 packet Italian seasoning mix
- 1 cup water
- ½ onion, sliced
- 1 tbsp. olive oil

Directions for Cooking:

1. Add olive oil into instant pot and set on Sauté mode.
2. Place meat into the pot and cook until brown for 5-6 minutes on each side.
3. Add remaining ingredients into the pot and stir well.
4. Seal pot with lid and select manual. Set timer for 55 minutes.
5. Quick release pressure then open the lid.
6. Shred the meat using a fork and serve.

Nutrition information per serving:

Calories: 630; Carbohydrates: 0.6g; Protein: 93.7g; Fat: 25.3g; Sugar: 0.3g; Sodium: 188mg

Spicy Beef Curry

(Servings: 4|Cooking Time: 20 minutes)

Ingredients:

- 1 lb. beef chuck roast, cut into pieces
- ½ tsp. cayenne pepper
- ½ cup fresh cilantro, chopped
- 4 garlic cloves, chopped
- 1 small onion, quarters
- 2 tomatoes, quarters
- 1 tsp. garam masala
- ½ tsp. ground coriander
- 1 tsp. ground cumin
- 1 tsp. salt

Directions for Cooking:

1. Add tomatoes, cilantro, garlic and onion into the blender, and blend until smooth.
2. Add cumin, cayenne, garam masala, coriander and salt. Blend until combined.
3. Place beef into instant pot then pour vegetable puree over the beef.
4. Seal pot with lid and cook on manual high pressure for 20 minutes.
5. Allow pressure to release naturally, then open lid.
6. Stir well and serve with rice.

Nutrition information per serving:

Calories: 437; Carbohydrates: 5.4g; Protein: 30.8g; Fat: 31.9g; Sugar: 2.4g; Sodium: 661mg

Apple Pork Tenderloin

(Servings: 6|Cooking Time: 7 minutes)

Ingredients:

- 2 pork tenderloins
- 1 cup chicken stock
- ¼ cup honey
- 2 cups apples, diced
- ½ tsp. nutmeg
- 1 tbsp. brown sugar
- 1 tbsp. cinnamon

Directions for Cooking:

1. Mix together all dry ingredients and rub over pork tenderloins.
2. Add stock, honey, apples and tenderloins into instant pot.

3. Seal pot with lid and select manual. Set timer for 7 minutes.
4. Quick release pressure then open the lid.
5. Slice and serve.

Nutrition information per serving:
Calories: 139; Carbohydrates: 24.5g; Protein: 8.1g; Fat: 1.6g; Sugar: 21g; Sodium: 149mg

Honey Garlic Teriyaki Pork Loin

(Servings: 4|Cooking Time: 45 minutes)

Ingredients:
- 2 lbs. pork loin
- 1 tsp. ground ginger
- 2 tbsp. brown sugar
- ½ cup water
- ¼ cup soy sauce
- 1 cup chicken stock
- 2 tbsp. honey
- 2 garlic cloves, crushed
- 1 tsp. onion powder

Directions for Cooking:
1. In a small bowl, mix together all ingredients except pork loin and stock.
2. Pour stock into instant pot.
3. Place pork into the pot then pour bowl mixture over the pork.
4. Seal pot with lid and cook select manual setting and set the timer for 45 minutes.
5. Allow pressure to release naturally, then open lid.
6. Serve and enjoy.

Nutrition information per serving:
Calories: 615; Carbohydrates: 15.8g; Protein: 63.4g; Fat: 31.8g; Sugar: 13.7g; Sodium: 1233mg

Beef Chili

(Servings: 8|Cooking Time: 35 minutes)

Ingredients:
- 1 lb. ground beef
- 6 oz. tomato paste
- ½ onion, chopped
- 3 tomatillos, chopped
- 1 lb. ground pork
- 1 tbsp. chili powder
- 1 tbsp. ground cumin
- 1 jalapeno pepper, chopped
- 1 tsp. garlic powder
- Salt

Directions for Cooking:
1. Set instant pot on Sauté mode.
2. Add beef and pork into the pot, and cook until brown.
3. Add remaining ingredients into the pot and stir well to combine.
4. Seal pot with lid and cook on manual high pressure for 35 minutes.
5. Allow pressure to release naturally, then open lid.
6. Stir and serve.

Nutrition information per serving:
Calories: 218; Carbohydrates: 6.6g; Protein: 33.5g; Fat: 6.1g; Sugar: 3.1g; Sodium: 121mg

Pork Sirloin Tip Roast

(Servings: 6|Cooking Time: 25 minutes)

Ingredients:
- 3 lbs. pork sirloin tip roast
- ¼ tsp. chili powder
- ½ tsp. garlic powder
- ½ tsp. onion powder

- ½ cup apple juice
- 1 cup water
- 1 tbsp. olive oil
- ½ tsp. black pepper
- ½ tsp. salt

Directions for Cooking:

1. Mix together all spices in a small bowl. Rub over pork.
2. Add oil into instant pot and set on Sauté mode.

3. Add pork into the pot and cook until brown.
4. Add remaining ingredients into the pot.
5. Seal pot with lid and cook on manual high pressure for 25 minutes.
6. Quick release pressure then open the lid.
7. Serve and enjoy.

Nutrition information per serving:

Calories: 234; Carbohydrates: 2.8g; Protein: 44.7g; Fat: 5.4g; Sugar: 2.1g; Sodium: 784mg

Chipotle Beef Chili

(Servings: 4|Cooking Time: 35 minutes)

Ingredients:

- 14 oz. can red kidney beans, rinsed and drained
- 1 lb. ground beef
- 2 tbsp. flour
- 1 can black beans
- 1 cup beef broth
- 1 tsp. garlic, minced
- ½ bell pepper, diced
- 1 tsp. chili powder
- 1 cup water
- ½ chipotle pepper, minced
- ½ onion, diced
- Salt

Directions for Cooking:

1. Turn instant pot to Sauté mode. Brown onion and ground beef until meat is no longer pink.
2. Add spices and garlic; sauté for a minute.
3. Add remaining ingredients except for flour and stir well.
4. Seal pot with lid. Select Meat/Stew setting and set timer for 35 minutes.
5. Quick release pressure then open the lid.
6. Whisk together flour and 3 tbsp. water; stir into instant pot.
7. Set pot on Sauté mode and cook until sauce thickens.
8. Stir well and serve.

Nutrition information per serving:

Calories: 425; Carbohydrates: 39.7g; Protein: 47.1g; Fat: 8.4g; Sugar: 4.5g; Sodium: 936mg

Pork Chops with Apple

(Servings: 4|Cooking Time: 15 minutes)

Ingredients:

- 1 ½ lbs. pork chops, boneless
- 5 tbsp. brown sugar
- 3 oz. bourbon
- 1 tbsp. honey
- ½ cup applesauce
- 1 tbsp. Worcestershire sauce
- 3 cups apple, diced
- ½ tsp. black pepper
- 1 tsp. sea salt

Directions for Cooking:

1. Place pork chops in instant pot then add diced apple, bourbon, Worcestershire sauce, applesauce, honey, brown sugar, sea salt and black pepper.
2. Seal pot with lid and select manual high pressure for 15 minutes.
3. Quick release pressure then open the lid.
4. Serve and enjoy.

Nutrition information per serving: Calories: 757; Carbohydrates: 42.8g; Protein: 38.8g; Fat: 42.6g; Sugar: 36.5g; Sodium: 634mg

Simple Flank Steak

(Servings: 2|Cooking Time: 25 minutes)

Ingredients:
- 1 lb. flank steak
- ½ tbsp. Worcestershire sauce
- 2 tbsp. apple cider vinegar
- 2 tbsp. onion soup mix
- ¼ cup olive oil

Directions for Cooking:
1. Place flank steak in instant pot and select Sauté mode. Brown the steak both the side.
2. Add olive oil, onion soup mix, vinegar and Worcestershire sauce over the steak.
3. Seal pot with lid and select manual high pressure for 25 minutes.
4. Allow pressure to release naturally, then open lid.
5. Stir and serve.

Nutrition information per serving: Calories: 678; Carbohydrates: 4.9g; Protein: 63.1g; Fat: 44.1g; Sugar: 2.8g; Sodium: 709mg

Potato Beef Roast

(Servings: 2|Cooking Time: 30 minutes)

Ingredients:
- 1 lbs. beef chunks, boneless
- 1 cups onion, diced
- 2 cups carrots, chunks
- 3 cups potato, peeled and cut into chunks
- 1 cups hot water
- 1 tbsp. onion soup mix, dried

Directions for Cooking:
1. Add beef chunks to instant pot.
2. In a mixing bowl, mix hot water and onion soup mix.
3. When completely dissolved, pour over the beef chunks.
4. Add diced onion, carrot and potato chunks into instant pot, and mix well.
5. Seal pot with lid and select Meat/Stew mode.
6. Quick release pressure, then open lid.
7. Serve and enjoy.

Nutrition information per serving: Calories: 470; Carbohydrates: 45.3g; Protein: 40.8g; Fat: 11.5g; Sugar: 11.3g; Sodium: 2943mg

Meatballs

(Servings: 8|Cooking Time: 5 minutes)

Ingredients:
- 1 lb. ground beef
- 2 cups water
- 2 bread slices, crumbled
- 1 small onion, minced
- ½ tsp. garlic salt
- 2 cups pasta sauce
- 1 egg, beaten
- 2 carrots, shredded
- Pepper
- Salt

Directions for Cooking:

1. In a mixing bowl, add ground beef, egg, carrots, crumbled bread, onion, garlic salt, pepper and salt. Mix well until combined.
2. Make round shape meatballs and set aside above mixture make 24 meatballs.
3. Pour 2 cups water and 2 cups pasta sauce into instant pot stir well to combine.
4. Add meatballs in tomato sauce mixture one by one.
5. Seal pot with lid and cook on manual high pressure for 5 minutes.
6. Allow pressure to release naturally, then open lid.
7. Serve meatballs with rice and enjoy.

Nutrition information per serving:
Calories: 184; Carbohydrates: 12.2g; Protein: 19.4g; Fat: 5.8g; Sugar: 6.8g; Sodium: 349mg

Delicious Mongolian Beef

(Servings: 4|Cooking Time: 30 minutes)

Ingredients:

- 1 ½ lbs. flank steak, sliced
- 3/4 cup coconut aminos
- ½ tsp. ginger powder
- 2 tbsp. olive oil
- ¼ cup arrowroot powder
- ½ cup carrot, grated
- 3/4 cup honey
- 3/4 cup water

Directions for Cooking:

1. Coat flank steak with arrowroot powder and set aside.
2. Add all other ingredients into instant pot and sauté for 5 minutes.
3. Add sliced beef and stir well.
4. Cover pot with lid and cook on high for 25 minutes.
5. Quick release pressure then open the lid carefully.
6. Stir and serve.

Nutrition information per serving:
Calories: 670; Carbohydrates: 70.9g; Protein: 47.6g; Fat: 21.2g; Sugar: 52.9g; Sodium: 160mg

Tasty Ground Beef

(Servings: 4|Cooking Time: 15 minutes)

Ingredients:

- 1 lb. ground beef
- ½ tsp. turmeric
- 1 tsp. garam masala
- 4 cardamom pods
- 3 cinnamon sticks
- 1 tbsp. garlic
- 1 tbsp. ginger, minced
- ¼ cup water
- ½ tsp. cumin
- ½ tsp. ground coriander
- ½ tsp. cayenne pepper
- 1 cup onion, chopped
- 1 tbsp. olive oil
- 1 tsp. salt

Directions for Cooking:

1. Add olive oil into instant pot and set on Sauté mode.
2. Add cinnamon and cardamom into the pot and sauté for 10 seconds.
3. Add ginger, garlic and onion. Sauté for 5 minutes.
4. Add ground beef and sauté for 4 minutes.
5. Add water and spices and stir well.
6. Seal pot with lid and cook on manual high pressure for 5 minutes.
7. Allow pressure to release naturally, then open lid carefully.

8. Stir well and serve.

Nutrition information per serving:

Calories: 263; Carbohydrates: 4.8g; Protein: 35.1g; Fat: 10.8g; Sugar: 1.3g; Sodium: 660mg

Easy Taco Meat

(Servings: 6|Cooking Time: 25 minutes)

Ingredients:
- 2 lbs. ground beef
- 2 tsp. onion powder
- 2 tsp. cumin
- 2 tsp. paprika
- 2 cups chicken stock
- ½ tsp. chipotle powder
- 1 tsp. ancho chili powder
- 2 tsp. garlic powder
- 1 tsp. salt

Directions for Cooking:
1. Add all ingredients into instant pot and stir well.
2. Seal pot with lid and cook on manual high pressure for 25 minutes.
3. Quick release pressure then open the lid carefully.
4. Stir well and serve.

Nutrition information per serving:
Calories: 295; Carbohydrates: 2.3g; Protein: 46.6g; Fat: 9.9g; Sugar: 0.8g; Sodium: 744mg

Thai Beef

(Servings: 8|Cooking Time: 45 minutes)

Ingredients:
- 3 lbs. chuck roast
- 1 tsp. curry powder
- 2 tbsp. olive oil
- ½ cup sweet chili sauce
- ½ cup orange juice
- 1 tsp. garlic powder
- Pepper
- Salt

Directions for Cooking:
1. Add olive oil into instant pot and set on Sauté mode.
2. Add roast into the pot and brown the roast for 2-3 minutes per side.
3. Add remaining ingredients into the pot and stir well.
4. Seal pot with lid and cook on manual high pressure for 45 minutes.
5. Quick release pressure then open the lid carefully.
6. Shred the meat using a fork.
7. Stir and serve.

Nutrition information per serving:
Calories: 436; Carbohydrates: 8g; Protein: 56.4g; Fat: 17.7g; Sugar: 7.4g; Sodium: 252mg

BBQ Short Ribs

(Servings: 4|Cooking Time: 28 minutes)

Ingredients:
- 1 lb. beef short ribs
- ½ cup BBQ sauce
- 1 cup water
- Pepper
- Salt

Directions for Cooking:
1. Season short ribs with pepper and salt. Place on dish in refrigerator for 30 minutes.
2. Pour water into instant pot then insert trivet.

3. Place ribs on top of the trivet.
4. Seal pot with lid and cook on manual high pressure for 28 minutes.
5. Allow pressure to release naturally, then open lid.
6. Place ribs on a baking tray and baste the ribs with BBQ sauce. Broil for 3 minutes.
7. Serve and enjoy.

Nutrition information per serving:
Calories: 279; Carbohydrates: 11.3g; Protein: 32.8g; Fat: 10.3g; Sugar: 8.1g; Sodium: 420mg

BBQ Shredded Pork

(Servings: 5|Cooking Time: 70 minutes)

Ingredients:
- 3 lbs. pork roast
- ½ cup BBQ sauce
- ½ cup chicken broth
- Pepper
- Salt

Directions for Cooking:
1. Season pork roast with pepper and salt.
2. Place season pork into instant pot.
3. Add BBQ sauce and broth over the pork; stir well.
4. Seal pot with lid and cook on manual high pressure for 70 minutes.
5. Allow pressure to release naturally, then open lid.
6. Using fork, shred the meat and stir well in pot sauce.
7. Serve and enjoy.

Nutrition information per serving:
Calories: 605; Carbohydrates: 9.2g; Protein: 78.1g; Fat: 25.9g; Sugar: 6.6g; Sodium: 540mg

Lemon Apple Pork Chops

(Servings: 2|Cooking Time: 10 minutes)

Ingredients:
- 2 pork chops, boneless
- 2 tbsp. lemon pepper
- ¼ cup apple juice

Directions for Cooking:
1. Season pork chops with lemon pepper.
2. Place seasoned pork chops into the pot and set on Sauté mode.
3. Sauté pork chops until lightly brown.
4. Pour apple juice over pork chops.
5. Seal pot with lid and cook on manual high pressure for 10 minutes.
6. Quick release pressure then open the lid carefully.
7. Transfer pork chops on serving dish then turn instant pot to Sauté mode until apple juice reduces.
8. Pour apple sauce over pork chops and serve.

Nutrition information per serving:
Calories: 286; Carbohydrates: 7.7g; Protein: 18.7g; Fat: 20.1g; Sugar: 3g; Sodium: 60mg

Delicious Beef Stew

(Servings: 4|Cooking Time: 30 minutes)

Ingredients:
- 2 ½ lbs. chuck roast, boneless
- 1 cup chicken stock
- ½ cup balsamic vinegar
- 1 tbsp. Worcestershire sauce

- 1 tbsp. soy sauce
- 1 tbsp. honey
- ½ tsp. red pepper flakes
- 4 garlic cloves, chopped

Directions for Cooking:
1. Add all ingredients into instant pot and stir well.
2. Seal pot with lid and cook on "Stew" high pressure for 30 minutes.
3. Allow pressure to release naturally, then open lid.
4. Serve and enjoy.

Nutrition information per serving:
Calories: 648; Carbohydrates: 7g; Protein: 94.3g; Fat: 23.7g; Sugar: 5.5g; Sodium: 647mg

Classic Lamb Leg

(Servings: 4 | Cooking Time: 15 minutes)

Ingredients:
- 2 lbs. leg of lamb, boneless and cut into chunks
- 2 tbsp. tomato paste
- ½ cup beef stock
- 1 tsp. oregano, chopped
- 2 tsp. thyme, chopped
- 1 tsp. rosemary, chopped
- 2 carrots, chopped
- 1 cup onion, chopped
- 1 cup red wine
- 4 garlic cloves, sliced
- 1 tbsp. olive oil
- Pepper
- Salt

Directions for Cooking:
1. Season meat with pepper and salt.
2. Add oil into instant pot and set on Sauté mode.
3. Add meat to the pot and sauté until brown.
4. Add garlic and sauté for 30 seconds.
5. Add red wine and stir well.
6. Add remaining ingredients to the pot and stir well.
7. Seal pot with lid and cook on manual high pressure for 15 minutes.
8. Allow pressure to release naturally, then open lid.
9. Serve and enjoy.

Nutrition information per serving:
Calories: 542; Carbohydrates: 10.6g; Protein: 65.3g; Fat: 20.4g; Sugar: 4.2g; Sodium: 343mg

Asian Pork

(Servings: 4 | Cooking Time: 10 minutes)

Ingredients:
- 1 ½ lbs. pork shoulder, boneless and cut into strips
- 1 cup scallions, chopped
- 1 tbsp. cornstarch
- 1 tbsp. water
- 3 cups cabbage, sliced
- 2 garlic cloves, minced
- 1 tbsp. sesame oil
- ¼ cup dry sherry
- ¼ cup soy sauce
- ½ cup chicken stock
- 0.5 oz. dried mushrooms, cut into pieces

Directions for Cooking:
1. Add meat into instant pot, along with garlic, oil, sherry, soy sauce, mushrooms and stock. Stir well.
2. Seal pot with lid and cook on manual high pressure for 8 minutes.
3. Allow pressure to release naturally, then open lid.

4. Add cabbage and stir well. Cook on Sauté mode until cabbage is softened.
5. In a small bowl, mix together cornstarch and 1 tablespoon of water. Pour into the pot. Stir until thickened, about 1-2 minutes.

6. Add scallions and stir well.
7. Serve and enjoy.

Nutrition information per serving:
Calories: 568; Carbohydrates: 8.6g; Protein: 42g; Fat: 40g; Sugar: 2.7g; Sodium: 1124mg

Salsa Pork

(Servings: 4|Cooking Time: 15 minutes)

Ingredients:
- 2 lbs. pork shoulder, boneless and cut into chunks
- ¼ cup fresh cilantro, chopped
- ½ cup chicken stock
- 1 tsp. dried oregano
- 1 tsp. ground cumin
- 1 tbsp. honey
- 14.5 oz. can tomatoes, drained and diced
- 16 oz. salsa
- Pepper
- Salt

Directions for Cooking:
1. Season meat with pepper and salt.

2. Add meat, stock, oregano, cumin, honey, tomatoes and salsa to the pot.
3. Seal pot with lid and cook on manual high pressure for 15 minutes.
4. Allow pressure to release naturally, then open lid.
5. Shred the meat using a fork.
6. Add cilantro and stir well.
7. Serve and enjoy.

Nutrition information per serving:
Calories: 735; Carbohydrates: 17.3g; Protein: 55.7g; Fat: 48.9g; Sugar: 11.4g; Sodium: 1189mg

BBQ Pork Ribs

(Servings: 6|Cooking Time: 30 minutes)

Ingredients:
- 1 cup water
- 3 lbs. pork ribs
- ¼ cup tomato sauce
- 1 cup BBQ sauce
- ½ tsp. black pepper
- ½ tsp. dried oregano
- 1 tsp. garlic powder
- 2 tsp. paprika
- 1 tbsp. brown sugar
- ½ tsp. salt

Directions for Cooking:
1. In a small bowl, mix together all spices.
2. In another bowl, mix together tomato sauce and ½ cup BBQ sauce.

3. Rub spice mixture over the pork ribs then toss ribs with sauce mixture.
4. Add pork ribs and water to the instant pot.
5. Seal pot with lid and cook on manual high pressure for 30 minutes.
6. Quick release pressure then open the lid.
7. Preheat the broiler. Place ribs on a baking tray and top with remaining BBQ sauce. Broil for 3-5 minutes.
8. Serve and enjoy.

Nutrition information per serving:
Calories: 694; Carbohydrates: 18.1g; Protein: 60.4g; Fat: 40.4g; Sugar: 12.9g; Sodium: 847mg

BBQ Pulled Pork

(Servings: 4 | Cooking Time: 15 minutes)

Ingredients:

- 2 lbs. pork shoulder, boneless and cut into chunks
- 1 cup beer
- 1 tbsp. vinegar
- ¾ cup BBQ sauce
- 1/8 tsp. cayenne pepper
- 1 tsp. black pepper
- ¼ tsp. oregano
- ½ tsp. onion powder
- 1 tsp. ground cumin
- 2 tsp. chili powder
- 2 tsp. paprika
- 1 tbsp. brown sugar
- 1 tsp. sea salt

Directions for Cooking:

1. In a small bowl, mix together all spices.
2. Add meat in a large bowl. Rub spice mixture all over the meat.
3. Pour vinegar and BBQ sauce over the meat and stir well.
4. Add beer and meat mixture into instant pot.
5. Seal pot with lid and cook on manual high pressure for 15 minutes.
6. Quick release pressure then open the lid.
7. Shred the meat using a fork and serve.

Nutrition information per serving:
Calories: 779; Carbohydrates: 23.5g; Protein: 53.6g; Fat: 49.2g; Sugar: 14.8g; Sodium: 1165mg

Pork Chops with Gravy

(Servings: 4 | Cooking Time: 18 minutes)

Ingredients:

- 2 ½ lbs. pork chops
- 1 tbsp. cornstarch
- 2 tbsp. water
- 1 cup chicken stock
- ½ tsp. thyme
- 2 tbsp. dried onion, minced
- 3 garlic cloves, smashed
- ¼ cup dry white wine
- 2 onions, sliced
- 2 tbsp. olive oil
- Pepper
- Salt

Directions for Cooking:

1. Season meat with pepper and salt; set aside.
2. Add oil into instant pot and set on Sauté mode.
3. Add onion to the pot and sauté for 10 minutes.
4. Add garlic and wine; stir well.
5. Add thyme, dried onion, seasoned pork chops and stock. Stir well to combine.
6. Seal pot with lid and cook on manual high pressure for 8 minutes.
7. Allow pressure to release naturally, then open the lid.
8. Remove pork chops from pot and place on a plate.
9. In a small bowl, mix together cornstarch and water. Pour into instant pot and cook on Sauté mode until gravy thickens.
10. Pour gravy over pork chops and serve.

Nutrition information per serving:
Calories: 636; Carbohydrates: 3.9g; Protein: 88.7g; Fat: 26.1g; Sugar: 0.6g; Sodium: 390mg

Spicy & Smoky Beef

(Servings: 4|Cooking Time: 15 minutes)

Ingredients:

- 1 ¾ lbs. flank steak, cut into strips
- ½ cup chicken stock
- ½ cup tomato sauce
- 1 onion, sliced
- 2 bell peppers, sliced
- ½ tsp. oregano
- 1 tsp. paprika
- 1 chipotle pepper in adobo sauce
- 3 garlic cloves, minced
- 2 tbsp. olive oil
- Pepper
- Salt

Directions for Cooking:

1. Season meat with pepper and salt.
2. Add oil into instant pot and set on Sauté mode.
3. Add meat to the pot and sauté until brown.
4. Add remaining ingredients into the pot and stir well to combine.
5. Seal pot with lid and cook on manual high pressure for 15 minutes.
6. Allow pressure to release naturally, then open lid.
7. Shred the meat using a fork and serve.

Nutrition information per serving:
Calories: 492; Carbohydrates: 10.2g; Protein: 57.1g; Fat: 24.2g; Sugar: 5.6g; Sodium: 490mg

Coconut Beef Curry

(Servings: 4|Cooking Time: 15 minutes)

Ingredients:

- 1 ½ lbs. beef, boneless and cut into chunks
- ½ cup basil, sliced
- 2 tbsp. brown sugar
- 2 tbsp. fish sauce
- ¼ cup chicken stock
- ¾ cup coconut milk
- 2 tbsp. curry paste
- 1 onion, sliced
- 1 bell pepper, sliced
- 1 sweet potato, peeled and cut into chunks

Directions for Cooking:

1. Add all ingredients except basil into instant pot and stir well.
2. Seal pot with lid and cook on manual high pressure for 15 minutes.
3. Allow pressure to release naturally, then open lid.
4. Add basil and stir well.
5. Serve over rice and enjoy.

Nutrition information per serving:
Calories: 538; Carbohydrates: 20.2g; Protein: 54.8g; Fat: 25.9g; Sugar: 10.8g; Sodium: 875mg

Classic Sirloin Tips with Gravy

(Servings: 4|Cooking Time: 10 minutes)

Ingredients:

- 1 ½ lbs. beef tips
- 1 tbsp. cornstarch
- 2 tbsp. water
- 1 cup chicken stock
- ¼ cup dry sherry
- 1 ½ tsp. thyme
- 2 tbsp. dried onion, minced
- 8 oz. mushrooms, sliced
- 2 onions, sliced
- Pepper
- Salt

Directions for Cooking:

1. In a small bowl, mix together cornstarch and water. Set aside
2. Season meat with pepper and salt.
3. Add meat to the pot along, with remaining ingredients and stir well.
4. Seal pot with lid and cook on manual high pressure for 10 minutes.
5. Allow pressure to release naturally, then open lid.
6. Remove meat from pot and place on a dish.
7. Add cornstarch mixture to the pot and cook on Sauté mode until gravy thickens.
8. Return meat to the pot and stir well.
9. Serve and enjoy.

Nutrition information per serving:

Calories: 426; Carbohydrates: 5.3g; Protein: 47.9g; Fat: 22.9g; Sugar: 1.7g; Sodium: 341mg

Moist & Tender Chuck Roast

(Servings: 6|Cooking Time: 20 minutes)

Ingredients:

- 3 lbs. beef chuck roast, boneless and cut into chunks
- 2 tbsp. parsley, chopped
- ½ cup red wine
- ½ cup chicken stock
- 1 tbsp. soy sauce
- 2 tbsp. tomato paste
- ½ tsp. thyme
- 3 garlic cloves, crushed
- 2 celery ribs, chopped
- 2 carrots, peeled and sliced
- 2 onions, chopped
- Pepper
- Salt

Directions for Cooking:

1. Season meat with pepper and salt; set aside.
2. Add onions, wine, stock, soy sauce, tomato paste, thyme, garlic, celery, carrots, pepper and salt to the pot; stir well. Place meat on top.
3. Seal pot with lid and cook on manual high pressure for 20 minutes.
4. Allow pressure to release naturally, then open lid.
5. Shred the meat using a fork.
6. Add parsley and stir well.
7. Serve and enjoy.

Nutrition information per serving:

Calories: 872; Carbohydrates: 7.9g; Protein: 60.5g; Fat: 63.3g; Sugar: 3.5g; Sodium: 409mg

Honey Pork Roast

(Servings: 2|Cooking Time: 35 minutes)

Ingredients:

- 1 lb. pork roast
- 1 tbsp. soy sauce
- 2 tbsp. grated parmesan cheese
- ½ tbsp. olive oil
- ½ tbsp. garlic, minced
- ½ cup chicken stock
- ½ tbsp. cornstarch
- ½ tbsp. basil
- 2 tbsp. honey
- Salt

Directions for Cooking:

1. Add all ingredients into instant pot and stir well.
2. Seal pot with lid and cook on meat mode for 35 minutes.
3. Allow pressure to release naturally, then open the lid.
4. Stir well and serve warm.

Nutrition information per serving:

Calories: 618; Carbohydrates: 20.6g; Protein: 68.5g; Fat: 27.3g; Sugar: 17.6g; Sodium: 968mg

Simple Meatballs

(Servings: 2|Cooking Time: 25 minutes)

Ingredients:

- 1 egg
- ¼ cup onion, chopped
- ¾ lb. ground pork
- ¾ tsp. brown sugar
- ¼ cup coconut milk
- 1 tbsp. breadcrumbs

Directions for Cooking:

1. In a bowl, combine together meat, breadcrumbs and egg.
2. Make small balls from meat mixture.
3. Add coconut milk and prepared meatballs into instant pot.
4. Add onion and brown sugar; stir well.
5. Seal pot with lid and cook on manual high pressure for 25 minutes.
6. Allow pressure to release naturally, then open lid.
7. Serve warm and enjoy.

Nutrition information per serving:

Calories: 367; Carbohydrates: 6.7g; Protein: 48.6g; Fat: 15.5g; Sugar: 3.1g; Sodium: 158mg

Shredded Thyme Pork

(Servings: 3|Cooking Time: 40 minutes)

Ingredients:

- 1 lb. pork belly, cut into cubes
- 1 tsp. thyme
- 1 ½ tsp. black pepper
- ½ cup onion, chopped
- ½ cup chicken stock
- 3 tbsp. water
- 1 tbsp. cornstarch
- ¼ tsp. salt

Directions for Cooking:

1. In a small bowl, mix together cornstarch and water; set aside.
2. Add remaining ingredients to the instant pot and stir well.
3. Seal pot with lid and cook on manual high pressure for 35 minutes.
4. Quick release pressure then open the lid.
5. Pour cornstarch mixture into instant pot and stir well.
6. Serve and enjoy.

Nutrition information per serving: Calories: 654; Carbohydrates: 7.2g; Protein: 19.6g; Fat: 60.2g; Sugar: 1g; Sodium: 1324mg

Pineapple Cinnamon Pork

(Servings: 2|Cooking Time: 25 minutes)

Ingredients:

- ½ lb. pork tenderloin, sliced
- ½ cup tomato puree
- ½ tsp. rosemary
- ¼ cup onion, chopped
- 2 cloves
- ½ tsp. cinnamon
- ½ tsp. nutmeg
- ½ cup pineapple, cut into chunks
- 1 cup pineapple juice

Directions for Cooking:

1. Add all ingredients except pineapple into instant pot and stir well.
2. Seal pot with lid and cook on manual high pressure for 25 minutes.
3. Quick release pressure then open the lid.
4. Add pineapple chunks and stir well.
5. Serve and enjoy.

Nutrition information per serving:
Calories: 284; Carbohydrates: 29.4g; Protein: 31.6g; Fat: 4.6g; Sugar: 20.3g; Sodium: 86mg

Spicy Celery Cauliflower Pork

(Servings: 4|Cooking Time: 20 minutes)

Ingredients:

- 2 lbs. pork ribs, cut into pieces
- 1 bay leaf
- ½ tsp. red pepper flakes
- 1 tsp. chili powder
- 3 tbsp. olive oil
- 4 cups chicken stock
- ¼ cup parsley, chopped
- 1 cup cauliflower florets
- 1 cup celery, chopped
- 1 onion, chopped
- 1 leek chopped
- 1 tsp. salt

Directions for Cooking:

1. Add oil into instant pot and set on Sauté mode.
2. Add meat to the pot and cook until brown. Remove meat from pot and set aside.
3. Add celery, onion, and salt and sauté for 4-5 minutes.
4. Return meat to the pot with remaining ingredients and stir well.
5. Seal pot with lid and cook on manual high pressure for 20 minutes.
6. Allow pressure to release naturally, then open lid.
7. Serve and enjoy.

Nutrition information per serving:
Calories: 744; Carbohydrates: 6.1g; Protein: 62g; Fat: 51.5g; Sugar: 2.9g; Sodium: 1514mg

Delicious Curried Pork

(Servings: 4|Cooking Time: 11 minutes)

Ingredients:

- 1 lb. pork, cut into strips
- 2 tsp. curry powder
- 1 tsp. fresh ginger, grated
- 2 tsp. sesame oil
- 1 tbsp. rice vinegar
- 1 spring onion, chopped

- 1 garlic clove, crushed
- 1 medium onion, sliced
- ¼ cup olive oil
- ½ tsp. salt

Directions for Cooking:

1. Add olive oil into instant pot and set on Sauté mode.
2. Add meat into the pot and sauté for 5 minutes. Remove meat from pot and set aside.

3. Add onion, spring onion and garlic. Sauté for 3-4 minutes.
4. Add ginger, curry powder and salt. Stir well and cook for 2 minutes more.
5. Drizzle with sesame oil and serve.

Nutrition information per serving:
Calories: 311; Carbohydrates: 4g; Protein: 30.3g; Fat: 19.1g; Sugar: 1.3g; Sodium: 358mg

Asian Pork with gravy

(Servings: 2|Cooking Time: 15 minutes)

Ingredients:

- 10 oz. pork, boneless and cut into strips
- 1 tsp. pepper
- 3 tbsp. sesame oil
- 2 tbsp. oyster sauce
- 2 tbsp. fish sauce
- 2 garlic cloves
- 1 cup mushrooms, chopped
- 2 spring onion, chopped
- 1 small onion, chopped
- ½ tsp. salt

Directions for Cooking:

1. Add oil into the pot and set on Sauté mode.

2. Add garlic, onion and meat. Sauté for 1-2 minutes.
3. Add spring onion and sauté for 2-3 minutes.
4. Add mushrooms and stir well.
5. Add oyster sauce and fish sauce. Stir well and cook for 2-3 minutes.
6. Season with pepper. Add ¼ cup of water and simmer for 10 minutes.
7. Serve and enjoy.

Nutrition information per serving:
Calories: 425; Carbohydrates: 8.3g; Protein: 40.1g; Fat: 25.6g; Sugar: 3.1g; Sodium: 2168mg

Simple Ground Pork

(Servings: 4|Cooking Time: 11 minutes)

Ingredients:

- 7 oz. ground pork
- 3 tbsp. butter
- 2 garlic cloves, crushed
- 4 eggs
- 1 onion, chopped
- 2 bacon slices, chopped
- ½ tsp. pepper
- ½ tsp. salt

Directions for Cooking:

1. Add butter into instant pot and set on Sauté mode.

2. Add onion to the pot and sauté for 2-3 minutes.
3. Add meat, garlic, bacon, pepper and salt. Cook for 5 minutes.
4. Add eggs and cook for 2-3 minutes. Stir well.
5. Serve hot and enjoy.

Nutrition information per serving:
Calories: 276; Carbohydrates: 3.7g; Protein: 22.6g; Fat:18.8g; Sugar: 1.5g; Sodium: 663mg

Pork with Veggies

(Servings: 3|Cooking Time: 20 minutes)

Ingredients:

- 1 lb. pork, cut into pieces
- ½ tsp. garlic powder
- 1 tsp. dried celery
- ½ tsp. pepper
- 4 cup chicken stock
- 1 tbsp. tomato paste
- 1 tbsp. Dijon mustard
- 1 chili pepper, chopped
- 2 spring onions, chopped
- 1 cup broccoli, chopped
- ¼ cup celery stalk, chopped
- 2 tbsp. apple cider vinegar
- 2 tbsp. butter
- 1 tsp. sea salt

Directions for Cooking:

1. Add butter into the pot and set on Sauté mode.
2. Season meat with pepper and salt, then add to pot.
3. Add vegetables, garlic powder, celery, tomato paste and stock; stir well.
4. Seal pot with lid and cook on manual high pressure for 20 minutes.
5. Allow pressure to release naturally, then open lid.
6. Serve hot and enjoy.

Nutrition information per serving:
Calories: 325; Carbohydrates: 6.1g; Protein: 42.3g; Fat: 14.1g; Sugar: 2.7g; Sodium: 1867mg

Broccoli Tomato Pork

(Servings: 4|Cooking Time: 15 minutes)

Ingredients:

- 1 lb. pork loin, chopped
- ¼ tsp. chili powder
- 1 fresh rosemary sprig
- ¼ cup olive oil
- 2 cups cherry tomatoes, chopped
- 1 cup broccoli, chopped
- 1 onion, chopped
- ½ tsp. pepper
- 1 tsp. salt

Directions for Cooking:

1. Season meat with pepper and salt.
2. Add oil to the pot and set on Sauté mode.
3. Place meat into the pot.
4. Add tomatoes, broccoli, onion and sauté for a minute. Season with rosemary and chili powder.
5. Seal pot with lid and cook on Meat/Stew.
6. Allow pressure to release naturally, then open the lid.
7. Discard rosemary and serve.

Nutrition information per serving:
Calories: 419; Carbohydrates: 7.8g; Protein: 32.8g; Fat: 28.7g; Sugar: 3.9g; Sodium: 666mg

Jalapeno Pork Verde

(Servings: 8|Cooking Time: 40 minutes)

Ingredients:

- 2 lbs. pork butt roast, cut into pieces
- 2 tsp. cumin powder
- 3 jalapeno peppers
- 3 tomatillos, husk removed
- 1 tbsp. fish sauce
- ¼ cup fresh cilantro, chopped
- 1 tomato, chopped
- 6 garlic cloves

- 2 poblano peppers

Directions for Cooking:

1. Add all ingredients except fish sauce and cilantro into instant pot; stir well.
2. Seal pot with lid and cook on manual high pressure for 30 minutes.
3. Allow pressure to release naturally for 10 minutes, then release using quick release method.
4. Remove pork from pot and place on a plate.

5. Add fish sauce and cilantro into the pot; stir well.
6. Puree the veggies using an immersion blender.
7. Return pork to pot and stir well.
8. Serve and enjoy.

Nutrition information per serving:
Calories: 229; Carbohydrates: 3.6g; Protein: 20.9g; Fat: 14.4g; Sugar: 1.1g; Sodium: 385mg

Balsamic Pork

(Servings: 4|Cooking Time: 6 minutes)

Ingredients:

- 2 ½ lbs. pork tenderloin
- 1 tbsp. mustard
- 1 tbsp. Worcestershire sauce
- 2 garlic cloves, minced
- ¼ cup balsamic vinegar
- ¼ cup honey
- 1 cup chicken stock
- 2 tbsp. olive oil
- ¼ cup water
- 3/4 tbsp. cornstarch
- 1 tsp. ground sage
- 1 tsp. ground black pepper
- 1 tsp. kosher salt

Directions for Cooking:

1. Add oil into instant pot and set on Sauté mode.

2. Add pork tenderloin into the pot and sauté until brown.
3. Add remaining ingredients except for water and cornstarch into the pot and stir well.
4. Seal pot with lid and cook on manual high pressure for 6 minutes.
5. Quick release pressure then open the lid.
6. Remove pork tenderloin from the pot and set aside.
7. Set instant pot on Sauté mode.
8. In a small bowl, whisk together water and cornstarch. Pour into the pot and cook until thickened.
9. Pour sauce over pork and serve.

Nutrition information per serving:
Calories: 562; Carbohydrates: 21.8g; Protein: 75.3g; Fat: 18g; Sugar: 18.6g; Sodium: 978mg

Flavorful Sirloin Tip Roast

(Servings: 6|Cooking Time: 25 minutes)

Ingredients:

- 3 lbs. pork sirloin tip roast
- ½ tsp. onion powder
- ½ cup apple juice
- 1 cup water
- 1 tbsp. olive oil
- ¼ tsp. chili powder
- ½ tsp. garlic powder
- ½ tsp. black pepper
- ½ tsp. salt

Directions for Cooking:

1. In a small bowl, mix together all spices.
2. Rub spice mixture over pork.
3. Add oil into instant pot and set on Sauté mode.

4. Add pork into the pot and cook until brown.
5. Add remaining ingredients into the pot.
6. Seal pot with lid and cook on manual high pressure for 25 minutes.

7. Quick release pressure then open the lid.
8. Serve and enjoy.

Nutrition information per serving:
Calories: 234; Carbohydrates: 2.8g; Protein: 44.7g; Fat: 5.4g; Sugar: 2.1g; Sodium: 784mg

Taco Pork Fajitas

(Servings: 6|Cooking Time: 16 minutes)

Ingredients:
- 1 ½ lbs. pork loin sirloin chops, cut into strips
- 1 tbsp. taco seasoning
- 2 bell peppers, cut into strips
- 15 oz. can salsa
- ½ cup chicken broth
- 1 tbsp. lime juice
- 1 onion, sliced

Directions for Cooking:
1. Add all ingredients into instant pot and stir well.

2. Seal pot with lid and select manual high pressure for 1 minute.
3. Allow pressure to release naturally for 15 minutes, then release using quick release method.
4. Stir well and serve.

Nutrition information per serving:
Calories: 271; Carbohydrates: 11g; Protein: 36.9g; Fat: 7.9g; Sugar: 3.2g; Sodium: 583mg

Pork Chops with Rice

(Servings: 4|Cooking Time: 21 minutes)

Ingredients:
- 4 pork chops
- ¼ cup green onions, sliced
- 1 tsp. butter
- 1 tsp. olive oil
- 1 ¼ cups water
- 1 cup rice
- Pepper
- Salt

Directions for Cooking:
1. Add olive oil into instant pot and set on Sauté mode.
2. Add pork chops into the pot and sauté until brown.

3. Add remaining ingredients to the pot and stir well.
4. Seal pot with lid and cook on manual high pressure for 6 minutes.
5. Allow pressure to release naturally for 15 minutes, then release using quick release method.
6. Serve and enjoy.

Nutrition information per serving:
Calories: 445; Carbohydrates: 37.5g; Protein: 21.4g; Fat: 22.3g; Sugar: 0.2g; Sodium: 107mg

Sun-dried Tomato Ribs

(Servings: 6|Cooking Time: 40 minutes)

Ingredients:
- 2 lbs. pork ribs, chopped
- ½ tsp. garlic powder
- ½ tsp. dried oregano
- 1 tsp. dried thyme

- 3 tbsp. swerve
- 4 cups chicken broth
- 4 tbsp. butter
- 1 onion, chopped
- 1 cup sun-dried tomatoes
- 2 cups cherry tomatoes
- 1 tsp. sea salt

Directions for Cooking:

1. Add pork ribs into instant pot. Pour broth over the ribs.
2. Seal pot with lid and cook on manual high pressure for 20 minutes.
3. Allow pressure to release naturally for 10 minutes, then release using quick release method. Open the lid.

4. Remove pork ribs from pot along with chicken broth.
5. Set pot on Sauté mode. Add butter and onion to the pot. Sauté until onion is softened.
6. Add tomatoes and remaining broth. Add garlic powder, oregano, thyme and swerve. Cook until tomatoes are softened. Stir well.
7. Return meat to the pot and stir well.
8. Turn off the Sauté mode and let sit meat in sauce for 10 minutes.
9. Serve and enjoy.

Nutrition information per serving:
Calories: 523; Carbohydrates: 4.9g; Protein:43.9 g; Fat: 35.5g; Sugar: 2.1g; Sodium: 965mg

Classic Pork Ribs with Sauerkraut

(Servings: 6|Cooking Time: 30 minutes)

Ingredients:

- 1 lb. pork ribs
- 24 oz. sauerkraut
- 14 oz. kielbasa, sliced
- 1 tbsp. olive oil
- 1/3 cup water
- 1 tbsp. brown sugar
- ¼ tsp. pepper
- ½ tsp. salt

Directions for Cooking:

1. Add olive oil into instant pot and set on Sauté mode.

2. Add pork ribs into the pot and sauté until brown. Season with pepper and salt.
3. Add remaining ingredients and stir well.
4. Seal pot with lid and cook on manual high pressure for 15 minutes.
5. Allow pressure to release naturally for 15 minutes, then release using quick release method.
6. Stir well and serve.

Nutrition information per serving:
Calorie: 403; Carbohydrates: 9g; Protein: 29.7 g; Fat: 27.5g; Sugar: 3.5g; Sodium: 1782mg

Spicy Lamb

(Servings: 4|Cooking Time: 35 minutes)

Ingredients:

- 1 lb. lamb, cut into pieces
- 1 tbsp. cumin powder
- 2 tsp. turmeric
- 2 tsp. garam masala
- 3 tbsp. chili powder
- 2 tbsp. apple cider
- 2 tbsp. lemon juice

- 1 cup fresh cilantro, chopped
- 2 onions, chopped
- 2 cups chicken stock
- 1 cup coconut milk
- 3 tbsp. butter
- 1 cup cherry tomatoes, chopped
- 1 tsp. salt

Directions for Cooking:

1. Set instant pot on Sauté mode. Season meat with pepper and salt, and place in the instant pot. Sauté meat for 5 minutes.
2. Add remaining ingredients to the pot and stir well.
3. Seal pot with lid and cook on manual high pressure for 15 minutes.
4. Allow pressure to release naturally for 15 minutes, then release using quick release method.
5. Stir well and serve.

Nutrition information per serving:
Calorie: 494; Carbohydrates: 16.3g; Protein: 35.9g; Fat: 33.2g; Sugar: 7.4g; Sodium: 1190mg

Beef Tomato Pepper Curry

(Servings: 5|Cooking Time: 45 minutes)

Ingredients:

- 1 lb. beef stew meat
- 2 tbsp. fresh ginger, grated
- 1 tsp. cumin powder
- 2 tsp. coriander powder
- 2 tsp. garam masala
- 1 tbsp. cayenne pepper
- 1 cup sun-dried tomatoes, diced
- 4 tbsp. butter
- ½ cup chicken stock
- 4 garlic cloves, crushed
- 3 green chili peppers, chopped
- 2 bell peppers, sliced

Directions for Cooking:

1. Add all ingredients into instant pot and stir well.
2. Seal pot with lid and cook on manual high pressure for 30 minutes.
3. Allow pressure to release naturally for 15 minutes, then release using quick release method.
4. Stir well and serve.

Nutrition information per serving:
Calorie: 290; Carbohydrates: 8.4g; Protein: 29.1g; Fat: 15.5g; Sugar: 3.8g; Sodium: 209mg

Lamb Zucchini Stew

(Servings: 3|Cooking Time: 30 minutes)

Ingredients:

- 1 lb. lamb loin, cut into pieces
- 1 zucchini, sliced
- ¼ tsp. dried thyme
- 1 tsp. oregano
- ½ tsp. chili powder
- 2 cups chicken stock
- 1 chili pepper, chopped
- 1 cup cabbage, shredded
- 3 tbsp. olive oil
- 3 garlic cloves, crushed
- 1 tsp. salt

Directions for Cooking:

1. Add oil into instant pot and set on Sauté mode. Add garlic and meat to the pot and sauté for a minute.
2. Season with thyme, oregano, chili powder, and salt. Stir everything well and cook for 5 minutes.
3. Add zucchini and cook for 3 minutes.
4. Add cabbage, chili pepper and stock. Stir well.
5. Seal pot with lid and cook on manual high pressure for 12 minutes.
6. Allow pressure to release naturally for 10 minutes, then release using quick release method. Open the lid.
7. Stir well and serve.

Nutrition information per serving:
Calorie: 456; Carbohydrates: 5.8g; Protein: 42.1g; Fat: 29.4g; Sugar: 2.5g; Sodium: 1400mg

Cauliflower Pepper Lamb Chops

(Servings: 5|Cooking Time: 35 minutes)

Ingredients:
- 5 lamb chops
- 2 bay leaves
- 1 cup chicken stock
- 1 bell pepper, chopped
- 1 cup cauliflower florets
- 1 cup onion, chopped
- 2 tbsp. olive oil
- ½ tsp. black pepper
- 1 tsp. sea salt

Directions for Cooking:
1. Add all ingredients into instant pot and stir well.
2. Seal pot with lid and cook on manual high pressure for 15 minutes.
3. Quick release pressure then open the lid.
4. Preheat the oven to 400°F.
5. Transfer lamb chops with vegetables onto a baking tray. Roast in preheated oven for 10 minutes on each side.
6. Serve and enjoy.

Nutrition information per serving:
Calorie: 392; Carbohydrates: 5.3g; Protein: 20.1g; Fat: 31.8g; Sugar: 2.8g; Sodium: 600mg

Asian Pork

(Servings: 6|Cooking Time: 35 minutes)

Ingredients:
- 2 lbs. pork belly, cut into cubes
- 2 tbsp. coconut aminos
- 1 tbsp. blackstrap molasses
- 3 tbsp. sherry
- 1 tbsp. ginger, grated
- 1/3 cup beef broth
- 2 tbsp. maple syrup
- 1 tsp. sea salt

Directions for Cooking:
1. Add all ingredients into instant pot and stir well.
2. Seal pot with lid and cook on manual high pressure for 25 minutes.
3. Allow pressure to release naturally for 10 minutes, then release using quick release method.
4. Set instant pot on Sauté mode and cook until sauce thicken.
5. Stir well and serve.

Nutrition information per serving:
Calorie: 735; Carbohydrates: 8.7g; Protein: 70.1g; Fat: 40.9g; Sugar: 5.9g; Sodium: 2805mg

Butter Ranch Pork Chops

(Servings: 6|Cooking Time: 15 minutes)

Ingredients:
- 6 pork chops, boneless
- ½ stick butter
- 1 tbsp. olive oil
- 1 cup water
- 1 packet ranch mix

Directions for Cooking:
1. Add oil into instant pot and set on Sauté mode.
2. Add pork chops into the pot and sauté until brown.
3. Add remaining ingredients into the pot.
4. Seal pot with lid and cook on manual high pressure for 5 minutes.
5. Allow pressure to release naturally for 10 minutes, then release using quick release method.
6. Serve and enjoy.

Nutrition information per serving: Calorie: 344; Carbohydrates: 0g; Protein: 18.1g; Fat: 29g; Sugar: 0g; Sodium: 156mg

Mushroom Lamb Shanks

(Servings: 4|Cooking Time: 35 minutes)

Ingredients:

- 4 lamb shanks
- 1 tsp. dried rosemary
- 1 tomato, chopped
- ¼ cup leeks, chopped
- 2 celery stalks, chopped
- 2 garlic cloves
- 1 onion, chopped
- ¼ cup apple cider vinegar
- 3 tbsp. olive oil
- 3 cups chicken broth
- 8 oz. mushrooms, sliced
- 2 tsp. sea salt

Directions for Cooking:

1. Add all ingredients into instant pot and stir well.
2. Seal pot with lid and cook on manual high pressure for 25 minutes.
3. Allow pressure to release naturally for 10 minutes, then release using quick release method.
4. Serve and enjoy.

Nutrition information per serving:
Calories: 536; Carbohydrates: 7.6g; Protein: 62.6g; Fat: 26g; Sugar: 3.5g; Sodium: 1771mg

Delicious Beef Stroganoff

(Servings: 4|Cooking Time: 30 minutes)

Ingredients:

- 1 lb. beef sirloin steak, cut into strips
- ½ cup sour cream
- ½ lb. mushrooms, sliced
- 1 cup chicken broth
- 3 tbsp. tomato paste
- 1 tsp. paprika
- 2 bacon slices, diced
- 2 garlic cloves, crushed
- 1 onion, diced

Directions for Cooking:

1. Add all ingredients except sour cream into instant pot and stir well.
2. Seal pot with lid and cook on manual high pressure for 20 minutes.
3. Allow pressure to release naturally for 10 minutes, then release using quick release method.
4. Add sour cream and stir well.
5. Serve and enjoy.

Nutrition information per serving:
Calories: 370; Carbohydrates: 9.1g; Protein: 42.8g; Fat: 17.7g; Sugar: 3.9g; Sodium: 517mg

Cabbage Beef Shawarma

(Servings: 4|Cooking Time: 10 minutes)

Ingredients:

- 1 lb. ground beef
- ½ tsp. ground coriander
- ½ tsp. cumin
- ¼ tsp. cayenne pepper
- ¼ tsp. allspice
- ½ tsp. cinnamon
- 1 tsp. dried oregano
- 2 cups cabbage, shredded
- 1 cup bell peppers, sliced
- 1 cup onion, chopped

- 1 tsp. salt

Directions for Cooking:
1. Add beef into instant pot and cook on Sauté mode for 2 minutes.
2. Add remaining ingredients and stir well.
3. Seal pot with lid and cook on manual high pressure for 2 minutes.

4. Allow pressure to release naturally for 5 minutes, then release using quick release method.
5. Stir well and serve.

Nutrition information per serving:
Calories: 244; Carbohydrates: 7g; Protein: 35.6g; Fat: 7.4g; Sugar: 3.9g; Sodium: 665mg

Salsa Pork Chops
(Servings: 8|Cooking Time: 15 minutes)

Ingredients:
- 3 lbs. pork chops
- ¾ tsp. garlic powder
- ½ tsp. ground cumin
- ¼ cup fresh lime juice
- ½ cup salsa
- 3 tbsp. butter
- ¾ tsp. salt

Directions for Cooking:
1. Mix together garlic powder, cumin, pepper and salt. Rub over pork chops.
2. Add butter into the pot and set on Sauté mode.

3. Add pork chops into the pot and sauté until brown.
4. Mix together lemon juice and salsa. Pour over pork chops.
5. Seal pot with lid and cook on manual high pressure for 15 minutes.
6. Quick release pressure then open the lid.
7. Serve and enjoy.

Nutrition information per serving:
Calories: 293; Carbohydrates: 1.7g; Protein: 32.3g; Fat: 18g; Sugar: 0.6g; Sodium: 785mg

Shredded Pork Shoulder
(Servings: 6|Cooking Time: 65 minutes)

Ingredients:
- 2 lbs. pork shoulder
- 1 tsp. paprika
- 2 tsp. ginger, grated
- 4 drops liquid stevia
- ¼ cup soy sauce
- 2 tbsp. garlic paste
- 1 tbsp. tomato paste
- ¼ cup tomato sauce
- 1 cup beef broth

Directions for Cooking:
1. Place meat in the instant pot.
2. Mix together remaining ingredients and pour over meat.

3. Seal pot with lid and cook on manual high pressure for 60 minutes.
4. Allow pressure to release naturally for 5 minutes, then release using quick release method.
5. Remove meat from pot and shred using a fork.
6. Return shredded meat to the pot and stir well.
7. Serve and enjoy.

Nutrition information per serving:
Calories: 412; Carbohydrates: 3.6g; Protein: 27.4g; Fat: 31.1g; Sugar: 1.2g; Sodium: 884mg

Jerk Seasoned Pork

(Servings: 8|Cooking Time: 45 minutes)

Ingredients:
- 2 lbs. pork shoulder
- ¼ cup chicken stock
- 2 tbsp. Jamaican jerk spice blend
- 1 tbsp. olive oil

Directions for Cooking:
1. Brush meat with oil and rub with Jamaican jerk spice blend.
2. Add meat to the pot and cook on Sauté mode until brown, about 2 minutes on each side.
3. Add broth. Seal pot with lid and cook on manual high pressure for 45 minutes.
4. Remove meat from pot and shred using a fork. Return shredded meat to the pot and stir well.
5. Serve and enjoy.

Nutrition information per serving:
Calories: 306; Carbohydrates: 0g; Protein: 19.1g; Fat: 24.9g; Sugar: 0g; Sodium: 99mg

Sirloin Pork with Tomatillo Salsa

(Servings: 4|Cooking Time: 45 minutes)

Ingredients:
- 2 lbs. sirloin pork, sliced
- 2 tsp. cumin
- 16 oz. tomatillo salsa
- 2 tsp. garlic powder
- 1 tbsp. olive oil
- ¼ tsp. salt

Directions for Cooking:
1. Add oil into the pot and set on Sauté mode.
2. Season meat with garlic powder, cumin, and salt.
3. Add meat to the pot and sauté until browned.
4. Pour salsa over the meat.
5. Seal pot with lid and cook on manual high pressure for 45 minutes.
6. Quick release pressure then open the lid.
7. Serve and enjoy.

Nutrition information per serving:
Calories: 483; Carbohydrates: 29g; Protein: 56.4g; Fat: 13g; Sugar: 0.4g; Sodium: 2009mg

Beef Meatballs

(Servings: 4|Cooking Time: 30 minutes)

Ingredients:
- 1 lb. ground beef
- ¼ tsp. garlic powder
- ½ cup tomato sauce
- ½ tsp. chili powder
- 2/3 cup salsa
- 1 egg
- ¼ cup arrowroot
- ¼ tsp. salt

Directions for Cooking:
1. In a bowl, combine together meat, chili powder, arrowroot, egg, pepper and salt.
2. Make small balls from meat mixture.
3. Add salsa, tomato sauce and garlic powder to the pot. Stir well.
4. Add meatballs to the pot. Seal pot with lid and cook on low for 30 minutes.
5. Quick release pressure then open the lid.
6. Serve and enjoy.

Nutrition information per serving:
Calories: 252; Carbohydrates: 5.8g; Protein: 37g; Fat: 8g; Sugar: 2.8g; Sodium: 663mg

Indian Lamb Curry

(Servings: 4|Cooking Time: 30 minutes)

Ingredients:

- 1 ½ lbs. lamb chunks
- 1 ½ tsp. ginger garlic paste
- 2 bay leaves
- 2 onion, chopped
- 1 tbsp. vegetable oil
- 1 ½ cups can tomatoes, chopped
- 3/4 tsp. fennel powder
- ½ tsp. coriander powder
- ½ tsp. garam masala
- ½ tsp. chili powder
- 3/4 tsp. cumin powder
- Salt

Directions for Cooking:

1. Add oil into instant pot and set on Sauté mode.
2. Add bay leaves and onion to the pot. Sauté for 5 minutes.
3. Add ginger garlic paste, meat and all spices. Stir well.
4. Add remaining ingredients and stir well to combine.
5. Seal pot with lid and cook on manual high pressure for 5 minutes.
6. Allow pressure to release naturally for 15 minutes, then release using quick release method.
7. Stir well and serve.

Nutrition information per serving:

Calories: 399; Carbohydrates: 11g; Protein: 49g; Fat: 16g; Sugar: 5.4g; Sodium: 400mg

Flavorful Lamb Korma

(Servings: 4|Cooking Time: 30 minutes)

Ingredients:

- 1 lb. lamb leg, cut into pieces
- ½ tsp. fresh lime juice
- 2 tbsp. cilantro, chopped
- ½ tsp. cardamom powder
- ½ cup coconut milk
- 2 tbsp. tomato paste
- 2 tbsp. ginger garlic paste
- 1 onion, chopped
- 1 tsp. chili powder
- 1 tsp. paprika
- ¼ tsp. cayenne pepper
- ½ tsp. turmeric
- 3 tsp. garam masala
- 3/4 cup water
- 1 tbsp. olive oil
- 1 tsp. salt

Directions for Cooking:

1. Add oil into instant pot and set on Sauté mode.
2. Add ginger garlic paste to the pot and sauté for a minute.
3. Add ¼ cup of water, tomato paste and all spices. Stir well.
4. Add coconut milk, remaining water and meat. Stir well.
5. Seal pot with lid and cook on manual high pressure for 15 minutes.
6. Allow pressure to release naturally for 15 minutes, then release using quick release method.
7. Add lime juice and stir well.
8. Garnish with cilantro and serve.

Nutrition information per serving:

Calories: 346; Carbohydrates: 8.3g; Protein: 33.9g; Fat: 19.8g; Sugar: 3.3g; Sodium: 742mg

Tomato Lamb Curry

(Servings: 6|Cooking Time: 58 minutes)

Ingredients:

- 2 lbs. lamb, cut into pieces
- ½ cup water
- 14 oz. can tomatoes, diced
- ½ tsp. cayenne
- 1 tsp. turmeric
- 1 tsp. paprika
- 1 tsp. garam masala
- 1 tsp. ground cumin
- 1 tbsp. coriander powder
- 1 bay leaf
- 3 cardamom pods
- 3 garlic cloves, minced
- 1 tbsp. ginger, minced
- 2 onions, diced
- 2 tbsp. olive oil
- 2 cloves
- 2 tsp. salt

Directions for Cooking:

1. Add oil into instant pot and set on Sauté mode.
2. Add meat to the pot and sauté until browned.
3. Add garlic, onion, spices and ginger. Sauté for 2-3 minutes.
4. Add water and tomatoes. Stir well.
5. Seal pot with lid and cook on manual high pressure for 45 minutes.
6. Allow pressure to release naturally for 10 minutes, then release using quick release method.
7. Stir well and serve.

Nutrition information per serving:

Calories: 360; Carbohydrates: 8.6g; Protein: 43.8g; Fat: 16.1g; Sugar: 3.9g; Sodium: 1035mg

Asian Lamb Curry

(Servings: 6|Cooking Time: 20 minutes)

Ingredients:

- 2 lbs. lamb meat, bone-in
- ½ tbsp. fish sauce
- 2 garlic cloves, crushed
- ½ cup chicken broth
- 4 oz. unsweetened coconut milk
- 2 tbsp. green curry paste
- ½ cup coconut cream
- ¼ cup cilantro, chopped
- ½ tbsp. lime juice
- 6 oz. green beans, chopped
- ½ tbsp. soy sauce
- 1 small onion, minced
- 1 tbsp. olive oil
- Pepper
- Salt

Directions for Cooking:

1. Season meat with pepper and salt.
2. Add oil into instant pot and set on Sauté mode.
3. Add garlic and onion to the pot. Sauté for 4 minutes.
4. Add curry paste and coconut cream. Cook for 5 minutes.
5. Add meat, fish sauce, soy sauce, broth and coconut milk. Stir well.
6. Seal pot with lid and cook on manual high pressure for 8 minutes.
7. Quick release pressure then open the lid.
8. Add lime juice and green beans and cook on Sauté mode for 2-3 minutes.
9. Garnish with cilantro and serve.

Nutrition information per serving:

Calories: 518; Carbohydrates: 10.7g; Protein: 45.6g; Fat: 32.5g; Sugar: 1.7g; Sodium: 602mg

Tasty Lamb Rogan Josh

(Servings: 4|Cooking Time: 35 minutes)

Ingredients:

- 1 lb. leg of lamb, cut into cubes
- 1 tsp. turmeric
- 1 tsp. paprika
- 2 tsp. garam masala
- ¼ cup cilantro, chopped
- 4 garlic cloves, minced
- ½ tsp. ground cinnamon
- 1 onion, diced
- 1 tbsp. tomato paste
- ¼ cup yogurt
- ¼ cup water
- ¼ tsp. cayenne pepper
- 2 tsp. ginger, minced
- 1 tsp. salt

Directions for Cooking:

1. Add all ingredients into the mixing bowl and stir well. Place bowl in refrigerator for 2 hours.
2. Add marinated meat with marinade into instant pot.
3. Seal pot with lid and cook on manual high pressure for 20 minutes.
4. Allow pressure to release naturally for 15 minutes, then release using quick release method.
5. Serve and enjoy.

Nutrition information per serving:
Calories: 248; Carbohydrates: 7g; Protein: 33.6g; Fat: 8.8g; Sugar: 2.9g; Sodium: 687mg

Parmesan Lamb Chops

(Servings: 3|Cooking Time: 18 minutes)

Ingredients:

- 3 lamb chops
- 1 cup water
- ¼ tsp. dried oregano, crushed
- ½ tsp. garlic powder
- 1 tbsp. olive oil
- ½ cup parmesan cheese
- ¼ tsp. dried basil, crushed
- Pepper
- Salt

Directions for Cooking:

1. Season lamb chops with pepper, garlic powder and salt.
2. Place seasoned lamb chops into instant pot and cook on Sauté mode for 4 minutes per side.
3. Remove lamb chops from pot and place on a dish.
4. Pour water into instant pot then insert trivet.
5. Place lamb chops on trivet.
6. Seal pot with lid and cook on manual high pressure for 10 minutes.
7. Quick release pressure then open the lid.
8. Serve and enjoy.

Nutrition information per serving:
Calories: 323; Carbohydrates: 1.4g; Protein: 32.2g; Fat: 21g; Sugar: 0.1g; Sodium: 585mg

Soy Garlic Lamb

(Servings: 6|Cooking Time: 17 minutes)

Ingredients:

- 2 lbs. lamb steak, cut into strips
- ½ cup soy sauce, low-sodium
- ½ cup water
- 3 garlic cloves, minced
- 1 tbsp. olive oil
- 2 scallions, chopped

- 3 tbsp. water
- 2 tbsp. arrowroot

Directions for Cooking:
1. Add oil into instant pot and set on Sauté mode.
2. Add meat to the pot and cook for 5 minutes.
3. Add the ginger and garlic. Cook for a minute.
4. Add remaining ingredients and stir well.
5. Seal pot with lid and cook on manual high pressure for 12 minutes.
6. Quick release pressure then open the lid.
7. Serve and enjoy.

Nutrition information per serving:
Calories: 318; Carbohydrates: 2.8g; Protein: 44.1g; Fat: 13.5g; Sugar: 0.5g; Sodium: 1315mg

Meatloaf

(Servings: 6|Cooking Time: 45 minutes)

Ingredients:
- 2 lbs. ground beef
- ½ tsp. sage
- 1 tsp. parsley
- 1 tsp. oregano
- 1 tsp. thyme
- 1 ½ cups water
- 2 eggs
- 3 tbsp. olive oil
- 1 tsp. garlic salt
- 1 tsp. rosemary

Directions for Cooking:
1. Pour water into instant pot and insert trivet.
2. Spray loaf pan with cooking spray.
3. Add all ingredients into the mixing bowl and mix until well combined.
4. Pour mixture into the prepared loaf pan and press down gently.
5. Place loaf pan on trivet. Seal pot with lid and cook on manual high pressure for 30 minutes.
6. Allow pressure to release naturally for 15 minutes, then release using quick release method.
7. Serve and enjoy.

Nutrition information per serving:
Calories: 366; Carbohydrates: 0.9g; Protein: 47.9g; Fat: 18g; Sugar: 0.2g; Sodium: 122mg

Mexican Cheese Beef

(Servings: 4|Cooking Time: 12 minutes)

Ingredients:
- 1 lb. ground beef
- 12 oz. Mexican cheese
- 1 tbsp. Cajun seasoning
- 1 tbsp. olive oil
- 2 tbsp. tomato paste
- 1 cup beef broth

Directions for Cooking:
1. Add oil into instant pot and set on Sauté mode.
2. Add meat to the pot and sauté until browned.
3. Add Cajun seasoning and tomato paste. Stir well.
4. Pour broth over meat. Seal pot with lid and cook on manual high pressure for 7 minutes.
5. Quick release pressure then open the lid.
6. Add cheese and stir well. Seal pot again and cook on high for 5 minutes.
7. Quick release pressure then open the lid.
8. Stir and serve.

Nutrition information per serving:
Calories: 561; Carbohydrates: 4.8g; Protein: 54.2g; Fat: 38.3g; Sugar: 1.1g; Sodium: 888mg

Green chili Chuck Roast

(Servings: 4|Cooking Time: 65 minutes)

Ingredients:

- 2 lbs. chuck roast
- 8 oz. can green chilies, chopped
- 2 lemon juice
- 1 onion, sliced
- ½ cup water
- ½ tsp. pepper
- 1 tbsp. oregano
- 1 tbsp. cumin
- 3 garlic cloves, minced

Directions for Cooking:

1. Add all ingredients into instant pot and stir well.
2. Seal pot with lid and cook on manual high pressure for 60 minutes.
3. Quick release pressure then open the lid.
4. Remove meat from pot and shred the meat using a fork.
5. Return shredded meat to the pot. Stir well and cook on Sauté mode for 5 minutes.
6. Serve and enjoy.

Nutrition information per serving:

Calories: 526; Carbohydrates: 7.5g; Protein: 76.2g; Fat: 19.5g; Sugar: 1.3g; Sodium: 380mg

Delicious Mozzarella Cheese Beef

(Servings: 4|Cooking Time: 22 minutes)

Ingredients:

- 1 lb. ground beef
- 1 tbsp. olive oil
- ½ onion, diced
- 1 carrot, sliced
- 14 oz. can tomatoes, diced
- ½ cup mozzarella cheese, shredded
- ½ cup tomato puree
- 1 tsp. basil
- 1 tsp. oregano

Directions for Cooking:

1. Add oil into instant pot and set on Sauté mode.
2. Add onion to the pot and sauté for 2 minutes.
3. Add meat and cook until browned.
4. Add can tomatoes, oregano, basil and tomato puree. Stir well.
5. Seal pot with lid and cook on manual high pressure for 15 minutes.
6. Quick release pressure then open the lid.
7. Set pot on Sauté mode. Add mozzarella cheese and cook for 5 minutes.
8. Serve and enjoy.

Nutrition information per serving:

Calories: 297; Carbohydrates: 11g; Protein: 37.1g; Fat: 11.3g; Sugar: 6.2g; Sodium: 327mg

Beef with Cabbage

(Servings: 8|Cooking Time: 35 minutes)

Ingredients:

- 3 lbs. corned beef, chopped
- 1 tbsp. butter
- 2 bacon slices, diced
- 3 lbs. cabbage, chopped
- 1 onion, chopped
- 1 celery stalk, chopped
- ½ tsp. cumin
- 1 tsp. garlic powder
- 3 cups chicken broth
- 1 carrot, sliced

- ½ tsp. salt

Directions for Cooking:

1. Add butter into instant pot and set on Sauté mode.
2. Add bacon to the pot and cook until crisp.
3. Add meat and cook until browned.
4. Add remaining ingredients and stir well.
5. Seal pot with lid and cook on manual high pressure for 35 minutes.
6. Quick release pressure then open the lid.
7. Stir and serve.

Nutrition information per serving:
Calories: 395; Carbohydrates: 12.7g; Protein: 28.9g; Fat: 25.4g; Sugar: 6.8g; Sodium: 2095mg

Broccoli Beef

(Servings: 4|Cooking Time: 25 minutes)

Ingredients:

- 1 lb. beef, chopped
- 1 tbsp. fish sauce
- 12 oz. broccoli, chopped
- 1 onion, chopped
- 1 tsp. ground ginger
- 1 tsp. garlic, minced
- ¼ cup coconut aminos
- Pepper
- Salt

Directions for Cooking:

1. Add all ingredients except broccoli into instant pot and stir well.
2. Seal pot with lid and cook on Meat/Stew mode for 20 minutes.
3. Quick release pressure then open the lid.
4. Add broccoli and cook on Sauté mode for 5 minutes.
5. Stir well and serve.

Nutrition information per serving:
Calories: 270; Carbohydrates: 12g; Protein: 37.4g; Fat: 7.4g; Sugar: 2.8g; Sodium: 507mg

Apple Cider Beef

(Servings: 6|Cooking Time: 90 minutes)

Ingredients:

- 3 lbs. chuck roast
- 1 tsp. oregano
- 4 garlic cloves
- ¼ cup apple cider vinegar
- 1 tsp. basil
- ½ tsp. ground ginger
- 1 tsp. marjoram
- 1 tsp. onion powder
- 1 cup chicken broth
- 1 tsp. salt

Directions for Cooking:

1. Using a knife, make slit cut on meat then press garlic inside the slit.
2. Mix together spices and herbs and rub over the meat.
3. Place meat into the pot. Pour broth and vinegar over the meat.
4. Seal pot with lid and cook on manual high pressure for 90 minutes.
5. Quick release pressure then open the lid.
6. Serve and enjoy.

Nutrition information per serving:
Calories: 504; Carbohydrates: 1.6g; Protein: 75.9g; Fat: 19g; Sugar: 0.3g; Sodium: 666mg

Jalapeno Pepper Beef

(Servings: 4|Cooking Time: 15 minutes)

Ingredients:

- 1 lb. lean minced beef
- 1 can tomato, chopped
- 2 tsp. Cajun seasoning
- 3 garlic cloves, minced
- 1 roasted red pepper, chopped
- 2 tsp. olive oil
- 1 tbsp. pickled jalapeno, chopped
- 1 onion, chopped
- ½ tsp. black pepper
- ½ tsp. sea salt

Directions for Cooking:

1. Add oil into instant pot and set on Sauté mode.
2. Add onion into the pot and sauté until softened.
3. Add Cajun seasoning and garlic. Sauté for a minute.
4. Add beef and peppers. Cook until meat is no longer pink.
5. Add water and tomatoes. Stir well.
6. Seal pot with lid and cook on manual high pressure for 15 minutes.
7. Quick release pressure then open the lid.
8. Serve and enjoy.

Nutrition information per serving:

Calories: 209; Carbohydrates: 7.6g; Protein: 25.5g; Fat: 8g; Sugar: 2g; Sodium: 304mg

Flavorful Taco Meat

(Servings: 6|Cooking Time: 18 minutes)

Ingredients:

- 1 ½ lbs. beef minced
- 1 onion, chopped
- ¼ tsp. smoked paprika
- ½ tsp. garlic powder
- ½ tsp. onion powder
- ½ tsp. dried basil
- 1 tsp. paprika
- 1 tsp. oregano
- 2 tomatoes, chopped
- 3 garlic cloves, minced
- 1 bell pepper, chopped
- ½ tbsp. olive oil
- ½ tsp. ground cumin
- ¼ tsp. black pepper
- 1 tsp. salt

Directions for Cooking:

1. Add oil into the pot and set on Sauté mode.
2. Add meat and sauté for 3 minutes.
3. Add remaining ingredients and stir well.
4. Seal pot with lid and cook on manual high pressure for 15 minutes.
5. Quick release pressure then open the lid.
6. Stir well and serve.

Nutrition information per serving:

Calories: 401; Carbohydrates: 33.4g; Protein: 10.1g; Fat: 24.1g; Sugar: 3.1g; Sodium: 392mg

Chapter 7 Instant Pot Soup &Stew Recipes

Carrot Peanut Butter Soup

(Servings: 4|Cooking Time: 15 minutes)

Ingredients:

- 8 carrots, peeled and chopped
- 1 onion, chopped
- 3 garlic cloves, peeled
- 14 oz. coconut milk
- 1 ½ cup chicken stock
- ¼ cup peanut butter
- 1 tbsp. curry paste
- Pepper
- Salt

Directions for Cooking:

1. Add all ingredients except salt and pepper into instant pot and stir well.
2. Seal pot with lid and cook on manual high pressure for 15 minutes.
3. Quick release pressure then open the lid.
4. Puree the soup using an immersion blender until smooth.
5. Season soup with pepper and salt.
6. Serve and enjoy.

Nutrition information per serving:
Calories: 416; Carbohydrates: 25.3g; Protein: 8.2g; Fat: 34.2g; Sugar: 12.3g; Sodium: 500mg

Healthy Chicken Vegetable Soup

(Servings: 6|Cooking Time: 14 minutes)

Ingredients:

- 2 chicken breasts, cut into cubes
- ½ tsp. red pepper flakes
- ¼ cup fresh parsley, chopped
- 1 tsp. garlic powder
- 3 cups chicken broth
- 14 oz. can tomatoes, diced
- ¼ cup cabbage, shredded
- 1 cup frozen green beans
- ¼ cup frozen peas
- ½ cup frozen corn
- 2 celery stalks, chopped
- 1 carrot, peeled and cubed
- ½ sweet potato, peeled and cubed
- 3 garlic cloves, minced
- ½ onion, chopped
- ½ tsp. pepper
- 1 tsp. salt

Directions for Cooking:

1. Add all ingredients into instant pot and stir well.
2. Seal pot with lid and cook on manual high pressure for 4 minutes.
3. Allow pressure to release naturally for 10 minutes, then release using quick release method.
4. Stir well and serve.

Nutrition information per serving:
Calories: 171; Carbohydrates: 13.9g; Protein: 18.9g; Fat: 4.6g; Sugar: 5.4g; Sodium: 977mg

Chicken Rice Noodle Soup

(Servings: 6|Cooking Time: 10 minutes)

Ingredients:

- 6 cups chicken, cooked and cubed
- 3 tbsp. rice vinegar
- 2 ½ cups cabbage, shredded
- 2 tbsp. fresh ginger, grated
- 2 tbsp. soy sauce
- 3 garlic cloves, minced
- 8 oz. rice noodles
- 1 bell pepper, chopped
- 1 large carrot, peeled and sliced
- 6 cups chicken stock
- 2 celery stalks, sliced
- 1 onion, chopped
- ½ tsp. black pepper

Directions for Cooking:

1. Add all ingredients into instant pot and stir well.
2. Seal pot with lid and cook on manual high pressure for 10 minutes.
3. Quick release pressure then open the lid.
4. Stir well and serve.

Nutrition information per serving:
Calories: 306; Carbohydrates: 18.7g; Protein: 43.1g; Fat: 5.1g; Sugar: 4.3g; Sodium: 1180mg

Creamy Squash Soup

(Servings: 4|Cooking Time: 15 minutes)

Ingredients:

- 4 lbs. butternut squash, peeled, seeded, and cubed
- 4 cups beef stock
- ½ tsp. sage
- 1 tsp. thyme
- 2 garlic cloves, minced
- 1 onion, chopped
- 2 tbsp. olive oil
- Pepper
- Salt

Directions for Cooking:
1. Add oil into instant pot and set on Sauté mode.
2. Add garlic and onion to the pot. Sauté for 5 minutes.
3. Add sage, thyme, pepper and salt. Stir for a minute.
4. Add squash and stock. Stir well.
5. Seal pot with lid and cook on manual high pressure for 10 minutes.
6. Quick release pressure then open the lid.
7. Puree the soup using an immersion blender until smooth and creamy.
8. Serve and enjoy.

Nutrition information per serving:
Calories: 295; Carbohydrates: 56.4g; Protein: 7.7g; Fat: 8.1g; Sugar: 11.2g; Sodium: 841mg

Spicy Mushroom Soup
(Servings: 2|Cooking Time: 11 minutes)

Ingredients:
- 1 cup mushrooms, chopped
- ½ tsp. chili powder
- 2 tsp. garam masala
- 3 tbsp. olive oil
- 1 tsp. fresh lemon juice
- 5 cups chicken stock
- ¼ cup fresh celery, chopped
- 2 garlic cloves, crushed
- 1 onion, chopped
- ½ tsp. black pepper
- 1 tsp. sea salt

Directions for Cooking:
1. Add oil into instant pot and set on Sauté mode.
2. Add garlic and onion to the pot. Sauté for 5 minutes.
3. Add chili powder and garam masala. Cook for a minute.
4. Add remaining ingredients and stir well.
5. Seal pot with lid and cook on manual high pressure for 5 minutes.
6. Quick release pressure then open the lid.
7. Puree the soup using a blender and serve.

Nutrition information per serving:
Calories: 244; Carbohydrates: 10.2g; Protein: 3.9g; Fat: 22.8g; Sugar: 5g; Sodium: 287mg

Kale Beef Soup
(Servings: 4|Cooking Time: 43 minutes)

Ingredients:
- 1 lb. beef stew meat
- 1 tsp. cayenne pepper
- 3 garlic cloves, crushed
- 4 cups chicken broth
- 2 tbsp. olive oil
- 1 cup kale, chopped
- 1 onion, sliced
- ¼ tsp. black pepper
- ½ tsp. salt

Directions for Cooking:
1. Add oil into instant pot and set on Sauté mode.
2. Add garlic and onion. Sauté for 3 minutes.
3. Add meat and sauté for 5 minutes.
4. Add broth and season with cayenne pepper, pepper and salt. Stir well.
5. Seal pot with lid and cook on manual high pressure for 25 minutes.
6. Quick release pressure then open the lid.
7. Add kale and stir well. Sit for 10 minutes.
8. Stir well and serve.

Nutrition information per serving:
Calories: 333; Carbohydrates: 6.3g; Protein: 40.3g; Fat: 15.6g; Sugar: 1.9g; Sodium: 1137mg

Creamy Cauliflower Soup

(Servings: 4|Cooking Time: 32 minutes)

Ingredients:

- 2 cups cauliflower florets
- 1 tsp. pumpkin pie spice
- 5 cups chicken broth
- 3 tbsp. olive oil
- 1 onion, chopped
- ¼ tsp. salt

Directions for Cooking:

1. Add oil into instant pot and set on Sauté mode.
2. Add onion to the pot and sauté for 5 minutes.
3. Add cauliflower and cook for a minute. Add broth and season with sea salt.
4. Seal pot with lid and cook on manual high pressure for 24 minutes.
5. Quick release pressure then open the lid.
6. Puree the soup using an immersion blender until smooth.
7. Add pumpkin pie spice and stir well. Cook on Sauté mode for 2 minutes.
8. Serve and enjoy.

Nutrition information per serving:

Calories: 163; Carbohydrates: 6.7g; Protein: 7.4g; Fat: 12.3g; Sugar: 3.3g; Sodium: 1118mg

Kale Cottage Cheese Soup

(Servings: 4|Cooking Time: 5 minutes)

Ingredients:

- 5 cups fresh kale, chopped
- 1 tbsp. olive oil
- 1 cup cottage cheese, cut into small chunks
- 3 cups chicken broth
- ½ tsp. black pepper
- ½ tsp. sea salt

Directions for Cooking:

1. Add all ingredients except cottage cheese into instant pot and stir well.
2. Seal pot with lid and cook on manual high pressure for 5 minutes.
3. Quick release pressure then open the lid.
4. Add cottage cheese and stir well.
5. Serve hot and enjoy.

Nutrition information per serving:

Calories: 152; Carbohydrates: 11.7g; Protein: 13.9g; Fat: 5.6g; Sugar: 0.7g; Sodium: 1072mg

Simple Kale Chicken Soup

(Servings: 4|Cooking Time: 15 minutes)

Ingredients:

- 2 cups chicken breast, cooked and chopped
- 2 tsp. garlic, minced
- ½ tsp. cinnamon
- 4 cups vegetable broth
- 1 onion, diced
- 12 oz. kale
- 1 tsp. salt

Directions for Cooking:

1. Add all ingredients into instant pot and stir well.
2. Seal pot with lid and cook on manual high pressure for 5 minutes.

3. Allow pressure to release naturally for 10 minutes, then release using quick release method.
4. Stir well and serve warm.

Nutrition information per serving:
Calories: 158; Carbohydrates: 13.1g; Protein: 19.7g; Fat: 2.8g; Sugar: 1.9g; Sodium: 1411mg

Mushroom Chicken Soup

(Servings: 4|Cooking Time: 25 minutes)

Ingredients:
- 1 lb. chicken breast, cut into chunks
- 1 tsp. Italian seasoning
- 2 ½ cups chicken stock
- 1 small yellow squash, chopped
- 2 cups mushrooms, sliced
- 2 garlic cloves, minced
- 1 onion, sliced
- 1 tsp. black pepper
- 1 tsp. salt

Directions for Cooking:
1. Add all ingredients into instant pot and stir well.
2. Seal pot with lid and cook on manual high pressure for 15 minutes.
3. Allow pressure to release naturally for 10 minutes, then release using quick release method.
4. Remove chicken from pot and puree the vegetable mixture using a blender.
5. Shred the chicken using a fork. Return shredded chicken to the pot and stir well.
6. Serve and enjoy.

Nutrition information per serving:
Calories: 166; Carbohydrates: 6.1g; Protein: 26.4g; Fat: 3.8g; Sugar: 2.8g; Sodium: 1123mg

Coconut Chicken Soup

(Servings: 4|Cooking Time: 15 minutes)

Ingredients:
- 1 lb. chicken thighs, boneless and cut into chunks
- 2 cups Swiss chard, chopped
- 1 ½ cups celery stalks, chopped
- 1 tsp. turmeric
- 1 tbsp. chicken broth base
- 10 oz. can tomato
- 1 cup coconut milk
- 1 tbsp. ginger, grated
- 4 garlic cloves, minced
- 1 onion, chopped

Directions for Cooking:
1. Add ½ cup of coconut milk, broth base, turmeric, tomatoes, ginger, garlic and onion to the blender; blend until smooth.
2. Transfer blended the mixture to the instant pot along with Swiss chard, celery and chicken. Stir well.
3. Seal pot with lid and cook on manual high pressure for 5 minutes.
4. Allow pressure to release naturally for 10 minutes, then release using quick release method.
5. Add remaining coconut oil and stir well.
6. Serve and enjoy.

Nutrition information per serving:
Calories: 473; Carbohydrates: 29.7g; Protein: 39.5g; Fat: 23.9g; Sugar: 4.7g; Sodium: 560mg

Taco Cheese Soup

(Servings: 8|Cooking Time: 25 minutes)

Ingredients:

- 1 lb. ground beef
- 1 lb. ground pork
- ½ cup Monterey Jack cheese, grated
- 2 tbsp. parsley, chopped
- 4 cups beef broth
- 20 oz. can tomatoes
- 16 oz. cream cheese
- 2 tbsp. taco seasonings

Directions for Cooking:

1. Add both the ground meats in the instant pot and sauté for 10 minutes.
2. Add taco seasonings, tomatoes and cream cheese. Stir to combine.
3. Seal pot with lid and cook on manual high pressure for 15 minutes.
4. Quick release pressure then open the lid.
5. Add parsley and stir well. Top with grated cheese and serve.

Nutrition information per serving:

Calories: 445; Carbohydrates: 5.7g; Protein: 41.1g; Fat: 28.1g; Sugar: 2.9g; Sodium: 808mg

Asparagus Garlic Ham Soup

(Servings: 4|Cooking Time: 50 minutes)

Ingredients:

- 1 ½ lbs. asparagus, chopped
- 4 cups chicken stock
- 2 tsp. garlic, minced
- 3 tbsp. olive oil
- 1 onion, diced
- ¾ cup ham, diced
- ½ tsp. thyme

Directions for Cooking:

1. Add oil into instant pot and set on Sauté mode.
2. Add onion and sauté for 4 minutes.
3. Add garlic and ham and cook for a minute.
4. Add stock and thyme. Stir well.
5. Seal pot with lid and cook on Soup mode for 45 minutes.
6. Quick release pressure then open the lid,
7. Stir well and serve.

Nutrition information per serving:

Calories: 188; Carbohydrates: 11.4g; Protein: 9g; Fat: 13.5g; Sugar: 5.1g; Sodium: 1099mg

Asian Pork Soup

(Servings: 5|Cooking Time: 30 minutes)

Ingredients:

- 1 lb. ground pork
- 1 tsp. ground ginger
- ¼ cup soy sauce
- 4 cups beef broth
- ½ cabbage head, chopped
- 2 carrots, peeled and shredded
- 1 onion, chopped
- 1 tbsp. olive oil
- Pepper
- Salt

Directions for Cooking:

1. Add oil into instant pot and set on Sauté mode.
2. Add meat to the pot and sauté for 5 minutes.
3. Add remaining ingredients and stir well.
4. Seal pot with lid and cook on manual high pressure for 25 minutes.

5. Quick release pressure then open the lid.
6. Stir well and serve hot.

Nutrition information per serving:
Calories: 229; Carbohydrates: 10.6g; Protein: 29.8g; Fat: 7.2g; Sugar: 5.2g; Sodium: 1443mg

Creamy Potato Soup

(Servings: 6|Cooking Time: 9 minutes)

Ingredients:
- 3 lbs. russet potatoes, peeled and diced
- 15 oz. can coconut milk
- 3 cups chicken broth
- ½ tsp. dried thyme
- 2 carrots, peeled and sliced
- 3 garlic cloves, minced
- 1 onion, chopped
- 2 tbsp. olive oil
- Pepper
- Salt

Directions for Cooking:
1. Add oil into instant pot and set on Sauté mode.
2. Add onion and garlic. Sauté for 3-4 minutes.
3. Add remaining ingredients except for coconut milk and stir well.
4. Seal pot with lid and cook on manual high pressure for 9 minutes.
5. Quick release pressure then open the lid.
6. Puree the soup using an immersion blender until smooth.
7. Add coconut milk and stir well.
8. Season soup with pepper and salt.
9. Serve and enjoy.

Nutrition information per serving:
Calories: 373; Carbohydrates: 42.3g; Protein: 20.7g; Fat: 20.7g; Sugar: 4.8g; Sodium: 447mg

Mexican Chicken Fajita Soup

(Servings: 4|Cooking Time: 24 minutes)

Ingredients:
- 1 lb. chicken breast, boneless
- 1 tsp. coriander powder
- 1 tsp. ground cumin
- 1 scallion, chopped
- 1 tbsp. fresh lemon juice
- 2 cups chicken stock
- 14 oz. can tomatoes, diced
- 2 cups bell pepper, chopped
- 1 tbsp. garlic, minced
- 1 jalapeno pepper, diced
- 1 cup onion, diced
- 1 tbsp. olive oil
- ¼ tsp. red pepper flakes
- 1 tsp. salt

Directions for Cooking:
1. Add oil to instant pot and set on Sauté mode.
2. Add garlic, onion, bell pepper and jalapeno. Sauté for 2 minutes.
3. Add chicken, spices, stock and tomatoes. Stir well.
4. Seal pot with lid and cook on manual high pressure for 12 minutes.
5. Allow pressure to release naturally for 10 minutes, then release using quick release method.
6. Remove chicken from pot and shred using a fork. Return shredded chicken to the pot and stir well.
7. Add lemon juice and stir well.
8. Garnish with scallions and serve.

Nutrition information per serving:
Calories: 224; Carbohydrates: 14.2g; Protein: 26.6g; Fat: 7g; Sugar: 8.3g; Sodium: 1238mg

Butternut Squash Garlic Soup

(Servings: 6|Cooking Time: 12 minutes)

Ingredients:

- 1 lb. butternut squash, cubed
- 2 cups chicken stock
- 1 tsp. paprika
- ½ tsp. dried thyme
- ¼ tsp. red pepper flakes
- 1 onion, diced
- 2 tsp. olive oil
- 3 garlic cloves, minced
- 1 lb. cauliflower, chopped
- ½ cup heavy cream
- ½ tsp. salt

Directions for Cooking:

1. Add oil into instant pot and set on Sauté mode.
2. Add onion and garlic to the pot. Sauté for 5 minutes.
3. Add paprika, thyme and red pepper flakes. Sauté for a minute.
4. Add squash and cook for 2 minutes. Add cauliflower and stock. Stir well.
5. Seal pot with lid and cook on manual high pressure for 5 minutes.
6. Quick release pressure then open the lid.
7. Puree the soup using an immersion blender until smooth.
8. Serve and enjoy.

Nutrition information per serving:

Calories: 115; Carbohydrates: 15.9g; Protein: 3.1g; Fat: 5.7g; Sugar: 4.6g; Sodium: 479mg

Tomato Almond Milk Soup

(Servings: 6|Cooking Time: 8 minutes)

Ingredients:

- 4 cups tomatoes, peeled, seeded and chopped
- ½ tsp. baking soda
- 1 cup chicken stock
- ½ cup heavy cream
- 1 ½ cups almond milk
- Pepper
- Salt

Directions for Cooking:

1. Add tomatoes and stock into the pot and stir well. Season with pepper and salt.
2. Seal pot with lid and cook on manual high pressure for 3 minutes.
3. Quick release pressure then open the lid.
4. Add baking soda to the pot and stir well.
5. Add heavy cream, almond milk, pepper and salt. Stir well.
6. Puree the soup using an immersion blender until smooth. Cook soup on Sauté mode for 5 minutes more.
7. Stir and serve.

Nutrition information per serving:

Calories: 196; Carbohydrates: 8.4g; Protein: 2.8g; Fat: 18.3g; Sugar: 5.3g; Sodium: 277mg

Squash Nutmeg Soup

(Servings: 6|Cooking Time: 18 minutes)

Ingredients:

- 6 cups butternut squash, peeled and cubed
- 1/8 tsp. nutmeg
- 3 cups chicken stock
- 1 onion, chopped
- 2 tbsp. olive oil
- 1/8 tsp. cayenne pepper
- 2 tsp. thyme
- ¼ cup heavy cream
- Pepper

- Salt

Directions for Cooking:

1. Add oil into instant pot and set on Sauté mode.
2. Add onion to the pot and sauté for 3 minutes.
3. Add squash, nutmeg, cayenne, thyme, stock, and salt. Stir well.
4. Seal pot with lid and cook on manual high pressure for 5 minutes.
5. Allow pressure to release naturally for 10 minutes, then release using quick release method.
6. Add heavy cream and stir well. Puree the soup using an immersion blender until smooth.
7. Season soup with pepper and salt.
8. Serve and enjoy.

Nutrition information per serving:
Calories: 134; Carbohydrates: 18.9g; Protein: 2.1g; Fat: 7g; Sugar: 4.2g; Sodium: 417mg

Tomato Basil Soup

(Servings: 6|Cooking Time: 36 minutes)

Ingredients:

- 28 oz. can tomatoes
- 1 3/4 cup coconut milk
- ½ cup fresh basil, chopped
- 1 fresh thyme sprig
- 1 cup carrots, diced
- 1 cup celery, diced
- 3 ½ cups chicken stock
- 1 cup onion, diced
- 1/3 cup cheddar cheese, grated
- 2 bay leaves
- 1 tbsp. butter
- 2 tbsp. olive oil
- Pepper
- Salt

Directions for Cooking:

1. Add olive oil and butter into the pot. Set on Sauté mode.
2. Add celery, onion and carrots. Sauté for 5 minutes.
3. Add remaining ingredients and stir well.
4. Seal pot with lid and cook on manual high pressure for 30 minutes.
5. Quick release pressure then open the lid.
6. Puree the soup using an immersion blender until smooth.
7. Stir well and serve.

Nutrition information per serving:
Calories: 296; Carbohydrates: 15.3g; Protein: 5.3g; Fat: 25.8g; Sugar: 9.2g; Sodium: 844mg

Tomato Cabbage Soup

(Servings: 4|Cooking Time: 16 minutes)

Ingredients:

- 3 cups cabbage, chopped
- ½ onion, sliced
- 4 garlic cloves, diced
- 13 oz. can tomatoes, diced
- 2 tbsp. olive oil
- 6 oz. tomato paste
- 13 oz. can stewed tomatoes
- 4 cups water
- ¼ tsp. pepper
- 1 ½ tsp. salt

Directions for Cooking:

1. Add oil into the pot and set on Sauté mode.
2. Add onion and garlic. Sauté for 2 minutes.
3. Add cabbage, water, tomato paste and tomatoes. Stir well.
4. Seal pot with lid and cook on manual high pressure for 4 minutes.
5. Allow pressure to release naturally for 10 minutes, then release using quick release method.

6. Season with pepper and salt.
7. Serve and enjoy.

Nutrition information per serving:
Calories: 162; Carbohydrates: 23.8g; Protein: 4.5g; Fat: 7.5g; Sugar: 13.8g; Sodium: 1331mg

Bacon Asparagus Soup

(Servings: 4|Cooking Time: 20 minutes)

Ingredients:

- 25 asparagus spears, trimmed and cut into pieces
- 5 bacon slices, cooked and chopped
- 1 medium onion, chopped
- 3 cups chicken broth
- 1 tbsp. olive oil
- Pepper
- Salt

Directions for Cooking:

1. Add oil into instant pot and set on Sauté mode.
2. Add onion to the pot and sauté for 2-3 minutes.
3. Add remaining ingredients except for bacon and stir well.
4. Seal pot with lid and cook on manual high pressure for 10 minutes.
5. Allow pressure to release naturally for 10 minutes, then release using quick release method.
6. Puree the using immersion blender until smooth.
7. Add bacon and stir well. Season with pepper and salt.
8. Serve and enjoy.

Nutrition information per serving:
Calories: 228; Carbohydrates: 9.4g; Protein: 16g; Fat: 14.7g; Sugar: 4.5g; Sodium: 1164mg

Creamy Celery Soup

(Servings: 4|Cooking Time: 30 minutes)

Ingredients:

- 6 cups celery stalk, chopped
- 2 cups chicken broth
- ½ tsp. dill
- 1 cup coconut milk
- 1 medium onion, chopped
- ¼ tsp. salt

Directions for Cooking:

1. Add all ingredients into instant pot and stir well.
2. Seal pot with lid and cook on Soup mode for 30 minutes.
3. Quick release pressure then open the lid.
4. Puree the soup using an immersion blender until smooth.
5. Stir well and serve.

Nutrition information per serving:
Calories: 193; Carbohydrates: 10.9g; Protein: 5.2g; Fat: 15g; Sugar: 5.6g; Sodium: 660mg

Parmesan Spinach Broccoli Soup

(Servings: 6|Cooking Time: 7 minutes)

Ingredients:

- 2 cups spinach
- 4 cups broccoli florets
- ½ cup parmesan cheese, shredded
- 1 cup cheddar cheese, shredded
- 1 onion, chopped
- 4 cups chicken broth
- 1 ½ tsp. dry mustard
- 2 garlic cloves, minced
- 2 tbsp. olive oil
- 1 ½ tsp. salt

Directions for Cooking:

1. Add oil into instant pot and set on Sauté mode.
2. Add garlic, onion and spices. Sauté for 2 minutes.
3. Add broccoli florets and stir to combine. Pour broth and stir well.
4. Seal pot with lid and cook on manual high pressure for 4 minutes.
5. Quick release pressure then open the lid.
6. Add spinach and cook on Sauté mode until spinach wilted.
7. Puree the soup using a blender until smooth.
8. Add cheese and stir again to combine.
9. Serve and enjoy.

Nutrition information per serving:
Calories: 232; Carbohydrates: 8g; Protein: 15.4g; Fat: 16g; Sugar: 2.5g; Sodium: 1462mg

Coconut Pumpkin Soup

(Servings: 6|Cooking Time: 16 minutes)

Ingredients:

- 2 cups pumpkin puree
- 2 cups coconut milk
- ¼ cup bell pepper, chopped
- 1/8 tsp. thyme, dried
- 1 onion, chopped
- 2 cups chicken broth
- ¼ tsp. nutmeg
- ½ tsp. salt

Directions for Cooking:

1. Add pumpkin puree, bell pepper, onion, broth, nutmeg, thyme, milk and salt in instant pot. Stir well.
2. Seal pot with lid and cook on manual high pressure for 6 minutes.
3. Allow pressure to release naturally for 10 minutes, then release using quick release method.
4. Serve and enjoy.

Nutrition information per serving:
Calories: 234; Carbohydrates: 13.5g; Protein: 4.6g; Fat: 19.8g; Sugar: 6.7g; Sodium: 465mg

Thai Zucchini Soup

(Servings: 6|Cooking Time: 10 minutes)

Ingredients:

- 10 cups zucchini, chopped
- 1 tbsp. Thai curry paste
- 32 oz. chicken broth
- 13 oz. coconut milk

Directions for Cooking:

1. Add all ingredients into instant pot and stir well.
2. Seal pot with lid and cook on manual high pressure for 10 minutes.
3. Quick release pressure then open the lid.

4. Puree the soup using an immersion blender until smooth.
5. Serve and enjoy.

Nutrition information per serving:
Calories: 198; Carbohydrates: 10.8g; Protein: 6.7g; Fat: 15.8g; Sugar: 5.9g; Sodium: 574mg

Curried Carrot Soup

(Servings: 4|Cooking Time: 17 minutes)

Ingredients:
- 1 ¼ lbs. carrot, chopped
- ½ tsp. curry powder
- 1 jalapeno pepper, chopped
- 1 medium onion, chopped
- ½ cup coconut milk
- ¼ tsp. cayenne pepper
- ¼ tsp. turmeric
- ¼ tsp. garam masala
- 1 tbsp. olive oil
- 1 tsp. garlic powder
- 1 tsp. sea salt
- 4 cups chicken broth
- 2 tsp. ginger, grated

Directions for Cooking:
1. Add oil into instant pot and set on Sauté mode.
2. Add onion into the pot and sauté for 5 minutes.
3. Add carrot and pepper. Sauté for a minute.
4. Add remaining ingredients except for coconut milk and stir well.
5. Seal pot with lid and select cook on high for 12 minutes.
6. Quick release pressure then open the lid.
7. Puree the soup using a blender until smooth. Stir in coconut milk.
8. Serve and enjoy.

Nutrition information per serving:
Calories: 215; Carbohydrates: 20.7g; Protein:7.3 g; Fat: 12.2g; Sugar: 10.2g; Sodium: 1335mg

Chicken Celery Soup

(Servings: 6|Cooking Time: 23 minutes)

Ingredients:
- 2 chicken breast, skinless and boneless
- 2 celery stalks, diced
- ½ onion, diced
- 14 oz. coconut milk
- 4 cups chicken broth
- 2 carrots, diced

Directions for Cooking:
1. Add 1 cup of broth and chicken into instant pot. Stir well.
2. Seal pot with lid and cook on Poultry mode for 8 minutes.
3. Quick release pressure then open the lid.
4. Add remaining ingredients and stir well.
5. Seal pot with lid and cook on Soup mode for 15 minutes.
6. Quick release pressure then open the lid.
7. Serve and enjoy.

Nutrition information per serving:
Calorie: 229; Carbohydrates:7.3g; Protein: 12.1 g; Fat: 17.5g; Sugar: 4.1g; Sodium: 555mg

Italian Leek Cabbage Soup

(Servings: 4|Cooking Time: 20 minutes)

Ingredients:

- ½ cabbage head, chopped
- 2 tbsp. olive oil
- 2 leeks, chopped
- 1 garlic clove, minced
- 2 carrots, diced
- 1 tsp. Creole seasoning
- 1 tsp. Italian seasoning
- 4 cups chicken broth
- 1 bell pepper, diced
- 3 celery ribs, diced
- 2 cups mixed salad greens
- Pepper
- Salt

Directions for Cooking:

1. Add coconut oil into instant pot and set on Sauté mode.
2. Add all ingredients except salad greens into the pot. Stir well.
3. Seal pot with lid and cook on Soup mode for 20 minutes.
4. Quick release pressure then open the lid.
5. Add salad greens and stir until wilted.
6. Serve and enjoy.

Nutrition information per serving:
Calorie: 191; Carbohydrates: 21.2g; Protein: 8.3g; Fat: 9.1g; Sugar: 8.8g; Sodium: 1161mg

Carrot Broccoli Soup

(Servings: 4|Cooking Time: 40 minutes)

Ingredients:

- 2 cups broccoli florets, chopped
- 32 oz. chicken broth
- 2 tbsp. olive oil
- 2 small carrots, diced
- 2 celery stalks, sliced
- 1 onion, diced
- 1 ½ cup heavy whipping cream
- ½ tsp. pepper
- ½ tsp. salt

Directions for Cooking:

1. Add oil into instant pot and set on Sauté mode.
2. Add onion, carrots, and celery and sauté for 4-5 minutes.
3. Add remaining ingredients except whipping cream and stir well.
4. Seal pot with lid and cook on Soup mode for 25 minutes.
5. Allow pressure to release naturally for 10 minutes, then release using quick release method.
6. Add heavy whipping cream and stir well.
7. Serve and enjoy.

Nutrition information per serving:
Calorie: 290; Carbohydrates: 10.6g; Protein: 7.4g; Fat: 25g; Sugar: 4g; Sodium: 1069mg

Spinach Chicken Curry Soup

(Servings: 6|Cooking Time: 20 minutes)

Ingredients:

- 1 lb. chicken thighs, skinless and boneless
- 4 oz. baby spinach
- ½ onion, diced
- 1 ½ cups coconut milk
- ¼ cup cilantro, chopped
- 1 tsp. garam masala
- ½ tsp. cayenne pepper
- 1 cup mushrooms, sliced
- 1 tsp. ginger, chopped

- 3 garlic cloves, crushed
- ½ tsp. turmeric
- 1 tsp. salt

Directions for Cooking:

1. Add all ingredients into instant pot and stir well.
2. Seal pot with lid and cook on manual high pressure for 10 minutes.
3. Allow pressure to release naturally for 10 minutes, then release quick.

4. Remove chicken from pot and shred using a fork.
5. Return shredded chicken to the pot and stir well.
6. Serve and enjoy.

Nutrition information per serving:
Calorie: 297; Carbohydrates: 6.2g; Protein: 24.4g; Fat: 20.1g; Sugar: 2.7g; Sodium: 479mg

Balsamic Onion Soup

(Servings: 6|Cooking Time: 35 minutes)

Ingredients:

- 8 cups onions, peel and slice
- 1 tbsp. balsamic vinegar
- 6 cups chicken broth
- 2 tbsp. olive oil
- 2 fresh thyme sprigs
- 2 bay leaves
- 1 tsp. salt

Directions for Cooking:

1. Add oil into instant pot and set on Sauté mode.
2. Add onion into the pot and cook until soft, about 15 minutes.

3. Add remaining ingredients and stir well.
4. Seal pot with lid and cook on manual high pressure for 10 minutes.
5. Allow pressure to release naturally for 10 minutes, then release quick.
6. Discard bay leaves and thyme from the soup.
7. Puree the soup using an immersion blender until smooth.
8. Serve and enjoy.

Nutrition information per serving:
Calorie: 140; Carbohydrates: 15.3g; Protein: 6.5g; Fat: 6.2g; Sugar: 7.2g; Sodium: 1157mg

Black Bean Sweet Potato Soup

(Servings: 4|Cooking Time: 23 minutes)

Ingredients:

- 1 lb. sweet potato, diced
- 14 oz. can black beans, rinsed
- 2 tsp. ground cumin
- 2 tbsp. fresh cilantro, chopped
- 1 tsp. paprika
- 1 tsp. ground coriander
- 1 onion, diced
- ½ lime juice
- 1 cube chicken stock
- 3 cups water
- 2 cups tomatoes, chopped
- ½ red chili, sliced

- 3 garlic cloves, diced
- 2 tbsp. olive oil
- 2 tsp. salt

Directions for Cooking:

1. Add olive oil into instant pot and set the instant pot on Sauté mode.
2. Add onion into the pot and sauté for 5 minutes.
3. Add garlic, cilantro, chili, spices and salt. Stir well.
4. Add sweet potatoes, stock cube, water, tomatoes and beans. Stir well.

5. Seal pot with lid and cook on manual high pressure for 3 minutes.
6. Allow pressure to release naturally for 15 minutes, then release quick.
7. Add lime juice and stir well.

8. Garnish with cilantro and serve.

Nutrition information per serving:
Calorie: 292; Carbohydrates: 48.8g; Protein: 9.3g; Fat: 8.2g; Sugar: 11.9g; Sodium: 1584mg

Potato Kale Soup

(Servings: 6|Cooking Time: 10 minutes)

Ingredients:
- 3 large potatoes, peeled and chopped
- 6 cups chicken broth
- 4 carrots, cut into pieces
- 4 cups kale, chopped
- Salt and Pepper

Directions for Cooking:
1. Add all ingredients except kale into instant pot and stir well.
2. Seal pot with lid and cook on manual high pressure for 9 minutes.
3. Quick release pressure then open the lid.
4. Add kale and stir well. Seal pot again and cook on manual high pressure for 1 minute.
5. Quick release pressure then open the lid.
6. Stir well and serve.

Nutrition information per serving:
Calorie: 204; Carbohydrates: 38.6g; Protein: 9.6g; Fat: 1.6g; Sugar: 4.8g; Sodium: 849mg

Corn Bean Soup

(Servings: 4|Cooking Time: 20 minutes)

Ingredients:
- 4 cups chicken stock
- 16 oz. salsa
- 4 cups can black beans
- 2 cups frozen corn
- 1 tsp. chili powder
- 1 tsp. cumin
- 1 tsp. salt

Directions for Cooking:
1. Add all ingredients except corn into instant pot and stir well.
2. Seal pot with lid and cook on manual high pressure for 5 minutes.
3. Allow pressure to release naturally for 15 minutes, then release using quick release method.
4. Stir in corn and serve.

Nutrition information per serving:
Calories: 350; Carbohydrates: 68.9g; Protein: 19.1g; Fat: 2.9g; Sugar: 8.7g; Sodium: 3004mg

Carrot Ham Pea Soup

(Servings: 6|Cooking Time: 33 minutes)

Ingredients:
- 2 cups yellow split peas, soak in hot water for 30 minutes
- 5 medium carrots, peeled and sliced
- 3 cups ham, cut into cube
- 1 tsp. coriander
- 1 tsp. chili powder
- 1 tsp. turmeric
- 2 tbsp. olive oil
- 6 cups water
- ½ tsp. salt

Directions for Cooking:

1. Add olive oil into instant pot and set on Sauté mode.
2. Add ham into the pot and sauté for 10 minutes.
3. Add remaining ingredients and stir well.
4. Seal pot with lid and cook on Soup mode for 13 minutes.
5. Allow pressure to release naturally for 15 minutes, then release using quick release method.
6. Stir well and serve.

Nutrition information per serving:
Calories: 397; Carbohydrates: 47.7g; Protein: 27.8g; Fat: 11.4g; Sugar: 7.8g; Sodium: 1130mg

Garlic Carrot Potato Soup

(Servings: 4|Cooking Time: 24 minutes)

Ingredients:
- 1 medium onion, diced
- 3 cups chicken broth
- 1 medium carrot, diced
- 3 cups red potatoes, cubed
- 2 garlic cloves, chopped
- 1 tbsp. olive oil
- 1 tsp. pepper

Directions for Cooking:
1. Add olive oil in instant pot and set on Sauté mode.
2. Add potatoes, onion and garlic. Sauté for 4 minutes.
3. Seal pot with lid and cook on manual high pressure for 10 minutes.
4. Allow pressure to release naturally for 10 minutes, then release using quick release method.
5. Serve and enjoy.

Nutrition information per serving:
Calories: 158; Carbohydrates: 23.5g; Protein: 6.4g; Fat: 4.8g; Sugar: 3.6g; Sodium: 591mg

Celery Carrot White Bean Soup

(Servings: 4|Cooking Time: 25 minutes)

Ingredients:
- 14 oz. can white beans, rinsed and drained
- 14 oz. can tomatoes crushed, drained
- 1 carrot, diced
- 2 celery stalks, diced
- 3 cups chicken stock
- 1 garlic cloves, minced
- 1 onion, diced
- 2 tbsp. olive oil
- Pepper
- Salt

Directions for Cooking:
1. Add oil in instant pot and set on Sauté mode.
2. Add onion, carrot, garlic and celery. Sauté until softened.
3. Add tomatoes and stir well. Add white beans and vegetable stock in pot. Stir.
4. Seal with lid and cook on manual high pressure for 10 minutes.
5. Allow pressure to release naturally for 10 minutes, then release using quick release method.
6. Season soup with pepper and salt.
7. Serve and enjoy.

Nutrition information per serving:
Calories: 291; Carbohydrates: 46.7g; Protein: 12.9g; Fat: 8.4g; Sugar: 3.3g; Sodium: 1168mg

Cheese Potato Onion Soup

(Servings: 8|Cooking Time: 10 minutes)

Ingredients:
- 8 cups chicken stock
- 5 cups potatoes, diced
- 6 garlic cloves, minced
- 1 cup onion, diced
- 1 tbsp. season salt
- ¼ cup cheddar cheese, shredded
- 16 oz. cream cheese

Directions for Cooking:

1. Add stock, potatoes, garlic, onion and season salt in instant pot. Stir well.
2. Seal with lid and cook on manual high pressure for 10 minutes.
3. Quick release pressure then open the lid.
4. Add cream cheese stir until well.
5. Top with shredded cheese and serve.

Nutrition information per serving:
Calories: 296; Carbohydrates: 19.1g; Protein: 7.7g; Fat: 21.6g; Sugar: 2.6g; Sodium: 1832mg

Red Lentil Carrot Soup

(Servings: 4|Cooking Time: 25 minutes)

Ingredients:
- 1 cup red lentils, dried
- 2 tsp. ground coriander
- 2 tsp. ground cumin
- 1/8 tsp. cayenne
- 2 carrots, sliced
- 1 tbsp. tomato paste
- 5 cups vegetable stock
- 1 tsp. ginger, grated
- 2 garlic cloves, crushed
- 1 onion, chopped
- 2 celery stalks, sliced
- 1 tbsp. olive oil
- Pepper
- Salt

Directions for Cooking:

1. Add oil into instant pot and set on Sauté mode.
2. Add onion, celery, ginger and garlic into the pot. Sauté until softened.
3. Add remaining ingredients into the pot and stir well.
4. Seal pot with lid and cook on manual high pressure for 10 minutes.
5. Allow pressure to release naturally for 15 minutes, then release using quick release method.
6. Stir well and serve.

Nutrition information per serving:
Calories: 248; Carbohydrates: 39.3g; Protein: 13.5g; Fat: 6.9g; Sugar: 6.8g; Sodium: 977mg

Chapter 8 Instant Pot Rice Recipes

Squash Risotto

(Servings: 6|Cooking Time: 17 minutes)

Ingredients:

- 1 ½ cups Arborio rice
- 2 tbsp. fresh parsley, chopped
- 3 tbsp. butter
- 2 oz. parmesan cheese, grated
- 14 oz. chicken broth
- 3 cups butternut squash, peeled and cubed
- 1 cup water
- ½ cup onion, chopped
- 2 tsp. olive oil
- ¼ tsp. black pepper
- ½ tsp. salt

Directions for Cooking:

1. Add oil into instant pot and set on Sauté mode.
2. Add onion and sauté for 5 minutes.
3. Add rice and stir for a minute. Add ½ cup of water, pepper and salt. Stir continuously until water is absorbed.
4. Add broth, squash and remaining water. Stir well.
5. Seal pot with lid and cook on low for 12 minutes.
6. Quick release pressure then open the lid.
7. Add parsley, butter and cheese. Stir well.
8. Serve and enjoy.

Nutrition information per serving:

Calories: 312; Carbohydrates: 47.6g; Protein: 8.5g; Fat: 10.1g; Sugar: 2.2g; Sodium: 541mg

Citrusy Flavored Basil Rice

(Servings: 4|Cooking Time: 12 minutes)

Ingredients:
- 1 cup basmati rice
- ¼ cup fresh basil, chopped
- 1 tsp. lemon zest
- 2 tbsp. orange juice
- 1 tbsp. lemon zest, grated
- 1 tbsp. orange zest, grated
- 2 tbsp. butter
- 1 ½ cups vegetable broth

Directions for Cooking:

1. Add all ingredients except basil to the instant pot and stir well.
2. Seal pot with lid and cook on low for 12 minutes.
3. Quick release pressure then open the lid.
4. Fluff the rice using a fork.
5. Add basil and stir well. Serve and enjoy.

Nutrition information per serving:
Calories: 241; Carbohydrates: 39g; Protein: 5.4g; Fat: 6.6g; Sugar: 1.1g; Sodium: 330mg

Corn Pea Risotto

(Servings: 4|Cooking Time: 12 minutes)

Ingredients:
- 1 cup Arborio rice
- ½ cup sweet corn
- ½ cup peas
- 1 red pepper, diced
- 1 tsp. mix herbs
- 3 cups chicken broth
- 1 tbsp. olive oil
- 2 garlic cloves, minced
- 1 onion, chopped
- ¼ pepper
- ½ tsp. salt

Directions for Cooking:

1. Add olive oil in instant pot and set on Sauté mode.
2. Add onion and garlic. Sauté for 4 minutes.
3. Add rice and stir well to combine.
4. Add remaining ingredients and stir well.
5. Seal pot with lid and cook on manual high pressure for 8 minutes.
6. Quick release pressure then open the lid.
7. Stir and serve.

Nutrition information per serving:
Calories: 284; Carbohydrates: 50g; Protein: 9.1g; Fat: 5.2g; Sugar: 4.9g; Sodium: 872mg

Creamy Avocado Rice

(Servings: 3|Cooking Time: 18 minutes)

Ingredients:
- 1 cup rice
- ½ avocado, cubed
- ¼ cup green hot sauce
- ½ cup fresh cilantro, chopped
- 1 ¼ cups chicken broth
- Pepper
- Salt

Directions for Cooking:
1. Add broth and rice in instant pot.
2. Seal pot with lid and cook on manual high pressure for 3 minutes.

3. Allow pressure to release naturally for 15 minutes, then release using quick release method.
4. Add green sauce, avocado and cilantro in a blender. Blend until smooth.
5. Add avocado mixture into the rice and stir well. Season with pepper and salt.
6. Serve and enjoy.

Nutrition information per serving:
Calories: 310; Carbohydrates: 52.7g; Protein: 7.1g; Fat: 7.5g; Sugar: 0.6g; Sodium: 375mg

Maple Syrup Brown Rice

(Servings: 2|Cooking Time: 23 minutes)

Ingredients:

- 1 cup brown rice
- 1 ½ cups water
- 2 tbsp. maple syrup

Directions for Cooking:

1. Add all ingredients into instant pot.
2. Seal pot with lid and cook on manual high pressure for 8 minutes.
3. Allow pressure to release naturally for 15 minutes, then release using quick release method.
4. Serve and enjoy.

Nutrition information per serving:
Calories: 396; Carbohydrates: 85.8g; Protein: 7.1g; Fat: 2.6g; Sugar: 11.9g; Sodium: 11mg

Simple Garlic Rice

(Servings: 4|Cooking Time: 12 minutes)

Ingredients:

- 1 cup rice, rinsed and drained
- 1 tsp. garlic, minced
- 1 ½ cups chicken broth
- 1/8 tsp. salt

Directions for Cooking:

1. Add rice to instant pot.
2. Add garlic, broth and salt. Stir well.
3. Seal pot with lid and cook on low for 12 minutes.
4. Quick release pressure then open the lid carefully.
5. Fluff with a fork and serve.

Nutrition information per serving:
Calories: 184; Carbohydrates: 37.6g; Protein: 5.2g; Fat: 0.8g; Sugar: 0.3g; Sodium: 362mg

Jalapeno Tomato Brown Rice

(Servings: 3|Cooking Time: 40 minutes)

Ingredients:

- 1 cup brown rice
- ¼ cup tomato paste
- 1 onion, chopped
- 1 tbsp. olive oil
- 1 cup water
- 1 jalapeno pepper, sliced
- 2 garlic cloves, minced
- ½ tsp. salt

Directions for Cooking:

1. Add oil and onion in instant pot. Sauté for 3-4 minutes.
2. Add garlic and sauté for a minute.
3. Add brown rice, jalapeno, tomato paste and salt. Stir well. Pour water and stir.
4. Seal pot with lid and cook on manual high pressure for 15 minutes.
5. Allow pressure to release naturally for 10 minutes, then release using quick release method.
6. Serve and enjoy.

Nutrition information per serving:
Calories: 306; Carbohydrates: 56.7g; Protein: 6.3g; Fat: 6.6g; Sugar: 4.4g; Sodium: 416mg

Easy Butter Rice

(Servings: 3|Cooking Time: 25 minutes)

Ingredients:

- 1 cup brown rice
- 3/4 cup onion soup

- 4 tbsp. butter
- 3/4 cup vegetable broth

Directions for Cooking:

1. Add all ingredients into instant pot and stir well.
2. Seal pot with lid and cook on manual high pressure for 15 minutes.
3. Allow pressure to release naturally for 10 minutes, then release using quick release method.
4. Stir well and serve.

Nutrition information per serving:
Calories: 403; Carbohydrates: 52.6g; Protein: 8g; Fat: 18.3g; Sugar: 1.9g; Sodium: 831mg

Tasty Potato Risotto

(Servings: 4|Cooking Time: 25 minutes)

Ingredients:

- 2 cups rice
- 4 cups chicken stock
- 1 medium potato, cubed
- 1 tbsp. olive oil
- 1 tbsp. tomato paste
- 4 tbsp. white wine
- 1 medium onion, chopped
- 1 tsp. salt

Directions for Cooking:

1. Add oil into instant pot and set on Sauté mode.
2. Add onion and sauté for 2-3 minutes
3. Add rice and stir for 2 minutes.
4. Add white wine and stir until the rice absorbs wine.
5. Add stock, potatoes, tomato paste and salt. Stir well.
6. Seal pot with lid and cook on manual high pressure for 5 minutes.
7. Allow pressure to release naturally for 15 minutes, then release using quick release method.
8. Serve and enjoy.

Nutrition information per serving:
Calories: 445; Carbohydrates: 87.7g; Protein: 8.8g; Fat: 4.8g; Sugar: 3g; Sodium: 1359mg

Garlic Bean Rice

(Servings: 6|Cooking Time: 50 minutes)

Ingredients:

- 2 cups rice
- 2 cups dried black beans, rinsed and drained
- 1 large onion, diced
- ½ tbsp. olive oil
- 9 cups water
- 3 garlic cloves, minced
- 1 tsp. salt

Directions for Cooking:

1. Add oil into instant pot and set on Sauté mode.
2. Add onion and garlic. Sauté until onion is softened.
3. Add all remaining ingredients and stir well.
4. Seal pot with lid and cook on manual high pressure for 27 minutes.
5. Allow pressure to release naturally, then open lid.
6. Stir well and serve.

Nutrition information per serving:
Calories: 468; Carbohydrates: 92.5g; Protein: 18.8g; Fat: 2.5g; Sugar: 2.5g; Sodium: 406mg

Butter Paprika Rice

(Servings: 6|Cooking Time: 30 minutes)

Ingredients:

- 2 cups rice
- 2 ½ cups chicken broth
- 2 cubes chicken bouillon
- 3 tsp. paprika
- 2 tbsp. butter
- ¼ tsp. pepper
- 1 tsp. salt

Directions for Cooking:

1. Add all ingredients into instant pot and stir well.
2. Seal pot with lid and cook on manual high pressure for 7 minutes.
3. Release pressure naturally, then open the lid.
4. Fluff rice using the fork.
5. Serve and enjoy.

Nutrition information per serving:
Calories: 281; Carbohydrates: 50.5g; Protein: 6.8g; Fat: 5.1; Sugar: 0.6g; Sodium: 737mg

Salsa Rice

(Servings: 4|Cooking Time: 37 minutes)

Ingredients:

- 2 cups brown rice
- ½ cup salsa
- 2 cups water
- 1 tsp. cumin
- 1 tbsp. garlic salt

Directions for Cooking:

1. Add all ingredients into instant pot and stir well.
2. Seal pot with lid and cook on manual high pressure for 22 minutes.
3. Allow pressure to release naturally for 15 minutes, then release using quick release method.
4. Fluff rice with a fork and serve.

Nutrition information per serving:
Calories: 362; Carbohydrates: 76.2g; Protein: 8.1g; Fat: 2.7g; Sugar: 1.5g; Sodium: 204mg

Saffron Risotto

(Servings: 6|Cooking Time: 25 minutes)

Ingredients:

- 1 ½ cups arborio rice
- ½ cup onion, chopped
- 2 tbsp. olive oil
- 2 tbsp. milk
- ½ tsp. saffron threads, crushed
- 1 cinnamon stick
- 1/3 cup dried currants
- 1/3 cup almonds, chopped
- 1 tbsp. honey
- 3 ½ cups water
- ½ tsp. sea salt

Directions for Cooking:

1. Whisk together milk and saffron. Set aside.
2. Add oil into instant pot and set on Sauté mode.
3. Add onion and sauté for 5 minutes. Add rice and stir for a minute.
4. Add remaining ingredients into the pot and stir well.
5. Seal pot with lid and cook on manual high pressure for 5 minutes.

6. Allow pressure to release naturally for 15 minutes, then release using quick release method.
7. Stir well and serve.

Nutrition information per serving:
Calories: 262; Carbohydrates: 43.8g; Protein: 4.7g; Fat: 7.7g; Sugar: 4.2g; Sodium: 167mg

Parmesan Butter Risotto

(Servings: 4|Cooking Time: 18 minutes)

Ingredients:
- 1 ½ cups Arborio rice
- ½ cup parsley, chopped
- 1 onion, diced
- 4 tbsp. butter
- 3 tbsp. parmesan cheese, grated
- 4 cups chicken broth
- 2 garlic cloves, minced
- ¼ tsp. black pepper
- ½ tsp. salt

Directions for Cooking:
1. Add butter into instant pot and set on Sauté mode.
2. Add onion and sauté for 5 minutes.
3. Add garlic and rice. Stir for 2-3 minutes.
4. Add remaining ingredients and stir well.
5. Seal pot with lid and cook on manual high pressure for 10 minutes.
6. Quick release pressure then open the lid.
7. Garnish with parsley and serve.

Nutrition information per serving:
Calories: 441; Carbohydrates: 61.2g; Protein: 12.6g; Fat: 15.1g; Sugar: 2g; Sodium: 1259mg

Squash Mushroom Risotto

(Servings: 4|Cooking Time: 38 minutes)

Ingredients:
- 1 ½ cups brown rice
- 1 cup peas
- 3 garlic cloves, minced
- ½ cup onion, diced
- 2 tsp. olive oil
- 1 tbsp. soy sauce
- 1 cup mushrooms, sliced
- 2 cup squash, cubed
- 2 ½ cups vegetable broth
- Salt and Pepper to taste

Directions for Cooking:
1. Add olive oil into instant pot and set on Sauté mode.
2. Add onion and garlic. Sauté for a minute.
3. Add remaining ingredients into the pot and stir well.
4. Seal pot with lid and cook on manual high pressure for 22 minutes.
5. Allow pressure to release naturally for 15 minutes, then release using quick release method.
6. Stir well and serve.

Nutrition information per serving:
Calories: 355; Carbohydrates: 65g; Protein: 12.1g; Fat: 5.4g; Sugar: 4.5g; Sodium: 754mg

Parsley Scallions Risotto

(Servings: 4|Cooking Time: 11 minutes)

Ingredients:
- 1 cup Arborio rice
- ¼ cup parsley, chopped
- 3 scallions, chopped
- 2 cups chicken stock
- 1/8 cup white wine
- 2 tbsp. butter

- ½ tsp. salt

Directions for Cooking:

1. Add butter into the pot and set on Sauté mode.
2. Add scallions and parsley. Sauté for 2 minutes.
3. Add remaining ingredients and stir well.

4. Seal pot with lid and cook on manual high pressure for 9 minutes.
5. Quick release pressure then open the lid.
6. Stir well and serve.

Nutrition information per serving:
Calories: 238; Carbohydrates: 39.4g; Protein: 3.9g; Fat: 6.3g; Sugar: 0.7g; Sodium: 721mg

Lentil Risotto

(Servings: 4|Cooking Time: 25 minutes)

Ingredients:

- 1 cup dry lentils, soaked overnight
- 1 tbsp. parsley, chopped
- 1 celery stalk, chopped
- 1 medium onion, chopped
- 3 ¼ cup vegetable stock
- 2 garlic cloves, mashed
- 1 cup Arborio rice
- 1 tbsp. olive oil

Directions for Cooking:

1. Add olive oil into instant pot and set on Sauté mode.
2. Add onion and sauté until softened.

3. Add parsley and celery. Sauté for a minute.
4. Add garlic, lentils, stock and rice. Stir well.
5. Seal pot with lid and cook on manual high pressure for 5 minutes.
6. Allow pressure to release naturally, then open lid.
7. Stir well and serve.

Nutrition information per serving:
Calories: 393; Carbohydrates: 71g; Protein: 16g; Fat: 6g; Sugar: 3g; Sodium: 596mg

Mushrooms Risotto

(Servings: 6|Cooking Time: 11 minutes)

Ingredients:

- 1 ½ cup Arborio rice
- 16 oz. mushrooms, sliced
- 4 garlic cloves, minced
- 1 medium onion, diced
- 1 tsp. dried parsley
- 1 cup parmesan cheese, grated
- 4 cups chicken broth
- 4 tbsp. butter
- 4 tbsp. olive oil
- Pepper
- Salt

Directions for Cooking:

1. Add 2 tbsp. butter and olive oil into instant pot. Set on Sauté mode.

2. Add garlic and onion into the pot. Sauté for 3-4 minutes.
3. Add mushrooms and rice. Stir well.
4. Pour chicken broth into instant pot and stir well.
5. Seal pot with lid and cook on manual high pressure for 7 minutes.
6. Quick release pressure then open the lid.
7. Add remaining butter, parsley, parmesan cheese, pepper and salt. Stir well.
8. Serve and enjoy.

Nutrition information per serving:
Calories: 425; Carbohydrates: 43.3g; Protein: 14.5g; Fat: 22.4g; Sugar: 2.6g; Sodium: 919mg

Tasty Spanish Rice

(Servings: 4|Cooking Time: 27 minutes)

Ingredients:
- 2 cups white rice, long grain
- 1 cup tomatoes, chopped
- 2 ½ cups water
- 1 tsp. garlic, minced
- 2 green onions, sliced
- 1 tsp. olive oil
- 2 tsp. taco seasoning
- 2 tbsp. tomato paste
- ½ small jalapeno pepper, minced
- ¼ cup cilantro, chopped
- 2 tsp. sea salt

Directions for Cooking:

1. Add olive oil into instant pot and set on Sauté mode.
2. Add garlic and green onions. Sauté for 2 minutes.
3. Add remaining ingredients and stir well.
4. Seal pot with lid and cook on manual high pressure for 10 minutes.
5. Allow pressure to release naturally for 15 minutes, then release using quick release method.
6. Fluff the rice using a fork and serve.

Nutrition information per serving:
Calories: 366; Carbohydrates: 78g; Protein: 7.6g; Fat: 1.9g; Sugar: 2.5g; Sodium: 957mg

Broccoli Rice

(Servings: 4|Cooking Time: 15 minutes)

Ingredients:
- 1 cup rice
- ¼ cup onion, chopped
- 1 cup cheddar cheese, shredded
- 4 oz. light cream cheese, cut into cubes
- 2 cups broccoli, chopped
- 2 ¼ cup water

Directions for Cooking:
1. Add all ingredients into instant pot and stir well.

2. Seal pot with lid and cook on manual high pressure for 15 minutes.
3. Quick release pressure then open the lid.
4. Stir well and serve.

Nutrition information per serving:
Calories: 400; Carbohydrates: 41.8g; Protein: 13.8g; Fat: 19.7g; Sugar: 1.3g; Sodium: 281mg

Delicious Rice Pilaf

(Servings: 4|Cooking Time: 18 minutes)

Ingredients:
- 1 cup rice
- 2 ¼ cup chicken stock
- ¼ cup spaghetti noodles, break into pieces
- 1 tbsp. fresh parsley, chopped
- 1/8 tsp. paprika
- 1 garlic clove, minced
- 4 mushrooms, sliced
- 2 celery stalks, chopped
- 1 onion, chopped
- 1 tbsp. butter
- ½ tsp. sea salt

Directions for Cooking:

1. Add butter into instant pot and set on Sauté mode.
2. Add mushrooms, celery and onion. Sauté for 5 minutes.
3. Add paprika, parsley, and garlic. Sauté for a minute.
4. Add remaining ingredients and stir well.
5. Seal pot with lid and cook on low for 12 minutes.
6. Quick release pressure then open the lid.
7. Fluff the rice using a fork and serve.

Nutrition information per serving:
Calories: 218; Carbohydrates: 41.2g; Protein: 4.7g; Fat: 3.6g; Sugar: 2.1g; Sodium: 696mg

Plain Jasmine Coconut Rice

(Servings: 3|Cooking Time: 15 minutes)

Ingredients:
- 1 cup jasmine rice, rinsed and drained
- ¾ cup vegetable stock
- ½ cup coconut milk
- ¼ tsp. sea salt

Directions for Cooking:
1. Add all ingredients into instant pot and stir well.
2. Seal pot with lid and cook on manual high pressure for 5 minutes.
3. Allow pressure to release naturally for 10 minutes, then release using quick release method.
4. Fluff the rice using a fork and serve.

Nutrition information per serving:
Calories: 308; Carbohydrates: 50.7g; Protein: 4.9g; Fat: 10g; Sugar: 1.8g; Sodium: 342mg

Mexican Brown Rice

(Servings: 4|Cooking Time: 33 minutes)

Ingredients:
- 2 cups brown rice, rinsed and drained
- 2 cups chicken broth
- ½ cup tomato sauce
- ½ tsp. ground cumin
- 2 garlic cloves, minced
- 1 small onion, chopped
- 2 tbsp. olive oil
- ½ tsp. salt

Directions for Cooking:
1. Add oil into instant pot and set on Sauté mode.
2. Add cumin, garlic and onion. Sauté for 2 minutes.
3. Add rice and stir for 4 minutes. Add remaining ingredients and stir well.
4. Seal pot with lid and cook on manual high pressure for 22 minutes.
5. Allow pressure to release naturally for 5 minutes, then release using quick release method.
6. Stir well and serve.

Nutrition information per serving:
Calories: 441; Carbohydrates: 76.7g; Protein: 10.3g; Fat: 10.4g; Sugar: 2.4g; Sodium: 838mg

Lime Rice

(Servings: 3|Cooking Time: 20 minutes)

Ingredients:
- 1 cup brown rice
- ¼ cup fresh cilantro, chopped
- 1 tsp. mirin
- 1 lime juice
- 1 lime zest
- 1 ¼ cups vegetable stock

Directions for Cooking:

1. Add rice and stock into instant pot. Stir well.
2. Seal pot with lid and cook on manual high pressure for 20 minutes.
3. Allow pressure to release naturally for 10 minutes, then release using quick release method.
4. Fluff the rice using a fork.
5. Add cilantro, mirin, lime zest and lime juice. Stir well.
6. Serve and enjoy.

Nutrition information per serving:
Calories: 240; Carbohydrates: 51.2g; Protein: 4.9g; Fat: 2.6g; Sugar: 1.6g; Sodium: 318mg

Cheese Bacon Rice

(Servings: 4|Cooking Time: 7 minutes)

Ingredients:

- 1 ½ cups white rice
- ½ cup bacon, shredded
- 4 oz. cheddar cheese, shredded
- 2 ¼ cups chicken stock
- Pepper
- Salt

Directions for Cooking:

1. Add rice and stock into instant pot. Stir well.
2. Seal pot with lid and cook on manual high pressure for 4 minutes.
3. Quick release pressure then open the lid.
4. Add bacon and cheese and stir well. Cook on Sauté mode for 2-3 minutes.
5. Season with pepper and salt.
6. Serve and enjoy.

Nutrition information per serving:
Calories: 459; Carbohydrates: 56.5g; Protein: 18.3g; Fat: 16.8g; Sugar: 0.6g; Sodium: 1015mg

Fried Rice

(Servings: 4|Cooking Time: 12 minutes)

Ingredients:

- 3 eggs, lightly beaten
- 1 cup cabbage, chopped
- ¼ cup frozen peas
- ¼ cup frozen carrots, chopped
- 3 tbsp. soy sauce
- 1 ½ cups water
- 1 cup white rice
- 1 tbsp. olive oil
- 1 tbsp. garlic, minced
- 1 small onion, diced

Directions for Cooking:

1. Add oil into instant pot and set on Sauté mode.
2. Add garlic and onion. Sauté until onion softens.
3. Add rice and water. Stir well.
4. Seal pot with lid and cook on manual high pressure for 4 minutes.
5. Quick release pressure then open the lid.
6. Set pot on Sauté mode. Add cabbage, carrots, peas and soy sauce. Stir well.
7. Make hole in center of the rice. Add eggs, stir well and cook until eggs are done.
8. Serve and enjoy.

Nutrition information per serving:
Calories: 277; Carbohydrates: 43.6g; Protein: 9.3g; Fat: 7.2g; Sugar: 2.6g; Sodium: 744mg

Broccoli Chicken Cheese Rice

(Servings: 4|Cooking Time: 10 minutes)

Ingredients:

- 1 cup white rice
- 1 cup cheddar cheese, shredded
- 4 cups broccoli florets
- 20 oz. skinless chicken thighs, boneless and cut into pieces
- 1 ½ cups chicken stock
- ¼ tsp. pepper
- ½ tsp. salt

Directions for Cooking:

1. Add all ingredients into instant pot and stir well.
2. Seal pot with lid and cook on manual high pressure for 10 minutes.
3. Quick release pressure then open the lid.
4. Stir well and serve.

Nutrition information per serving:
Calories: 587; Carbohydrates: 43.7g; Protein: 54.2g; Fat: 20.7g; Sugar: 2g; Sodium: 907mg

Cumin Seed Rice

(Servings: 3|Cooking Time: 11 minutes)

Ingredients:

- 1 cup basmati rice
- 1 ¼ cups water
- 1 tsp. cumin seeds
- 2 green cardamom
- 2 cloves
- 1 green chili, sliced
- 1 bay leaf
- 1 tbsp. ghee

Directions for Cooking:

1. Add ghee into instant pot and set on Sauté mode.
2. Add cumin seeds, cardamom, cloves, green chili and bay leaf. Sauté for a minute.
3. Add rice and water. Stir well.
4. Seal pot with lid and cook on manual high pressure for 5 minutes.
5. Allow pressure to release naturally for 5 minutes, then release using quick release method.
6. Fluff the rice using a fork and serve.

Nutrition information per serving:
Calories: 265; Carbohydrates: 49.6g; Protein: 4.5g; Fat: 4.8g; Sugar: 0.1g; Sodium: 7mg

Curry Coconut Rice

(Servings: 4|Cooking Time: 12 minutes)

Ingredients:

- 1 cup jasmine rice
- 2 tsp. curry powder
- ½ cup chicken broth
- 13.5 oz. coconut milk
- 1 tsp. sea salt

Directions for Cooking:

1. Add all ingredients into instant pot and stir well.
2. Seal pot with lid and cook on manual high pressure for 5 minutes.
3. Allow pressure to release naturally for 10 minutes, then release using quick release method.
4. Stir well and serve.

Nutrition information per serving:
Calories: 388; Carbohydrates: 42g; Protein: 5.9g; Fat: 23.1g; Sugar: 3.3g; Sodium: 578mg

Pineapple Rice

(Servings: 3|Cooking Time: 13 minutes)

Ingredients:

- 1 cup white rice
- 1 tbsp. butter
- 8 oz. can pineapple, crushed
- ¼ cup pineapple juice
- 1 cup water

Directions for Cooking:

1. Add all ingredients into instant pot and stir well.
2. Seal pot with lid and cook on manual high pressure for 7 minutes.
3. Quick release pressure then open the lid.
4. Stir well and serve.

Nutrition information per serving:

Calories: 310; Carbohydrates: 62.1g; Protein: 4.8g; Fat: 4.3g; Sugar: 9.7g; Sodium: 33mg

Chapter 9 Instant Pot Vegetable Recipes

Sweet Potato Mash

(Servings: 4|Cooking Time: 10 minutes)

Ingredients:

- 1 ½ lbs. sweet potatoes, scrubbed
- ½ tsp. paprika
- 2 tbsp. light brown sugar
- 2 tbsp. butter, melted
- 1 cup water
- ¼ tsp. salt

Directions for Cooking:

1. Pour 1 cup of water into instant pot then insert trivet.
2. Place sweet potatoes on top of the trivet.
3. Seal pot with lid and cook on manual high pressure for 14 minutes.
4. Quick release pressure then open the lid.
5. Remove sweet potatoes from pot and set aside to cool.
6. Peel the sweet potatoes and place in a bowl. Mash sweet potatoes with a masher until smooth. Add remaining ingredients and stir well.
7. Serve and enjoy.

Nutrition information per serving:
Calories: 269; Carbohydrates: 52g; Protein: 2.7g; Fat: 6.1g; Sugar: 5.3g; Sodium: 207mg

Sautéed Veggies

(Servings: 3|Cooking Time: 11 minutes)

Ingredients:

- 1 onion, sliced
- 1 zucchini, cut into cubes
- 2 bell pepper, sliced
- ¼ tsp. dried oregano
- ½ tsp. dried thyme
- 2 tbsp. sesame oil
- 2 tbsp. tamari sauce
- ½ cup sour cream
- ¼ cup feta cheese
- ¼ cup mushrooms, sliced
- 3 tbsp. water
- 1 tsp. sea salt

Directions for Cooking:

1. Add oil into instant pot and set on Sauté mode.
2. Add zucchini to the pot and season with salt. Cook for 5 minutes.
3. Add onion, bell peppers, tamari sauce and stir well. Season with oregano, thyme and salt.
4. Add mushrooms and feta cheese and cook for 2-3 minutes.

5. Add water and stir well. Cook for 3 minutes.
6. Turn off the instant pot. Add sour cream and stir well.
7. Serve and enjoy.

Nutrition information per serving:
Calories: 255; Carbohydrates: 14.8g; Protein: 6.5g; Fat: 20.2g; Sugar: 7.6g; Sodium: 1465mg

Vegetable Curry

(Servings: 6|Cooking Time: 10 minutes)

Ingredients:
- 10 cherry tomatoes, cut in half
- ½ cup vegetable stock
- 2 zucchini, peeled and diced
- 1 onion, diced
- 1 bell pepper, diced
- 6 carrots, diced
- 2 tbsp. curry powder
- ½ tsp. sea salt

Directions for Cooking:

1. Add all ingredients except tomatoes into instant pot and stir well.
2. Seal pot with lid and cook on manual high pressure for 10 minutes.
3. Quick release pressure then open the lid.
4. Stir in cherry tomatoes and serve.

Nutrition information per serving:
Calories: 94; Carbohydrates: 20.8g; Protein: 3.8g; Fat: 1.1g; Sugar: 11.5g; Sodium: 277mg

Balsamic Braised Parsnips

(Servings: 4|Cooking Time: 3 minutes)

Ingredients:
- 1 ½ lbs. parsnips, peeled and sliced
- ¼ cup vegetable stock
- 2 tbsp. maple syrup
- 3 tbsp. balsamic vinegar
- 1/8 tsp. pepper
- ½ tsp. salt

Directions for Cooking:
1. Add parsnips, vinegar and stock into instant pot.

2. Seal pot with lid and cook on manual high pressure for 3 minutes.
3. Quick release pressure then open the lid.
4. Stir in maple syrup. Season with pepper and salt.
5. Serve and enjoy.

Nutrition information per serving:
Calories: 157; Carbohydrates: 37.6g; Protein: 2.1g; Fat: 0.7g; Sugar: 14.3g; Sodium: 354mg

Zucchini Tomato Melange

(Servings: 4|Cooking Time: 8 minutes)

Ingredients:
- 1 lb. cherry tomatoes
- 1 cup water
- 1 tbsp. olive oil
- 1 onion, chopped
- 3 zucchini, chopped
- 2 garlic cloves, minced
- 1 tsp. salt

Directions for Cooking:
1. Add olive oil into instant pot and set on Sauté mode.
2. Add onion and sauté for 3 minutes.

3. Add zucchini, water, and cherry tomatoes. Stir well.
4. Seal pot with lid and cook on manual high pressure for 5 minutes.
5. Quick release pressure then open the lid.
6. Add garlic and stir well.

7. Stir and serve.

Nutrition information per serving:
Calories: 87; Carbohydrates: 12.4g; Protein: 3.2g; Fat: 4g; Sugar: 6.7g; Sodium: 605mg

Ratatouille

(Servings: 8|Cooking Time: 7 minutes)

Ingredients:

- 28 oz. can tomatoes, crushed
- 4 zucchini, sliced
- 2 eggplants, peeled and sliced
- 2 garlic cloves, crushed
- 12 oz. red pepper, roasted, drained and sliced
- 1 onion, sliced
- 1 tbsp. olive oil
- 1 tsp. salt

Directions for Cooking:

1. Add olive oil into instant pot and set on Sauté mode.
2. Add vegetables into the pot and sauté for 3 minutes. Season with salt.
3. Add crushed tomatoes and stir well.
4. Seal pot with lid and cook on manual high pressure for 4 minutes.
5. Quick release pressure then open the lid.
6. Stir well and serve.

Nutrition information per serving:
Calories: 150; Carbohydrates: 31.4g; Protein: 5.4g; Fat: 2.6g; Sugar: 18.8g; Sodium: 520mg

Vegetable Lasagna

(Servings: 4|Cooking Time: 3 minutes)

Ingredients:

- 24 oz. jar spaghetti sauce
- 3 cups Padron peppers, stem cut and halved
- 3 zucchini, sliced
- 3 eggplants, sliced
- 2 tomatoes, sliced

Directions for Cooking:

1. Layer zucchini, tomato, eggplant, peppers and sauce into instant pot.

2. Seal pot with lid and cook on manual high pressure for 3 minutes.
3. Quick release pressure then open the lid.
4. Serve and enjoy.

Nutrition information per serving:
Calories: 243; Carbohydrates: 48.5g; Protein: 9g; Fat: 5.1g; Sugar: 30.9g; Sodium: 785mg

Balsamic Mushrooms

(Servings: 4|Cooking Time: 4 minutes)

Ingredients:

- 1 lb. fresh mushrooms, sliced
- 3 tbsp. white wine
- 3 garlic cloves, minced
- 1/3 cup olive oil
- Salt and Pepper to taste

Directions for Cooking:

1. Add oil into instant pot and set on Sauté mode
2. Add garlic and mushrooms. Sauté for 2-3 minutes.

3. Add vinegar and white wine. Stir well. Seal pot with lid and cook on low for 1 minute.
4. Quick release pressure then open the lid.
5. Season with pepper and salt.
6. Serve and enjoy.

Nutrition information per serving:
Calories: 181; Carbohydrates: 4.8g; Protein: 3.7g; Fat: 17.1g; Sugar: 2.1g; Sodium: 46mg

Butter Mushrooms

(Servings: 2|Cooking Time: 17 minutes)

Ingredients:
- 1 lb. button mushrooms
- 2 tbsp. butter
- 2 tbsp. olive oil
- ½ tsp. thyme
- 2 tsp. garlic, minced
- Salt

Directions for Cooking:
1. Add olive oil into instant pot and set on Sauté mode.
2. Add mushrooms and cook for 5 minutes.
3. Add thyme, garlic, butter and salt. Stir well.
4. Seal pot with lid and cook on manual high pressure for 12 minutes.
5. Quick release pressure then open the lid.
6. Serve and enjoy.

Nutrition information per serving:
Calories: 275; Carbohydrates: 8.6g; Protein: 7.4g; Fat: 26.2g; Sugar: 3.9g; Sodium: 173mg

Spiced Eggplant

(Servings: 4|Cooking Time: 14 minutes)

Ingredients:
- 1 eggplant, cut into cubes
- ½ tsp. red pepper
- 1 tsp. garlic powder
- 2 tbsp. olive oil
- ½ cup water
- ¼ cup tomato paste
- ½ tsp. Italian seasoning
- 1 tsp. paprika
- 1 tsp. salt

Directions for Cooking:
1. Pour water into instant pot. Insert steamer basket.
2. Add eggplant into steamer basket.
3. Seal pot with lid and cook on manual high pressure for 5 minutes.
4. Quick release pressure then open the lid.
5. Remove eggplant from the pot and drain all liquid from the pot.
6. Add oil into the pot and set on Sauté mode.
7. Add tomato paste, Italian seasoning, paprika, red pepper and garlic powder to the pot and sauté for 3-4 minutes.
8. Add cooked eggplant pieces and salt. Stir well and cook on Sauté mode for 5 minutes more.
9. Serve and enjoy.

Nutrition information per serving:
Calories: 112; Carbohydrates: 7.6g; Protein: 2.2g; Fat: 7.6g; Sugar: 6.5g; Sodium: 602mg

Creamy Herbed Mushrooms

(Servings: 4|Cooking Time: 4 minutes)

Ingredients:

- 24 oz. Bella mushrooms, clean
- 2 bay leaves
- ¼ tsp. dried thyme
- ½ tsp. dried oregano
- ½ tsp. dried basil
- 4 garlic cloves, minced
- 2 tbsp. parsley, chopped
- 2 tbsp. butter
- ¼ cup half and half
- 1 cup vegetable broth
- Pepper
- Salt

Directions for Cooking:

1. Add all ingredients except parsley, butter and half and half into instant pot. Stir well.
2. Seal pot with lid and cook on manual high pressure for 4 minutes.
3. Quick release pressure then open the lid.
4. Add parsley, half and half and butter. Stir well.
5. Serve and enjoy.

Nutrition information per serving:
Calories: 135; Carbohydrates: 7g; Protein: 6.9g; Fat: 7.9g; Sugar: 0.3g; Sodium: 278mg

Squash Puree

(Servings: 6|Cooking Time: 20 minutes)

Ingredients:

- 2 lbs. butternut squash, peeled and diced
- ½ tsp. baking soda
- 4 tbsp. butter
- 2 tbsp. honey
- 1 sprig sage
- ½ cup water
- 2 tsp. sea salt

Directions for Cooking:

1. Add butter into instant pot and set on Sauté mode.
2. Add squash; sprinkle with baking soda and salt. Stir in water and sage.
3. Seal pot with lid and cook on manual high pressure for 20 minutes.
4. Quick release pressure then open the lid.
5. Discard sage and using immersion blender puree until smooth.
6. Add honey and salt. Stir well.
7. Serve and enjoy.

Nutrition information per serving:
Calories: 147; Carbohydrates: 21.8g; Protein: 1.6g; Fat: 9g; Sugar: 5.8g; Sodium: 1215mg

Simple Green Beans

(Servings: 4|Cooking Time: 5 minutes)

Ingredients:

- 1 lb. fresh green beans
- 2 tbsp. butter
- 1 cup water
- 1 garlic clove, minced
- Pepper
- Salt

Directions for Cooking:

1. Add all ingredients into instant pot and stir well.
2. Seal pot with lid and cook on low pressure for 5 minutes.
3. Quick release pressure then open the lid.
4. Stir well and serve.

Nutrition information per serving:
Calories: 87; Carbohydrates: 8.4g; Protein: 2.2g; Fat: 5.9g; Sugar: 1.6g; Sodium: 88mg

Garlic Kale

(Servings: 4|Cooking Time: 6 minutes)

Ingredients:

- 1 lb. kale, wash and stems trimmed
- 3 garlic cloves, sliced
- 1 tbsp. olive oil
- ½ lemon juice
- ½ cup water
- ½ tsp. kosher salt

Directions for Cooking:

1. Add oil into instant pot and set on Sauté mode.
2. Add garlic sauté for 30 seconds.
3. Add kale, salt and water into the pot. Stir well.
4. Seal pot with lid and cook on manual high pressure for 5 minutes.
5. Quick release pressure then open the lid.
6. Add lemon juice and stir well.
7. Serve and enjoy.

Nutrition information per serving:
Calories: 91; Carbohydrates: 12.7g; Protein: 3.6g; Fat: 3.6g; Sugar: 0.1g; Sodium: 342mg

Healthy Kale

(Servings: 4|Cooking Time: 3 minutes)

Ingredients:

- 2 large kale heads, ribs removed and cut into pieces
- 2 tbsp. olive oil
- 1/3 cup water
- 1/8 tsp. red pepper flakes
- 3/4 tsp. salt

Directions for Cooking:

1. Add all ingredients into instant pot.
2. Seal pot with lid and cook on manual high pressure for 3 minutes.
3. Quick release pressure then open the lid.
4. Stir well and serve.

Nutrition information per serving:
Calories: 81; Carbohydrates: 4.5g; Protein: 1.3g; Fat: 7g; Sugar: 0g; Sodium: 457mg

Cauliflower Rice Mac & Cheese

(Servings: 4|Cooking Time: 15 minutes)

Ingredients:

- 2 cups cauliflower rice
- 2 tbsp. cream cheese
- ½ cup sharp cheddar cheese, shredded
- ½ cup half and half
- 1 ½ cups water
- Pepper
- Salt

Directions for Cooking:

1. Add all ingredients into the heat-safe bowl and cover bowl with foil.
2. Pour water into instant pot then insert trivet.
3. Place bowl on top of the trivet. Seal pot with lid and cook on manual high pressure for 5 minutes.
4. Allow pressure to release naturally for 10 minutes, then release using quick release method.
5. Stir well and serve.

Nutrition information per serving:
Calories: 126; Carbohydrates: 4.3g; Protein: 5.8g; Fat: 10g; Sugar: 1.3g; Sodium: 169mg

Mint Carrots

(Servings: 4|Cooking Time: 3 minutes)

Ingredients:
- 16 oz. baby carrots
- 1 tbsp. mint leaves, chopped
- 1 cup water
- 1 tbsp. butter
- Sea salt

Directions for Cooking:
1. Add carrots and water into instant pot.
2. Seal pot with lid and cook on manual high pressure for 2 minutes.
3. Quick release pressure then open the lid.
4. Pour carrots into the strainer and drain well. Clean the instant pot.
5. Add butter and mint into the pot and sauté for 30 seconds.
6. Return carrots to the pot and season with salt.
7. Stir well and serve.

Nutrition information per serving:
Calories: 66; Carbohydrates: 9.5g; Protein: 0.8g; Fat: 3g; Sugar: 5.4g; Sodium: 111mg

Zucchini Noodles

(Servings: 2|Cooking Time: 2 minutes)

Ingredients:
- 2 zucchini, spiralized into noodles
- ½ lemon zest
- 2 garlic cloves, chopped
- 4 tbsp. parmesan cheese, grated
- 1 tbsp. mint, sliced
- 1/3 fresh lemon juice
- 2 tbsp. olive oil
- ½ tsp. sea salt

Directions for Cooking:
1. Add oil into instant pot and set on Sauté mode.
2. Add lemon zest, garlic and salt in the pot. Stir for a minute.
3. Add zucchini noodles and lemon juice. Stir well. Seal pot with lid and cook on low for 1 minute.
4. Quick release pressure then open the lid.
5. Add parmesan cheese and mint. Stir well and serve.

Nutrition information per serving:
Calories: 232; Carbohydrates: 7.8g; Protein: 8.7g; Fat: 18.9g; Sugar: 3.4g; Sodium: 789mg

Braised Cabbage

(Servings: 2|Cooking Time: 8 minutes)

Ingredients:
- 1 ½ lbs. cabbage, sliced into strips
- 3 oz. bacon, cubed
- 1 onion, sliced
- ½ cup vegetable broth
- 1 tbsp. butter

Directions for Cooking:
1. Add butter into the pot and set on Sauté mode.
2. Add bacon and onion. Sauté for 5 minutes.
3. Add cabbage and broth. Stir well.
4. Seal pot with lid and cook on manual high pressure for 3 minutes.
5. Quick release pressure then open the lid.
6. Stir well and serve.

Nutrition information per serving:
Calories: 398; Carbohydrates: 25.7g; Protein: 22g; Fat: 24.3g; Sugar: 13.4g; Sodium: 1277mg

Herb Carrots

(Servings: 4|Cooking Time: 5 minutes)

Ingredients:

- 1 lb. baby carrots
- 1 tsp. garlic powder
- 2 tbsp. butter
- 1 cup water
- ½ tsp. oregano
- ½ tsp. thyme
- Pepper
- Salt

Directions for Cooking:

1. Pour water into instant pot and insert steamer basket.
2. Add baby carrots into steamer basket.
3. Seal pot with lid and cook on Steam mode for 2 minutes.
4. Quick release pressure then open the lid.
5. Transfer carrots to the bowl and remove instant pot water.
6. Add butter into the pot and set on Sauté mode.
7. Return carrots in the pot with remaining ingredients and cook on Sauté mode for 2-3 minutes.
8. Stir well and serve.

Nutrition information per serving:
Calories: 94; Carbohydrates: 10g; Protein: 0.9g; Fat: 6g; Sugar: 5.6g; Sodium: 170mg

Cajun Seasoned Zucchini

(Servings: 4|Cooking Time: 1 minute)

Ingredients:

- 4 zucchinis, sliced
- 2 tbsp. Cajun seasoning
- ½ cup water
- 1 tbsp. butter
- 1 tsp. garlic powder
- 1 tsp. paprika

Directions for Cooking:

1. Add all ingredients into instant pot and stir well.
2. Seal pot with lid and cook on low for 1 minute.
3. Quick release pressure then open the lid.
4. Stir well and serve.

Nutrition information per serving:
Calories: 61; Carbohydrates: 7.4g; Protein: 2.7g; Fat: 3.3g; Sugar: 3.6g; Sodium: 116mg

Cauliflower Broccoli Macaroni

(Servings: 6|Cooking Time: 9 minutes)

Ingredients:

- 2 cups cauliflower florets
- 1 oz. American cheese, cut into pieces
- 3/4 cup coconut milk
- 1 cup cheddar cheese, shredded
- 8 oz. elbow macaroni
- 2 cups broccoli florets
- 3 cups water
- ½ tsp. salt

Directions for Cooking:

1. Add water, macaroni, cauliflower, broccoli and salt into instant pot. Stir well.
2. Seal pot with lid and cook on manual high pressure for 4 minutes.
3. Quick release pressure then open the lid.
4. Set instant pot on Sauté mode. Add American cheese, coconut milk and cheddar cheese. Stir well and cook for 5 minutes.

5. Serve and enjoy.

Nutrition information per serving:

Calories: 319; Carbohydrates: 34.3g; Protein: 12.7g; Fat: 15.3g; Sugar: 3.8g; Sodium: 401mg

Squash with Farro

(Servings: 4|Cooking Time: 14 minutes)

Ingredients:

- 1 medium butternut squash, peeled and cut into cubes
- ¼ cup feta cheese, crumbled
- ¼ cup walnuts, chopped
- ½ tsp. dried thyme
- 2 cups vegetable broth
- 1 cup farro, uncooked
- 1 onion, chopped
- 2 tsp. olive oil
- ¼ tsp. pepper
- ¼ tsp. salt

Directions for Cooking:

1. Add oil into instant pot and set on Sauté mode.
2. Add onion and sauté for 3 minutes.
3. Add farro and cook for 2-3 minutes. Add broth and stir well.
4. Place steaming rack over farro mixture and place squash on the rack. Season with pepper, thyme and salt.
5. Seal pot with lid and cook on manual high pressure for 8 minutes.
6. Quick release pressure then open the lid.
7. Spoon squash into a bowl.
8. Add farro and stir well. Sprinkle with cheese and walnuts.
9. Serve and enjoy.

Nutrition information per serving:

Calories: 225; Carbohydrates: 18g; Protein: 10g; Fat: 13g; Sugar: 4.4g; Sodium: 799mg

Cauliflower & Chickpeas

(Servings: 4|Cooking Time: 69 minutes)

Ingredients:

- 3/4 cup dried chickpeas, rinsed and drained
- 2 tbsp. curry powder
- 1 medium cauliflower head, cut into florets
- 1 ½ cups vegetable broth
- 2 garlic cloves, minced
- 2 tbsp. ginger, minced
- 1 bell pepper, chopped
- 1 onion, chopped
- 2 tsp. olive oil
- 3 cups water
- ¼ tsp. salt

Directions for Cooking:

1. Add chickpeas and water into instant pot.
2. Seal pot with lid and cook on manual high pressure for 45 minutes.
3. Allow pressure to release naturally for 15 minutes, then release quick.
4. Drain chickpeas well and place in a bowl.
5. Add oil into instant pot and set on Sauté mode.
6. Add onion bell pepper, garlic and ginger and sauté for 3 minutes.
7. Add cauliflower, broth, chickpeas, curry powder and salt. Stir well.
8. Seal pot with lid and cook on manual high pressure for 3 minutes.
9. Quick release pressure then open the lid.
10. Serve and enjoy.

Nutrition information per serving:

Calories: 249; Carbohydrates: 39.8g; Protein: 13.3g; Fat: 6g; Sugar: 10.6g; Sodium: 496mg

Cauliflower Rice

(Servings: 4|Cooking Time: 3 minutes)

Ingredients:

- 1 medium cauliflower head, cut into florets
- ¼ tsp. cumin
- ½ tsp. dried parsley
- 2 tbsp. olive oil
- ¼ tsp. paprika
- ¼ tsp. turmeric
- 1 cup water
- ¼ tsp. salt

Directions for Cooking:

1. Pour water into instant pot. Insert steamer basket.
2. Add cauliflower florets into steamer basket.
3. Seal pot with lid and cook on manual high for 1 minute.
4. Quick release pressure then open the lid.
5. Remove cauliflower from pot and place on a dish.
6. Remove water from the instant pot.
7. Add olive oil into the pot and set on Sauté mode.
8. Add cooked cauliflower florets to the instant pot and stir well.
9. Break the cauliflower using potato masher into the small pieces.
10. Add remaining ingredients and stir well. Cook on Sauté mode for 1-2 minutes.
11. Serve and enjoy.

Nutrition information per serving:
Calories: 97; Carbohydrates: 7.9g; Protein: 2.9g; Fat: 7.2g; Sugar: 3.5g; Sodium: 191mg

Quinoa Stuff Bell Pepper

(Servings: 4|Cooking Time: 14 minutes)

Ingredients:

- 4 bell peppers, cut off the top
- 1 cup white beans, soaked overnight
- 2 tbsp. garlic powder
- 3 cups vegetable broth
- 1 cup cheese, shredded
- 1 cup quinoa

Directions for Cooking:

1. Add vegetable broth, garlic powder, quinoa and beans in instant pot.
2. Seal pot with lid and cook on manual high pressure for 8 minutes.
3. Quick release pressure then open the lid.
4. Stuffed bell pepper with bean and quinoa mixture. Top with shredded cheese.
5. Place stuffed bell peppers in the pot and cook on Sauté mode for 6 minutes.
6. Serve and enjoy.

Nutrition information per serving:
Calories :519; Carbohydrates: 70.8g; Protein: 304g; Fat: 13g; Sugar: 8.8g; Sodium: 762mg

Chili Garlic Cabbage

(Servings: 6|Cooking Time: 3 minutes)

Ingredients:

- 1 cabbage head, chopped
- ½ tsp. paprika
- ½ tsp. garlic salt
- 1 cup vegetable stock
- 2 tbsp. olive oil
- ½ tsp. chili powder
- 3 tbsp. low sodium soy sauce
- ½ onion, diced
- ½ tsp. salt

Directions for Cooking:

1. Add olive oil into instant pot and set on Sauté mode.
2. Add chopped cabbage into instant pot and stir well.
3. Add remaining ingredients and stir well to combine.
4. Seal pot with lid and cook on manual high pressure for 3 minutes.
5. Release pressure using quick release method.
6. Stir well and serve.

Nutrition information per serving:
Calories: 82; Carbohydrates: 9.3g; Protein: 2.2 g; Fat: 5.2g; Sugar: 4.8g; Sodium: 638mg

Coconut Cabbage

(Servings: 4|Cooking Time: 19 minutes)

Ingredients:
- 1 medium cabbage, shredded
- 1 carrot, sliced
- 1 tbsp. turmeric powder
- 1 tbsp. curry powder
- 1 tbsp. mustard seeds
- 1/3 cup water
- 1 tbsp. olive oil
- ½ cup desiccated coconut
- 2 tbsp. lemon juice
- ½ red chili, sliced
- 2 garlic cloves, diced
- 1 onion, sliced
- 1 tbsp. coconut oil
- 1 ½ tsp. salt

Directions for Cooking:
1. Add coconut oil, onion and salt into instant pot and Sauté for 2-3 minutes.
2. Add spices, chili, garlic, carrots, cabbage, olive oil, coconut and lime juice. Stir well.
3. Pour water into the pot and stir well.
4. Seal pot with lid and cook on manual high pressure for 5 minutes.
5. Allow pressure to release naturally for 10 minutes, then release using quick release method.
6. Stir and serve.

Nutrition information per serving:
Calorie: 162; Carbohydrates: 20.9g; Protein: 4.5 g; Fat: 8.4g; Sugar: 9.6g; Sodium: 929mg

Delicious Roasted Potatoes

(Servings: 4|Cooking Time: 12 minutes)

Ingredients:
- 1 ½ lbs. russet potatoes, cut into wedges
- 1 cup vegetable broth
- ¼ tsp. paprika
- ¼ tsp. pepper
- 1 tsp. garlic powder
- ½ tsp. onion powder
- 4 tbsp. olive oil
- 1 tsp. sea salt

Directions for Cooking:

1. Add olive in instant pot and set on Sauté mode.
2. Add potatoes and cook for 5-6 minutes.
3. Add remaining ingredients into the pot and mix well.
4. Seal pot with lid and cook on manual high pressure for 6 minutes.
5. Quick release pressure then open the lid,
6. Serve and enjoy.

Nutrition information per serving:
Calorie: 251; Carbohydrates: 27g; Protein: 4g; Fat: 14g; Sugar: 2g; Sodium: 669mg

Cheese Artichokes

(Servings: 4|Cooking Time: 10 minutes)

Ingredients:

- 4 artichokes, wash and trim
- 4 tsp. olive oil
- 2 tsp. garlic, minced
- ½ cup vegetable stock
- ¼ cup parmesan cheese, grated

Directions for Cooking:

1. Discard step, top and outer leaves of artichoke.
2. Add garlic on top of artichoke and drizzle with oil.
3. Sprinkle each artichoke with grated cheese.
4. Place artichoke into instant pot insert. Pour in stock.
5. Seal pot with lid and cook on Steam mode for 10 minutes.
6. Quick release pressure then open the lid.
7. Serve and enjoy.

Nutrition information per serving:

Calorie: 269; Carbohydrates: 17g; Protein: 17g; Fat: 14 g; Sugar: 1.9g; Sodium: 843mg

Mushroom Beans Gumbo

(Servings: 4|Cooking Time: 18 minutes)

Ingredients:

- 3 garlic cloves, chopped
- 1 cup mushrooms, sliced
- 1 cup kidney beans, soaked overnight
- 1 bell pepper, chopped
- 2 tbsp. tamari sauce
- 2 medium zucchini, sliced
- 2 tbsp. olive oil
- 2 cups vegetable stock

Directions for Cooking:

1. Add all ingredients into instant pot and stir well.
2. Seal pot with lid and cook on manual high pressure for 8 minutes,
3. Allow pressure to release naturally for 10 minutes, then release quick.
4. Stir well and serve.

Nutrition information per serving:

Calorie: 247; Carbohydrates: 35g; Protein: 12g; Fat: 7g; Sugar: 4.5g; Sodium: 17mg

Ranch Cauliflower Mashed

(Servings: 4|Cooking Time: 15 minutes)

Ingredients:

- 1 head cauliflower, cut into florets
- 3 tbsp. dry ranch dressing mix
- 1 cup water
- 2 tbsp. cream
- 4 tbsp. butter

Directions for Cooking:

1. Pour water into instant pot and insert steamer basket.
2. Add cauliflower florets into steamer basket.
3. Seal pot with lid and cook on manual high pressure for 15 minutes.
4. Quick release pressure then open the lid.
5. Remove cauliflower florets from pot and place into the large bowl.
6. Add remaining ingredients to the bowl and mash until smooth.
7. Serve and enjoy.

Nutrition information per serving:

Calorie: 126; Carbohydrates: 4g; Protein: 1g; Fat: 12g; Sugar: 2g; Sodium: 169mg

Spinach Dip

(Servings: 8|Cooking Time: 4 minutes)

Ingredients:

- 1 lb. fresh spinach
- 1 tsp. onion powder
- ½ cup sour cream
- ½ cup vegetable broth
- 1 tbsp. olive oil
- 1 cup mozzarella cheese, shredded
- 8 oz. cream cheese, cubed
- ½ cup mayonnaise
- 3 garlic cloves, minced
- ¼ tsp. pepper
- ½ tsp. salt

Directions for Cooking:

1. Add oil into instant pot and set on Sauté mode.
2. Add spinach and garlic. Sauté until cooked. Drain excess liquid.
3. Add remaining ingredients to the pot and stir well.
4. Seal pot with lid and cook on manual high pressure for 4 minutes.
5. Quick release pressure then open the lid.
6. Stir well and serve.

Nutrition information per serving:
Calorie: 230; Carbohydrates: 7.8g; Protein: 5.8g; Fat: 20.5g; Sugar: 1.4g; Sodium: 457mg

Squash Kale Curry

(Servings: 6|Cooking Time: 6 hours)

Ingredients:

- 1 cup kale, chopped
- 2 cups coconut milk
- 2 cups butternut squash, cubed
- 1 tbsp. garlic powder
- 1 cup chickpeas, soaked overnight
- 1 tsp. chili powder
- 1 tbsp. cumin powder
- 2 cups vegetable broth
- 3 garlic cloves, chopped
- 1 medium onion, chopped
- 3 tbsp. olive oil
- 1 tsp. pepper

Directions for Cooking:

1. Add all ingredients into instant pot and stir well.
2. Seal pot with lid and cook on slow cooker mode for 6 hours.
3. Stir well and serve.

Nutrition information per serving:
Calorie: 425; Carbohydrates: 35g; Protein: 11g; Fat: 28g; Sugar: 8g; Sodium: 289mg

Lentil Spinach Curry

(Servings: 6|Cooking Time: 15 minutes)

Ingredients:

- 4 cups baby spinach, chopped
- 1 medium onion, chopped
- 2 tbsp. olive oil
- 3 cups vegetable stock
- 3 garlic cloves, minced
- ¼ tsp. cayenne pepper
- 1 ½ cups red lentils, dried
- 1 tsp. ground coriander
- 1 tsp. ground cumin
- ¼ cup cilantro, chopped
- 1 medium potato, diced
- 1 tsp. ground turmeric
- ½ tsp. salt

Directions for Cooking:

1. Add oil into the pot and set on Sauté mode.
2. Add onion, garlic, cayenne pepper, turmeric, coriander and cumin and sauté for 5 minutes.
3. Add potato, vegetable stock, lentils and salt. Stir well.
4. Seal pot with lid and cook on manual high pressure for 10 minutes.
5. Quick release pressure then open the lid.
6. Add cilantro and spinach. Stir well.
7. Serve and enjoy.

Nutrition information per serving:
Calories: 254; Carbohydrates: 38g; Protein: 14g; Fat: 5.5g; Sugar: 2.2g; Sodium: 217mg

Tomato Salsa

(Servings: 6|Cooking Time: 30 minutes)

Ingredients:

- 12 cups fresh tomatoes, peeled, seeded and diced
- 6 oz. tomato paste
- ½ cup jalapeno peppers, seeded and chopped
- 3 onion, chopped
- 2 tbsp. sugar
- 2 large green peppers, chopped
- 4 tbsp. cilantro
- 2 tbsp. cayenne pepper
- 1 ½ tbsp. garlic powder
- ½ cup vinegar
- 1 tbsp. salt

Directions for Cooking:

1. Add all ingredients into instant pot and stir well to combine.
2. Seal pot with lid and cook on manual high pressure for 30 minutes.
3. Allow pressure to release naturally, then open the lid.
4. Serve and enjoy.

Nutrition information per serving:
Calories: 155; Carbohydrates: 34g; Protein: 6g; Fat: 1.4g; Sugar: 20g; Sodium: 1359mg

Artichoke Dip

(Servings: 6|Cooking Time: 10 minutes)

Ingredients:

- 10 oz. frozen spinach, chopped
- 1 cup mozzarella cheese, shredded
- ½ cup parmesan cheese, grated
- 8 oz. cream cheese, cut into cubes
- ½ cup onion, chopped
- 1 tsp. Worcestershire sauce
- 14 oz. can artichoke hearts, drained and chopped
- 2 garlic cloves, minced
- Pepper
- Salt

Directions for Cooking:

1. Add all ingredients into the large mixing bowl and mix until well combined.
2. Transfer bowl mixture into the baking dish and cover with aluminum foil.
3. Pour 1 cup water into instant pot and insert trivet.
4. Place dish on top of the trivet.
5. Seal pot with lid and cook on manual high pressure for 10 minutes.
6. Quick release pressure then open the lid.
7. Serve and enjoy.

Nutrition information per serving:
Calories: 282; Carbohydrates: 7.6g; Protein: 14.8g; Fat: 20.2g; Sugar: 1.4g; Sodium: 829mg

Chickpea Curry

(Servings: 4|Cooking Time: 10 minutes)

Ingredients:

- 2 potatoes, peeled and cubed
- 1 cup chickpeas, cooked
- ½ tbsp. cumin seeds
- 1 tsp. turmeric
- 1 cup tomatoes, diced
- 1 onion, chopped
- 1 tbsp. olive oil
- ¼ tsp. ground ginger
- 1 tsp. ground coriander
- ½ tsp. salt

Directions for Cooking:

1. Add oil, cumin and onion in instant pot. Select Sauté mode for 3 minutes.
2. Add ginger, coriander, turmeric, tomatoes, salt and potatoes. Sauté for another 2 minutes.
3. Pour water into the pot and stir well.
4. Seal pot with lid and cook on manual high pressure for 5 minutes.
5. Quick release pressure then open the lid.
6. Serve and enjoy.

Nutrition information per serving:
Calories: 310; Carbohydrates: 52.2g; Protein: 12g; Fat: 7g; Sugar: 9g; Sodium: 314mg

Parmesan Brussels Sprouts

(Servings: 4|Cooking Time: 5 minutes)

Ingredients:

- 1 lb. Brussels sprouts, trimmed and washed
- ¼ cup parmesan cheese, grated
- 1 lemon juice
- 2 tbsp. butter
- 1 cup water

Directions for Cooking:

1. Pour water into instant pot.
2. Add Brussels sprouts into steamer basket.
3. Seal pot with lid and cook on manual high pressure for 2 minutes.
4. Quick release pressure then open the lid.
5. Remove Brussels sprouts from instant pot and place on a dish.
6. Drain water from the pot.
7. Add butter into the pot and set on Sauté mode.
8. Add cooked Brussels sprouts and lemon juice. Sauté for 3 minutes.
9. Garnish with parmesan cheese and serve.

Nutrition information per serving:
Calories: 140; Carbohydrates: 10.6g; Protein: 7g; Fat: 8.5g; Sugar: 2.7g; Sodium: 223mg

Sweet Red Cabbage

(Servings: 4|Cooking Time: 12 minutes)

Ingredients:

- 6 cups red cabbage, sliced
- 1 tbsp. apple cider vinegar
- 1 onion, chopped
- 1 tbsp. olive oil
- ½ cup applesauce
- 1 cup water
- 2 garlic cloves, minced
- Pepper
- Salt

Directions for Cooking:

1. Add oil in instant pot and set on Sauté mode.
2. Add onion and garlic. Sauté for 2 minutes.

3. Add all remaining ingredients and stir well.

4. Seal pot with lid and cook on manual high pressure for 10 minutes.

5. Quick release pressure then open the lid carefully.

6. Stir well and serve.

Nutrition information per serving:

Calories: 83; Carbohydrates: 12g; Protein: 1.8g; Fat: 3.7g; Sugar: 7g; Sodium: 62mg

Chapter 10 Instant Pot Pasta & Side Dishes Recipes

Coconut Lentils

(Servings: 6|Cooking Time: 20 minutes)

Ingredients:

- 1 ½ cups lentils
- 15 oz. can coconut milk
- 2 tbsp. tomato paste
- 15 oz. tomato sauce
- 1 tsp. dried oregano
- 1 tsp. dried basil
- ¼ cup water
- ¼ tsp. garlic salt

Directions for Cooking:

1. Add all ingredients into instant pot and stir well.
2. Seal pot with lid and cook on manual high pressure for 20 minutes.
3. Quick release pressure then open the lid.
4. Stir well and serve over rice.

Nutrition information per serving:
Calories: 332; Carbohydrates: 35.9g; Protein: 15g; Fat: 15g; Sugar: 4.7g; Sodium: 389mg

Rosemary Potatoes

(Servings: 4|Cooking Time: 4 minutes)

Ingredients:

- 1 lb. potatoes, scrubbed and sliced
- ¼ tsp. rosemary, dried
- 2 garlic cloves, sliced
- 1 tbsp. olive oil
- 1 cup water
- Salt

Directions for Cooking:

1. Pour water into instant pot and place steamer basket into the pot.
2. Add sliced potatoes to the steamer basket.
3. Seal pot with lid and cook on manual high pressure for 4 minutes.
4. Quick release pressure then open the lid.

5. Add olive oil, garlic and rosemary into the oven-safe dish. Microwave for 1 minute.
6. Add sliced potatoes into the dish and stir to coat.

7. Serve and enjoy.

Nutrition information per serving:
Calories: 111; Carbohydrates: 18g; Protein: 2g; Fat: 0.5g; Sugar: 1.3g; Sodium: 46mg

Creamy Squash Apple Mash

(Servings: 4|Cooking Time: 8 minutes)

Ingredients:
- 1 lb. butternut squash, cut into 2" pieces
- 2 apples, cored and sliced
- 1 cup water
- 2 tbsp. coconut oil
- 1 onion, sliced
- ¼ tsp. ground cinnamon
- 1/8 tsp. ginger powder
- ¼ tsp. salt

Directions for Cooking:
1. Pour water into instant pot and place steamer basket into the pot.
2. Toss apples, butternut squash and onion together. Put in a steamer basket. Season with salt.
3. Seal pot with lid and cook on manual high pressure for 8 minutes.
4. Quick release pressure then open the lid.
5. Transfer apple and squash mixture into the bowl. Mash until smooth.
6. Add coconut oil, ginger and cinnamon. Mix well to combine.
7. Serve and enjoy.

Nutrition information per serving:
Calories: 179; Carbohydrates: 31.4g; Protein: 1.8g; Fat: 7.1g; Sugar: 15g; Sodium: 156mg

Parmesan Asparagus

(Servings: 2|Cooking Time: 8 minutes)

Ingredients:
- 25 asparagus spears, ends trimmed and cut into pieces
- 3 garlic cloves, minced
- 3 tbsp. butter
- 3 tbsp. parmesan cheese, grated
- 1 cup water

Directions for Cooking:
1. Pour water into instant pot then insert trivet.
2. Place asparagus on foil piece, and top with garlic and butter. Curve the edges of foil.
3. Place foil on trivet. Seal pot with lid and cook on manual high pressure for 8 minutes.
4. Quick release pressure then open the lid.
5. Sprinkle with parmesan cheese and serve.

Nutrition information per serving:
Calories: 232; Carbohydrates: 4.6g; Protein: 6.7g; Fat: 13.2g; Sugar: 1.6g; Sodium: 309mg

Turnip Mash

(Servings: 4 | Cooking Time: 25 minutes)

Ingredients:
- 4 medium turnips, peeled and diced
- ¼ cup sour cream
- ½ cup vegetable broth
- 1 onion, diced
- Pepper
- Salt

Directions for Cooking:
1. Add turnips, broth and onion into instant pot. Seal pot with lid and cook on manual high pressure for 5 minutes.
2. Allow pressure to release naturally for 10 minutes, then release quick.
3. Drain turnips well and transfer in mixing bowl. Mash turnips until smooth.
4. Add sour cream and stir well. Season with pepper and salt.
5. Serve and enjoy.

Nutrition information per serving:
Calories: 82; Carbohydrates: 11g; Protein: 2.4g; Fat: 3.2g; Sugar: 6.3g; Sodium: 223mg

Braised Parsnips

(Servings: 4 | Cooking Time: 3 minutes)

Ingredients:
- 1 ½ lbs. parsnips, peeled and sliced
- 3 tbsp. balsamic vinegar
- ¼ cup vegetable broth
- 2 tbsp. maple syrup
- 1/8 tsp. pepper
- ½ tsp. salt

Directions for Cooking:
1. Add parsnips, vinegar and broth into instant pot.
2. Seal pot with lid and cook on manual high pressure for 3 minutes.
3. Quick release pressure then open the lid.
4. Add maple syrup and stir well. Season with pepper and salt.
5. Serve and enjoy.

Nutrition information per serving:
Calories: 159; Carbohydrates: 37g; Protein: 2.4g; Fat: 0.6g; Sugar: 14.2g; Sodium: 357mg

Turmeric Mushrooms

(Servings: 4 | Cooking Time: 6 minutes)

Ingredients:
- 24 oz. Bella mushrooms, sliced
- 1 tbsp. olive oil
- 3 tbsp. water
- ½ tsp. mustard seeds
- 1 tsp. cumin seeds
- ¼ tsp. turmeric powder
- 3 curry leaves
- 2 tsp. salt

Directions for Cooking:
1. Add olive oil into instant pot and set on Sauté mode.
2. Add cumin seeds and mustard seeds into pot. Let them pop.
3. Add sliced mushrooms, turmeric, curry leaves and salt. Stir well.
4. Add water and stir. Seal pot with lid and cook on Steam mode for 2 minutes.
5. Quick release pressure then open the lid.
6. Set instant pot on Sauté mode. Stir mushrooms and simmer for 3-4 minutes.
7. Serve and enjoy.

Nutrition information per serving:
Calories: 83; Carbohydrates: 5.3g; Protein: 5.1g; Fat: 3.8g; Sugar: 0g; Sodium: 1164mg

Pumpkin Spice Butternut Squash

(Servings: 4|Cooking Time: 3 minutes)

Ingredients:
- 2 lbs. butternut squash, chopped
- 1 onion, chopped
- 3/4 cup water
- 1 tsp. garlic powder
- 1 tsp. chili powder
- 1 tbsp. pumpkin pie spice
- 1 tsp. dried oregano

Directions for Cooking:

1. Add all ingredients into instant pot and stir well.
2. Seal pot with lid and select manual high for 3 minutes.
3. Quick release pressure then open the lid.
4. Stir and serve.

Nutrition information per serving:
Calories: 123; Carbohydrates: 31g; Protein: 2.9g; Fat: 0.6g; Sugar: 6.5g; Sodium: 19mg

Green Pea Mash

(Servings: 3|Cooking Time: 18 minutes)

Ingredients:
- 1 cup green peas, frozen and thawed
- 1 cup vegetable stock
- 1 cup heavy cream
- 2 tbsp. butter
- Salt and Pepper

Directions for Cooking:
1. Add butter into instant pot and set on Sauté mode.
2. Add peas and sauté for 2 minutes.
3. Add stock, heavy cream and salt. Stir well.
4. Seal pot with lid and cook on manual high pressure for 6 minutes.
5. Allow pressure to release naturally for 10 minutes, then release using quick release method.
6. Puree the pea's mixture using an immersion blender until smooth.
7. Serve and enjoy.

Nutrition information per serving:
Calories: 248; Carbohydrates: 8.8g; Protein: 3.5g; Fat: 23g; Sugar: 3.5g; Sodium: 363mg

Black Eyed Peas

(Servings: 3|Cooking Time: 25 minutes)

Ingredients:
- ½ cup dry black-eyed peas
- 1 tbsp. butter
- ½ cup onion, chopped
- 1 cup Swiss chard
- 1 ¼ cup vegetable stock
- ½ cup can tomatoes
- ½ tsp. pepper
- ½ tsp. salt

Directions for Cooking:
1. Add all ingredients except butter into the pot and stir well.
2. Add butter on top. Seal pot with lid and cook on manual high pressure for 15 minutes.
3. Allow pressure to release naturally for 10 minutes, then release using quick release method.
4. Stir well and serve.

Nutrition information per serving:
Calories: 117; Carbohydrates: 20.6g; Protein: 6.9g; Fat: 4.7g; Sugar: 3.8g; Sodium: 835mg

Cauliflower Risotto

(Servings: 4|Cooking Time: 14 minutes)

Ingredients:

- 1 medium cauliflower head, cut into florets
- 2 tbsp. coconut aminos
- 3 garlic cloves, minced
- 1 lb. mushrooms, sliced
- 1 small onion, diced
- 2 tbsp. tapioca starch
- ¼ cup nutritional yeast
- 1 cup chicken broth
- 1 cup coconut milk
- 1 tbsp. coconut oil
- ½ tsp. sea salt

Directions for Cooking:

1. Add cauliflower florets into the food processor and process until it looks like rice.
2. Add coconut oil into instant pot and set on Sauté mode.
3. Add garlic, mushrooms and onion into the pot. Sauté for 7 minutes.
4. Add coconut aminos and stir for 5 minutes.
5. Add cauliflower rice, nutritional yeast, broth, coconut milk and salt. Stir well.
6. Seal pot with lid and cook on manual high pressure for 2 minutes.
7. Quick release pressure then open the lid.
8. Sprinkle tapioca starch and stir until thickened.
9. Serve and enjoy.

Nutrition information per serving:

Calories: 300; Carbohydrates: 26.1g; Protein: 13.9g; Fat: 19.1g; Sugar: 8.5g; Sodium: 491mg

Dijon White Beans

(Servings: 3|Cooking Time: 30 minutes)

Ingredients:

- 15 oz. can cannellini beans, rinsed
- 1 tsp. Dijon mustard
- 1 tbsp. olive oil
- 1 tsp. fresh thyme
- ¼ small onion, sliced
- ½ bell pepper, chopped
- 1 tbsp. vinegar
- Pepper
- Salt

Directions for Cooking:

1. Add beans into instant pot. Season with pepper and salt.
2. Seal pot with lid and cook on manual high pressure for 20 minutes.
3. Allow pressure to release naturally for 10 minutes, then release using quick release method.
4. Add remaining ingredients and stir well.
5. Serve and enjoy.

Nutrition information per serving:

Calories: 183; Carbohydrates: 25g; Protein: 9g; Fat: 4.8g; Sugar: 2.4g; Sodium: 180mg

Baked Potato

(Servings: 2|Cooking Time: 20 minutes)

Ingredients:

- 2 large sweet potatoes
- 4 tbsp. olive oil
- 1 cup water
- Salt and Pepper to taste

Directions for Cooking:

1. Pour water into instant pot and place steamer basket into the pot.
2. Cut sweet potatoes in half and season with pepper and salt.

3. Rub olive oil into the flesh of sweet potatoes.
4. Place sweet potato into the steamer basket.
5. Seal pot with lid and cook on manual high pressure for 20 minutes.

6. Quick release pressure then open the lid.
7. Serve and enjoy.

Nutrition information per serving:
Calories: 370; Carbohydrates: 33g; Protein: 2g; Fat: 28g; Sugar: 7g; Sodium: 123mg

Spiced Potatoes

(Servings: 4|Cooking Time: 10 minutes)

Ingredients:

- 1 lb. potatoes, cut into 1-inch cubes
- 2 tbsp. Moroccan spice mix
- 2 tbsp. coconut oil
- 1 cup water
- ½ lemon juice

Directions for Cooking:

1. Pour water into instant pot and place steamer basket into the pot.
2. Place potatoes into the steamer basket. Seal pot with lid and cook on manual high pressure for 5 minutes.
3. Quick release pressure then open the lid.

4. Transfer potatoes on a plate and clean the instant pot.
5. Add oil into the pot and set on Sauté mode.
6. Return potatoes to the pot and sprinkle with the spice mix and cook until brown, about 5 minutes.
7. Transfer on serving dish and drizzle with lemon juice.
8. Serve and enjoy.

Nutrition information per serving:
Calories: 137; Carbohydrates: 17.8g; Protein: 1.9g; Fat: 6.9g; Sugar: 1.3g; Sodium: 7mg

Creamy Turnips Potato Mash

(Servings: 4|Cooking Time: 9 minutes)

Ingredients:

- 3 cups turnip, cubed
- 3 large potatoes, peeled and diced
- ¼ cup chicken broth
- 2 tbsp. coconut milk
- 1 cup water
- 3 tbsp. butter
- 2 garlic cloves, chopped
- 1 cup water
- Pepper
- Salt

Directions for Cooking:

1. Pour water into instant pot and place steamer basket into the pot.
2. Place potatoes and turnips into the steamer basket.

3. Seal pot with lid and cook on manual high pressure for 9 minutes.
4. Quick release pressure then open the lid.
5. Transfer potatoes and turnips into the large bowl.
6. Clean the instant pot. Add butter and garlic to the pot. Sauté until brown.
7. Transfer garlic butter mixture into the potato-turnip bowl and mash until smooth.
8. Add broth, coconut milk, pepper and salt. Stir well.
9. Serve and enjoy.

Nutrition information per serving:
Calories: 317; Carbohydrates: 50.8g; Protein: 6.2g; Fat: 10.9g; Sugar: 7.2g; Sodium: 233mg

Potato Pumpkin Mash

(Servings: 6|Cooking Time: 8 minutes)

Ingredients:

- 8 potatoes, diced
- 1 tsp. garlic powder
- 4 tbsp. butter
- 1 ½ cups vegetable stock
- 15 oz. can pumpkin puree
- 2 tsp. fresh thyme
- ¼ tsp. black pepper
- 1 tsp. salt

Directions for Cooking:

1. Add broth and potatoes into instant pot. Stir well.
2. Seal pot with lid and cook on manual high pressure for 8 minutes.
3. Quick release pressure then open the lid.
4. Mash the potatoes until smooth.
5. Add remaining ingredients into the pot and stir well.
6. Serve and enjoy.

Nutrition information per serving:
Calories: 374; Carbohydrates: 70.7g; Protein: 7.5g; Fat: 8.5g; Sugar: 13.9g; Sodium: 652mg

Dill Butter Potato

(Servings: 4|Cooking Time: 15 minutes)

Ingredients:

- 1 lb. baby potatoes
- 2 tbsp. butter
- 4 fresh dill sprigs
- 1 cup water
- 1 tbsp. Celtic salt

Directions for Cooking:

1. Pour water into instant pot and place steamer basket into the pot.
2. Place baby potatoes into the steamer basket. Seal pot with lid and cook on manual high pressure for 5 minutes.
3. Allow pressure to release naturally for 10 minutes, then release using quick release method.
4. Transfer potatoes into the large bowl.
5. Add remaining ingredients and toss well.
6. Serve and enjoy.

Nutrition information per serving:
Calories: 117; Carbohydrates: 14.1g; Protein: 3g; Fat: 5.9g; Sugar: 0g; Sodium: 52mg

Cauliflower Turmeric Rice

(Servings: 4|Cooking Time: 3 minutes)

Ingredients:

- 1 lb. cauliflower, cut into florets
- ½ tbsp. parsley, dried
- 2 tbsp. olive oil
- ¼ tsp. cumin
- 1 lime juice
- ¼ tsp. paprika
- ¼ tsp. turmeric
- 4 tbsp. cilantro, chopped
- 1 cup water
- ¼ tsp. salt

Directions for Cooking:

1. Add all cauliflower florets into the steamer basket and place basket into instant pot.
2. Pour water into instant pot.
3. Seal pot with lid and cook on manual high pressure for 1 minute.

4. Quick release pressure then open the lid.
5. Transfer cauliflower on a plate.
6. Add olive oil in instant pot and set on Sauté mode.
7. Add cauliflower florets into instant pot and using masher break cauliflower into the small pieces.
8. Add turmeric, cumin, paprika, parsley, and salt. Sauté for 2 minutes.
9. Add lime juice and serve.

Nutrition information per serving:
Calories: 90; Carbohydrates: 6.3g; Protein: 2.3g; Fat: 7.2g; Sugar: 2.7g; Sodium: 182mg

Coconut Cauliflower Rice

(Servings: 4|Cooking Time: 1 minute)

Ingredients:
- 16 oz. cauliflower rice
- 1 ½ tsp. arrowroot
- 1 cup coconut milk
- ½ tsp. sea salt

Directions for Cooking:
1. Add coconut milk, cauliflower rice and sea salt into instant pot. Mix well.
2. Seal pot with lid and cook on manual high pressure for 1 minute.
3. Quick release pressure then open the lid.
4. Add arrowroot and stir until thickened.
5. Serve and enjoy.

Nutrition information per serving:
Calories: 167; Carbohydrates: 9.5g; Protein: 3.7g; Fat: 14.4g; Sugar: 4.7g; Sodium: 277mg

Delicious Spaghetti Noodles

(Servings: 2|Cooking Time: 15 minutes)

Ingredients:
- 6 oz. spaghetti noodles
- ½ tsp. dried oregano
- ½ tsp. dried basil
- 1 garlic clove, minced
- ½ onion, diced
- ½ lb. ground beef
- 2 tbsp. parmesan cheese
- 1 ¼ cups chicken stock
- 2 tbsp. tomato paste
- 1 cup jar spaghetti sauce
- 1 tbsp. olive oil
- ½ tsp. salt

Directions for Cooking:
1. Set instant pot on Sauté mode and olive oil into the pot.
2. Add ground beef and sauté for 3 minutes, stir and break meat apart with a spoon.
3. Add onion and cook for 4 minutes.
4. Stir in garlic, oregano, basil, spaghetti sauce, chicken stock, tomato paste, parmesan cheese, pepper and salt. Stir well.
5. Turn off the pot. Break noodles in half and layer them in the meat mixture.
6. Seal instant pot with lid and cook on high for 8 minutes.
7. Quick release pressure then open the lid.
8. Stir well and serve.

Nutrition information per serving:
Calories: 572; Carbohydrates: 57.5g; Protein: 46.2g; Fat: 17g; Sugar: 5.9g; Sodium: 1468mg

Chicken Pasta

(Servings: 4|Cooking Time: 27 minutes)

Ingredients:

- 1 lb. chicken breasts, skinless, boneless, and cut into chunks
- 3/4 cup heavy cream
- 8 oz. pasta
- 2 tbsp. butter
- ½ tbsp. olive oil
- 2 tbsp. parmesan cheese
- 1 ½ cups cheddar cheese, shredded
- ½ tbsp. mustard
- 1 cup hot water
- ¼ tsp. pepper
- ½ tsp. sea salt

Directions for Cooking:

1. Add olive oil into instant pot and set on Sauté mode.
2. Add chicken chunks and sauté for 4-5 minutes.
3. Add remaining ingredients except for cheeses and heavy cream. Stir well.
4. Seal pot with lid and cook on manual high pressure for 12 minutes.
5. Allow pressure to release naturally for 10 minutes, then release using quick release method.
6. Add cheddar cheese, parmesan cheese and heavy cream. Stir well until cheese is melted.
7. Serve and enjoy.

Nutrition information per serving:

Calories: 704; Carbohydrates: 32.4g; Protein: 51.3g; Fat: 40.3g; Sugar: 0.2g; Sodium: 703mg

Cheeseburger Macaroni

(Servings: 3|Cooking Time: 14 minutes)

Ingredients:

- 1 cup elbow macaroni, uncooked
- ½ tsp. basil
- ½ onion, chopped
- 1 ½ cups chicken broth
- ½ cup cheddar cheese, shredded
- ½ lb. ground beef
- 1 tbsp. Italian seasoning
- 14 oz. can tomatoes, diced
- 7.5 oz. can tomato sauce
- 1 ½ tsp. garlic, minced
- ½ tbsp. seasoning salt

Directions for Cooking:

1. Set instant pot on Sauté mode. Add onion and ground beef. Sauté until meat is no longer pink.
2. Add garlic, seasoning salt, Italian seasoning and basil. Sauté for 5 minutes.
3. Add tomatoes, tomato sauce and broth. Stir well.
4. Add macaroni and stir well. Seal pot with lid and cook on manual high pressure for 4 minutes.
5. Quick release pressure then open the lid.
6. Stir in cheese and serve.

Nutrition information per serving:

Calories: 408; Carbohydrates: 34.9g; Protein: 36.1g; Fat: 13.6g; Sugar: 36.1g; Sodium: 2368mg

Garlic Cheese Ziti

(Servings: 4|Cooking Time: 16 minutes)

Ingredients:

- 8 oz. ziti pasta
- 1 tsp. garlic, minced
- 1 cup heavy cream
- 1 ½ cups chicken broth
- ½ cup mozzarella cheese, shredded
- 1 cup parmesan cheese, shredded
- 1 cup pasta sauce
- Pepper
- Salt

Directions for Cooking:

1. Add chicken broth, heavy cream, garlic, pepper, salt and noodles to the instant pot.
2. Seal pot with lid and select high pressure for 6 minutes.
3. Allow pressure to release naturally for 10 minutes, then release using quick release method.
4. Add pasta sauce and stir well. Add cheese and stir until cheese melts and sauce thickens.
5. Serve and enjoy.

Nutrition information per serving:
Calories: 430; Carbohydrates: 41.9g; Protein: 18.6g; Fat: 20.7g; Sugar: 5.8g; Sodium: 968mg

Spinach Chicken Florentine

(Servings: 4|Cooking Time: 12 minutes)

Ingredients:

- 8 oz. linguine noodles, break in half
- 1 tsp. garlic, minced
- 1 ½ cups heavy cream
- 2 cups chicken broth
- 3 cups baby spinach
- 1 cup parmesan cheese, shredded
- 1 chicken breast, cut into chunks
- Pepper
- Salt

Directions for Cooking:

1. Add broth, garlic, heavy cream, pepper and salt into instant pot. Stir well.
2. Add chicken and stir well. Add noodles and stir well to coat.
3. Seal pot with lid and cook on manual high pressure for 6 minutes.
4. Allow pressure to release naturally for 6 minutes, then release using quick release method.
5. Add parmesan cheese and stir until cheese melt.
6. Add spinach stir for a minute.
7. Serve and enjoy.

Nutrition information per serving:
Calories: 693; Carbohydrates: 86.8g; Protein: 31.4g; Fat: 25.6g; Sugar: 4.5g; Sodium: 809mg

Creamy Alfredo

(Servings: 4|Cooking Time: 6 minutes)

Ingredients:

- ½ lb. dry linguine noodles, break in half
- 1 ½ cups heavy cream
- 1 ½ cups vegetable broth
- 3/4 cup parmesan cheese, shredded
- 1 tsp. garlic, minced
- Pepper
- Salt

Directions for Cooking:

1. Add vegetable broth, heavy cream, garlic, pepper, salt and noodles to the instant pot.
2. Seal pot with lid and cook on manual high pressure for 6 minutes.
3. Quick release pressure then open the lid.

4. Add parmesan cheese and stir until cheese melts.
5. Serve and enjoy.

Nutrition information per serving:
Calories: 258; Carbohydrates: 7.6g; Protein: 9.3g; Fat: 21.4g; Sugar: 0.6g; Sodium: 597mg

Spinach Tomato Pasta

(Servings: 3|Cooking Time: 14 minutes)

Ingredients:

- ½ small onion, diced
- 12 oz. pasta sauce
- 6 oz. spiral pasta
- 1 cup vegetable stock
- ½ bell pepper, chopped
- 1 cup spinach, chopped
- ½ tomato, diced
- ½ medium yellow squash, chopped

Directions for Cooking:

1. Add vegetables, pasta sauce and stock. Stir well.
2. Seal pot with lid and cook on manual high pressure for 4 minutes.
3. Allow pressure to release naturally for 10 minutes, then release using quick release method.
4. Stir well and serve.

Nutrition information per serving:
Calories: 321; Carbohydrates: 63.2g; Protein: 7.7g; Fat: 5g; Sugar: 14.2g; Sodium: 729mg

Creamy Zucchini Pasta

(Servings: 3|Cooking Time: 4 minutes)

Ingredients:

- 16 oz. ziti pasta
- 1 cup frozen peas
- 2 cups zucchini, chopped
- 1 cup heavy cream
- 1 cup mozzarella cheese
- 2 cups vegetable broth
- 1 cup white wine
- 3 garlic cloves, minced

Directions for Cooking:

1. Add pasta, garlic, vegetables, broth and white wine into instant pot. Stir well.

2. Seal pot with lid and cook on manual high pressure for 4 minutes.
3. Quick release pressure then open the lid.
4. Set pot on Sauté mode. Add heavy cream and cheese. Stir until cheese is melted.
5. Serve and enjoy.

Nutrition information per serving:
Calories: 749; Carbohydrates: 98.1g; Protein: 27.7 g; Fat: 21.2g; Sugar: 4.9g; Sodium: 670mg

Parmesan Pasta

(Servings: 3|Cooking Time: 4 minutes)

Ingredients:

- 8 oz. pasta
- 2 tbsp. parsley, chopped
- ½ cup heavy cream
- ½ cup chicken broth

- 1 garlic clove, minced
- 4 oz. parmesan cheese, grated
- ½ cup water
- 1 tbsp. butter

Directions for Cooking:
1. Add butter into instant pot and set on Sauté mode.
2. Once butter is melted, add garlic and stir for 30 seconds.
3. Add pasta, water, heavy cream and broth. Stir well.
4. Seal pot with lid and cook on manual high pressure for 3 minutes.
5. Quick release pressure then open the lid.
6. Add cheese and stir until cheese is melted.
7. Garnish with parsley and serve.

Nutrition information per serving:
Calorie: 451; Carbohydrates: 43.9g; Protein: 22.1 g; Fat: 21.3g; Sugar: 0.2g; Sodium: 535mg

Tuna Capers Pasta

(Servings: 4|Cooking Time: 7 minutes)

Ingredients:
- 2 cups pasta
- 15 oz. can tomatoes, diced
- 2 tbsp. olive oil
- 2 garlic cloves, sliced
- 2 tbsp. capers
- 3.5 oz. can tuna
- Pepper
- Salt

Directions for Cooking:
1. Add oil into the pot and set on Sauté mode.
2. Add garlic and sauté for a minute. Add remaining ingredients and stir well.
3. Seal pot with lid and cook on manual high pressure for 6 minutes.
4. Quick release pressure then open the lid.
5. Stir well and serve.

Nutrition information per serving:
Calorie: 302; Carbohydrates: 47.8g; Protein: 11.4g; Fat: 8.3g; Sugar: 3.7g; Sodium: 407mg

Spinach Mushroom Pasta

(Servings: 4|Cooking Time: 18 minutes)

Ingredients:
- ½ lb. pasta
- 8 oz. mushrooms, sliced
- 3 garlic cloves, minced
- 3 tbsp. coconut amino
- 2 cups vegetable broth
- 2 carrots, peeled and chopped
- 1 tsp. ground ginger
- 2 cups baby spinach, chopped
- 1 cup peas
- ¼ green onion, sliced
- ¼ tsp. red chili flakes
- ¼ tsp. pepper
- ½ tsp. salt

Directions for Cooking:
1. Add all ingredients except spinach into instant pot and stir well.
2. Seal pot with lid and cook on manual high pressure for 4 minutes.
3. Allow releasing pressure naturally for 10 minutes, then release using quick release method.
4. Add spinach and stir for 4 minutes.
5. Serve and enjoy.

Nutrition information per serving:
Calorie: 257; Carbohydrates: 45.8g; Protein: 13.5g; Fat: 2.4g; Sugar: 5g; Sodium: 738mg

Chicken Fajita Pasta

(Servings: 4|Cooking Time: 10 minutes)

Ingredients:

- 1 lb. chicken breasts, boneless and skinless, cut into pieces
- 4 garlic cloves, minced
- 1 medium onion, diced
- 1 cup chicken stock
- 2 bell peppers, seeded and diced
- 8 oz. penne pasta, dry
- 3 tbsp. fajita seasoning, divided into half
- 13.5 oz. can tomatoes with juice
- 2 tbsp. olive oil

Directions for Cooking:

1. Add olive oil in instant pot and set on Sauté mode.
2. Add chicken and half fajita seasoning. Sauté for 2 minutes.
3. Add garlic, bell pepper, onions and remaining fajita seasoning. Stir well and sauté for 2 minutes.
4. Add tomatoes with juice, chicken stock and pasta. Stir well.
5. Seal pot with lid and cook on manual high pressure for 6 minutes.
6. Quick release pressure then open the lid.
7. Serve and enjoy.

Nutrition information per serving:
Calorie: 516; Carbohydrates: 48.1g; Protein: 41.2g; Fat: 17.1g; Sugar: 7.8g; Sodium: 957mg

Corn Quinoa

(Servings: 6|Cooking Time: 8 minutes)

Ingredients:

- 3 tbsp. cottage cheese, crumbled
- 2 tbsp. fresh lime juice
- 2 green onions, chopped
- ½ cup fresh cilantro, chopped
- 1 ¼ cups water
- ½ tsp. chili powder
- 1 jalapeno pepper, chopped
- 1 cup quinoa, rinsed and drained
- 16 oz. frozen corn
- 2 tsp. olive oil
- ¼ tsp. salt

Directions for Cooking:

1. Add oil into instant pot and set on Sauté mode.
2. Add corn to the pot and sauté for 4-5 minutes.
3. Add quinoa, chili powder, jalapeno, water and salt. Stir well.
4. Seal pot with lid and cook on manual high pressure for 3 minutes.
5. Quick release pressure then open the lid.
6. Add lime juice, green onions and half cilantro. Stir well.
7. Sprinkle with cheese and remaining cilantro. Serve.

Nutrition information per serving:
Calorie: 480; Carbohydrates: 96.5g; Protein: 18.5g; Fat: 8.3g; Sugar: 13.6g; Sodium: 194mg

Quick Mac & Cheese

(Servings: 4|Cooking Time: 4 minutes)

Ingredients:

- 8 oz. macaroni noodles
- ¼ cup sour cream
- ¼ cup heavy whipping cream

- 8 oz. Colby & Monetary Jack blend cheese
- 2 cups water
- Pepper
- Salt

Directions for Cooking:

1. Add water and macaroni into instant pot. Seal pot with lid and cook on manual high pressure for 4 minutes.
2. Quick release pressure then open the lid.

3. Add remaining ingredients and stir until cheese melts.
4. Season with pepper and salt.
5. Serve and enjoy.

Nutrition information per serving:
Calorie: 490; Carbohydrates: 44.6g; Protein: 21.5g; Fat: 24.9g; Sugar: 1.8g; Sodium: 399mg

Pesto Chicken Pasta

(Servings: 8|Cooking Time: 3 minutes)

Ingredients:

- 2 cups broccoli, chopped
- 1 onion, diced
- 1 red pepper, diced
- 9 oz. jar pesto
- 1 cup parmesan cheese, grated
- 1 lb. rotini pasta
- 4 cups water
- 2 garlic cloves, minced
- 2 chicken breasts, diced
- 1 tbsp. olive oil
- ½ tsp. salt

Directions for Cooking:

1. Add oil, pasta, water, garlic, and chicken into instant pot. Stir well.

2. Seal pot with lid and cook on manual high pressure for 3 minutes.
3. Allow pressure to release naturally for 15 minutes, then release using quick release method.
4. Add broccoli, onion, red pepper, pesto, parmesan cheese and salt. Stir well and cover the pot with lid. Let sit for 10 minutes.
5. Serve and enjoy.

Nutrition information per serving:
Calorie: 376; Carbohydrates: 22g; Protein: 21g; Fat: 22g; Sugar: 2g; Sodium: 622mg

Butter Ranch Potatoes

(Servings: 4|Cooking Time: 8 minutes)

Ingredients:

- 3 potatoes, peeled and cubed
- ½ cup water
- 2 tbsp. butter
- 2 tbsp. ranch seasoning
- Pepper
- Salt

Directions for Cooking:

1. Add all ingredients into instant pot and stir well.

2. Seal pot with lid and cook on manual high pressure for 8 minutes.
3. Quick release pressure then open the lid.
4. Stir well and serve.

Nutrition information per serving:
Calories: 176; Carbohydrates: 25.1g; Protein: 2.7g; Fat: 5.9g; Sugar: 1.8g; Sodium: 426mg

Cheese Ranch Potatoes

(Servings: 4|Cooking Time: 6 minutes)

Ingredients:

- 2 lbs. potatoes, peeled and chopped
- ½ cup chicken broth
- ½ cup water
- 1 cup parmesan cheese, shredded
- 1 oz. ranch seasoning
- ½ tsp. salt

Directions for Cooking:

1. Add all ingredients except cheese into instant pot and stir well.
2. Seal pot with lid and cook on manual high pressure for 7 minutes.
3. Quick release pressure then open the lid.
4. Add cheese and stir until cheese melts.
5. Serve and enjoy.

Nutrition information per serving:

Calories: 266; Carbohydrates: 36.4g; Protein: 12g; Fat: 5.9g; Sugar: 2.7g; Sodium: 1236mg

Corn Cob

(Servings: 4|Cooking Time: 5 minutes)

Ingredients:

- 4 ears of corn, remove husks
- 4 tsp. parmesan cheese, grated
- 4 tsp. ranch seasoning
- ¼ cup butter, melted

Directions for Cooking:

1. Pour 1 ½ cups water into instant pot then insert trivet.
2. Place corn on top of the trivet. Seal pot with lid and cook on manual high pressure for 5 minutes.
3. Quick release pressure then open the lid.
4. In a small bowl, mix together ranch seasoning and melted butter.
5. Brush butter and ranch mixture all over the corn and serve.

Nutrition information per serving:

Calories: 256; Carbohydrates: 29g; Protein: 6.1g; Fat: 14.1g; Sugar: 5g; Sodium: 379mg

Cabbage with Butter

(Servings: 4|Cooking Time: 12 minutes)

Ingredients:

- 1 medium cabbage head, chopped
- 1 cup chicken broth
- ½ cup butter
- Pepper
- Salt

Directions for Cooking:

1. Add all ingredients into instant pot and stir well.
2. Seal pot with lid and cook on manual high pressure for 6 minutes.
3. Quick release pressure then open the lid.
4. Stir well and serve.

Nutrition information per serving:

Calories: 270; Carbohydrates: 13.4g; Protein: 4.4g; Fat: 23.6g; Sugar: 7.5g; Sodium: 434mg

Ginger Honey Carrots

(Servings: 6|Cooking Time: 3 minutes)

Ingredients:

- 6 carrots, peeled and sliced
- 1/3 cup water
- 1 tsp. ground ginger
- 3 tbsp. honey
- 1 tsp. salt

Directions for Cooking:

1. Add all ingredients into instant pot and stir well.
2. Seal pot with lid and cook on manual high pressure for 6 minutes.
3. Quick release pressure then open the lid.
4. Serve and enjoy.

Nutrition information per serving:

Calories: 58; Carbohydrates: 14.9g; Protein: 0.6g; Fat: 0g; Sugar: 11.6g; Sodium: 431mg

Simple Chicken Noodles

(Servings: 5|Cooking Time: 15 minutes)

Ingredients:

- ½ lb. egg noodles
- 4 cups chicken broth
- 1 tsp. poultry seasoning
- 1 ¼ lbs. chicken tenders
- Pepper
- Salt

Directions for Cooking:

1. Add all ingredients into instant pot and stir well to combine.
2. Seal pot with lid and cook on manual high pressure for 5 minutes.
3. Allow pressure to release naturally for 10 minutes, then release using quick release method.
4. Stir and serve.

Nutrition information per serving:

Calories: 310; Carbohydrates: 12.4g; Protein: 38.8g; Fat: 10.5g; Sugar: 0.8g; Sodium: 741mg

Chapter 11 Instant Pot Stocks & Sauces Recipes

Cranberry Sauce

(Servings: 8|Cooking Time: 14 minutes)

Ingredients:
- 12 oz. fresh cranberries
- 1 tsp. lemon zest
- 1 tsp. vanilla extract
- ¾ cup Swerve
- ¼ cup water

Directions for Cooking:
1. Add cranberries and water to the pot. Seal pot with lid and cook on manual high pressure for 1 minute.
2. Allow pressure to release naturally for 10 minutes, then release using quick release method.
3. Set pot on Sauté mode. Add remaining ingredients and cook for 2-3 minutes.
4. Allow to cool completely. Transfer in a jar and refrigerate.

Nutrition information per serving:
Calories: 25; Carbohydrates: 4.2g; Protein: 0g; Fat: 0g; Sugar: 1.6g; Sodium: 0mg

Apple Sauce

(Servings: 8|Cooking Time: 18 minutes)

Ingredients:
- 8 apple, peeled, cored, and diced
- 2 tsp. ground cinnamon
- 1 cup water

Directions for Cooking:
1. Add water and apple into the pot. Seal pot with lid and cook on manual high pressure for 8 minutes.
2. Allow pressure to release naturally for 10 minutes, then release using quick release method.
3. Blend until smooth.
4. Add cinnamon and stir well. Transfer to a glass jar.
5. Place in the refrigerator and serve chilled.

Nutrition information per serving:
Calories: 95; Carbohydrates: 25g; Protein: 0.5g; Fat: 0.3g; Sugar: 18g; Sodium: 2mg

Slow Cooked jam

(Servings: 6|Cooking Time: 6 hours)

Ingredients:
- 3 cups fresh blackberries
- 5 tbsp. butter
- ¼ cup chia seeds
- 4 tbsp. erythritol
- ¼ cup fresh lemon juice

Directions for Cooking:
1. Add all ingredients into instant pot and stir well.
2. Seal pot with lid and cook on Slow Cook mode for 6 hours.
3. Serve and enjoy.

Nutrition information per serving:
Calories: 235; Carbohydrates: 33g; Protein: 2.9g; Fat: 11g; Sugar: 0g; Sodium: 81mg

Hot Sauce

(Servings: 50|Cooking Time: 17 minutes)

Ingredients:
- 1 lb. jalapeno pepper, chopped
- ½ cup water
- 1 ¼ cups apple cider vinegar
- 5 garlic cloves, peeled
- 1 bell pepper, roasted and chopped
- Salt

Directions for Cooking:
1. Add all ingredients into instant pot and stir well.
2. Seal pot with lid and cook on manual high pressure for 2 minutes.
3. Allow pressure to release naturally for 15 minutes, then release using quick release method.
4. Once jalapeno mixture is cool completely then blend until smooth.
5. Strain sauce into the jar and store in the refrigerator.

Nutrition information per serving:
Calories: 5; Carbohydrates: 0.9g; Protein: 0.2g; Fat: 0.1g; Sugar: 0.5g; Sodium: 4mg

Spicy Garlic Pepper Sauce

(Servings: 50|Cooking Time: 17 minutes)

Ingredients:

- 1 lb. cayenne peppers, trimmed and chopped
- 1 tbsp. paprika
- ½ cup water
- 1 ¼ cups apple cider vinegar
- 5 garlic cloves, peeled
- 1 red bell pepper, roasted and chopped
- ¼ cup carrot, peeled and shredded
- Salt

Directions for Cooking:

1. Add all ingredients into instant pot and stir well.
2. Seal pot with lid and cook on manual high pressure for 2 minutes.
3. Allow pressure to release naturally for 15 minutes, then release using quick release method.
4. Once sauce mixture is cooled then blend until smooth.
7. Strain sauce into the jar and store in the refrigerator.

Nutrition information per serving:

Calories: 32; Carbohydrates: 5.6g; Protein: 1.2g; Fat: 1.6g; Sugar: 1.1g; Sodium: 8mg

Vegan Cheese Sauce

(Servings: 25|Cooking Time: 5 minutes)

Ingredients:

- 2 cups water
- 1 tsp. turmeric
- ½ cup nutritional yeast
- ½ cup cashews
- 2 garlic cloves, peeled
- ½ cup onion, chopped
- 1 cup carrot, chopped
- 2 cups potato, peeled and chopped
- 1 tsp. salt

Directions for Cooking:

1. Add all ingredients into instant pot and stir well.
2. Seal pot with lid and cook on manual high pressure for 5 minutes.
3. Quick release pressure then open the lid.
4. Once sauce mixture is cool, blend until smooth and creamy.
5. Store and serve.

Nutrition information per serving:

Calories: 35; Carbohydrates: 4.2g; Protein: 2.1g; Fat: 1.5g; Sugar: 0.5g; Sodium: 100mg

Sweet Caramel Sauce

(Servings: 9|Cooking Time: 6 hours)

Ingredients:

- ½ cup erythritol
- 2 tbsp. water
- ¼ tsp. xanthan gum
- ½ cup almond milk
- 4 tbsp. butter

Directions for Cooking:

1. Add all ingredients into instant pot and stir well.
2. Seal pot with lid and cook on Slow Cook mode for 6 hours.
3. Quick release pressure then open the lid.
4. Serve and enjoy.

Nutrition information per serving:

Calories: 76; Carbohydrates: 0.7g; Protein: 0.4g; Fat: 8.3g; Sugar: 0g; Sodium: 43mg

BBQ Sauce

(Servings: 50|Cooking Time: 25 minutes)

Ingredients:

- 1 tbsp. Dijon mustard
- 1 tbsp. liquid smoke
- 2 tbsp. corn syrup
- 2 tbsp. molasses
- ¼ cup butter
- ½ cup brown sugar
- ¼ cup apple cider vinegar
- ¼ cup tomato paste
- 2/3 cup ketchup
- 1 cup tomato sauce
- ½ cup onion, peeled and diced

Directions for Cooking:

1. Add all ingredients into instant pot and stir well.
2. Seal pot with lid and cook on manual high pressure for 15 minutes.
3. Allow pressure to release naturally for 10 minutes, then release using quick release method, then open lid.
4. Allow to cool completely and store in the refrigerator.

Nutrition information per serving:
Calories: 24; Carbohydrates: 4.1g; Protein: 0.2g; Fat: 1g; Sugar: 3.2g; Sodium: 74mg

Hawaiian BBQ Sauce

(Servings: 50|Cooking Time: 25 minutes)

Ingredients:

- 1 cup fresh pineapple, diced
- ½ tsp. red pepper flakes
- ½ cup onion, minced
- 2 tbsp. Dijon mustard
- 1 tsp. dry mustard powder
- 2 garlic cloves
- ¼ cup Worcestershire sauce
- 1/3 cup soy sauce
- 1/3 cup apple cider vinegar
- 7 dates, pitted
- 6 oz. pineapple juice
- 1 ½ cups ketchup
- ½ tsp. pepper
- 1 tsp. garlic salt

Directions for Cooking:

1. Add all ingredients except pineapple into instant pot and stir well.
2. Seal pot with lid and cook on manual high pressure for 15 minutes.
3. Allow pressure to release naturally for 10 minutes, then release using quick release method, then open lid.
4. Blend until smooth.
5. Add pineapple and stir well. Transfer sauce to the jar and store in the refrigerator.

Nutrition information per serving:
Calories: 18; Carbohydrates: 4.2g; Protein: 0.4g; Fat: 0.1g; Sugar: 3.4g; Sodium: 197mg

Fudge Sauce

(Servings: 9|Cooking Time: 5 hours)

Ingredients:

- 1 cup whipping cream
- ½ tsp. vanilla
- 2.5 oz. unsweetened chocolate
- 1/3 cup Swerve

Directions for Cooking:

1. Add all ingredients into instant pot and stir well.

2. Seal pot with lid and cook on Slow Cook mode for 5 hours.
3. Stir well and serve.

Nutrition information per serving:
Calories: 126; Carbohydrates: 3.7g; Protein: 1.7g; Fat: 14.8g; Sugar: 0g; Sodium: 19mg

Tomato Pepper Sauce

(Servings: 6|Cooking Time: 6 minutes)

Ingredients:
- 1 cup basil
- 2 tomatoes, sliced
- 1 green pepper, sliced
- 2 yellow pepper, sliced
- 2 red peppers, sliced
- 2 garlic cloves
- 1 onion, sliced
- 1 tbsp. olive oil
- Pepper
- Salt

Directions for Cooking:

1. Add oil into the pot and set on Sauté mode.
2. Add garlic and onion. Sauté for 3 minutes.
3. Add tomatoes, peppers, basil, pepper and salt. Stir well.
4. Seal pot with lid and cook on manual high pressure for 3 minutes.
5. Quick release pressure then open the lid.
6. Stir well and serve.

Nutrition information per serving:
Calories: 64; Carbohydrates: 9.9g; Protein: 1.8g; Fat: 2.7g; Sugar: 3.2g; Sodium: 33mg

Tomato Sauce

(Servings: 8|Cooking Time: 15 minutes)

Ingredients:
- 10 basil leaves
- 6 lbs. tomatoes, quartered
- 1 celery stalk, chopped
- 2 large carrots, peeled and chopped
- 2 onions, sliced
- ¼ cup olive oil

Directions for Cooking:
1. Add oil into instant pot and set on Sauté mode.
2. Add onion and sauté for 5 minutes. Add carrots and celery. Sauté for 5 minutes.

3. Add tomatoes and stir well. Seal pot with lid and cook on manual high pressure for 5 minutes.
4. Quick release pressure then open the lid.
5. Using blender puree the sauce until smooth.
6. Transfer sauce to the jar and store in the refrigerator.

Nutrition information per serving:
Calories: 134; Carbohydrates: 17.7g; Protein: 3.5g; Fat: 7g; Sugar: 11g; Sodium: 32mg

Fish Stock

(Servings: 6|Cooking Time: 62 minutes)

Ingredients:
- 2 salmon heads, quartered
- 1 cup carrots, chopped
- 2 lemongrass stalks, chopped
- 2 tsp. garlic, minced
- 1 tbsp. olive oil
- 1 cup celery, chopped

Directions for Cooking:
1. Add oil into instant pot and set on Sauté mode.

2. Add salmon and cook for 2 minutes. Add remaining ingredients and stir well.
3. Pour 8 cups water into the pot.
4. Seal pot with lid and cook on Soup mode for 45 minutes.
5. Allow pressure to release naturally for 10 minutes, then release using quick release method.
6. Strain and store.

Nutrition information per serving:
Calories: 78; Carbohydrates: 2.6g; Protein: 6.9g; Fat: 4.5g; Sugar: 1.1g; Sodium: 41mg

Chicken Cauliflower Stock

(Servings: 6|Cooking Time: 4 hours)

Ingredients:
- 2 lbs. chicken, bone-in and skin on
- 3 tbsp. fresh parsley, chopped
- 2 baby carrots, sliced
- 1 cup broccoli, chopped
- 1 onion, chopped
- 1 cup cauliflower, chopped
- 1 tsp. black pepper
- 1 tsp. salt

Directions for Cooking:
1. Add all ingredients into instant pot and stir well.
2. Pour in enough water to cover the ingredients.
3. Seal pot with lid and cook on Slow Cook mode for 4 hours.
4. Allow pressure to release naturally, then open the lid.
5. Strain stock and store.

Nutrition information per serving:
Calories: 26; Carbohydrates: 4.2g; Protein: 1.5g; Fat: 0.7g; Sugar: 1.6g; Sodium: 497mg

Beef Stock

(Servings: 6|Cooking Time: 20 minutes)

Ingredients:
- 2 lbs. beef bones
- 1 tsp. peppercorn
- 1 cup tomatoes, chopped
- 1 onion, cut into wedges
- 2 celery stalks, chopped
- 1 cup apple cider vinegar
- 1 cup sauerkraut
- 1 tsp. black pepper
- 1 tsp. salt

Directions for Cooking:
1. Add all ingredients into instant pot and pour in enough water to cover.
2. Seal pot with lid and cook on manual high pressure for 20 minutes.
3. Quick release pressure then open the lid.
4. Strain the stock and store.

Nutrition information per serving:
Calories: 28; Carbohydrates: 4.9g; Protein: 2.9g; Fat: 0.6g; Sugar: 2.2g; Sodium: 660mg

Fish Bones Stock

(Servings: 6|Cooking Time: 2 hours 10 minutes)

Ingredients:
- 1 lb. fish bones
- ½ tsp. red pepper flakes
- ½ tsp. pepper
- 3 tbsp. fresh parsley, chopped

- 1 carrot, sliced
- 1 celery stalk, chopped
- 1 onion, sliced
- 7 cups water
- 1 tsp. sea salt

Directions for Cooking:
1. Add 1 cup water, carrot, celery, onion and fish bones into instant pot. Cook on Sauté mode for 10 minutes.

2. Add remaining ingredients along with remaining water.
3. Seal pot with lid and cook on Slow Cook mode for 2 hours.
4. Quick release pressure then open the lid.
5. Strain the stock and store.

Nutrition information per serving:
Calories: 38; Carbohydrates: 0.1g; Protein: 3.9g; Fat: 1.3g; Sugar: 1.4g; Sodium: 323mg

Apple Pear Sauce

(Servings: 30|Cooking Time: 19 minutes)

Ingredients:
- 2 large apples, peeled, cored and quartered
- 1 tsp. cinnamon
- ¼ cup water
- 8 pears, peeled, cored and quartered

Directions for Cooking:
1. Add apple, cinnamon, pear and water into instant pot. Stir well to combine.
2. Seal pot with lid and cook on manual high pressure for 4 minutes.

3. Allow pressure to release naturally for 15 minutes, then release using quick release method.
4. Blend the sauce until smooth.
5. Store and serve.

Nutrition information per serving:
Calories: 40; Carbohydrates: 10.6g; Protein: 0.2g; Fat: 0.1g; Sugar: 7g; Sodium: 1mg

Chunky Apple Pear Sauce

(Servings: 16|Cooking Time: 22 minutes)

Ingredients:
- 4 pears, diced
- 4 apples, peeled, cored and diced
- 2 tsp. vanilla
- 2 tbsp. cinnamon
- 1/3 cup maple syrup
- ¾ cup water

Directions for Cooking:
1. Add all ingredients into instant pot and stir well.

2. Seal pot with lid and cook on manual high pressure for 12 minutes.
3. Allow pressure to release naturally for 10 minutes then release using quick release method.
4. Blend the sauce using a blender until getting a chunky consistency.
5. Serve and enjoy.

Nutrition information per serving:
Calories: 80; Carbohydrates: 20.8g; Protein: 0.4g; Fat: 0.2g; Sugar: 14.9g; Sodium: 2mg

Orange Cranberry Sauce

(Servings: 30|Cooking Time: 5 minutes)

Ingredients:

- 12 oz. cranberries
- ½ tsp. orange zest
- 1 cup sugar
- 1 cup orange juice

Directions for Cooking:

1. Add all ingredients into instant pot and stir well.
2. Seal pot with lid and cook on manual high pressure for 5 minutes.
3. Quick release pressure then open the lid.
4. Allow to cool completely then store.

Nutrition information per serving:

Calories: 35; Carbohydrates: 8.6g; Protein: 0.1g; Fat: 0g; Sugar: 7.8g; Sodium: 0mg

Apple Cranberry Sauce

(Servings: 8|Cooking Time: 10 minutes)

Ingredients:

- 1 apple, peeled, cored and chopped
- ½ cup maple syrup
- ½ cup apple cider
- 1 orange zest
- 1 orange juice
- 12 oz. fresh cranberries, rinsed

Directions for Cooking:

1. Add all ingredients into instant pot and stir well.
2. Seal pot with lid and cook on manual high pressure for 5 minutes.
3. Allow pressure to release naturally for 5 minutes, then release using quick release method.
4. Allow to cool completely and store.

Nutrition information per serving:

Calories: 101; Carbohydrates: 23.9g; Protein: 0.2g; Fat: 0.1g; Sugar: 18.8g; Sodium: 3mg

Rosemary Cranberry Apple Sauce

(Servings: 16|Cooking Time: 5 minutes)

Ingredients:

- 2 lbs. apples, cored and diced
- 2 tbsp. maple syrup
- 1 fresh rosemary sprig
- 1 cup apple cider
- 12 oz. cranberries

Directions for Cooking:

1. Add all ingredients into instant pot and stir well.
2. Seal pot with lid and cook on manual high pressure for 5 minutes.
3. Quick release pressure then open the lid.
4. Discard rosemary from the sauce and mash until desired consistency.
5. Allow to cool completely then store.

Nutrition information per serving:

Calories: 40; Carbohydrates: 9.3g; Protein: 0.1g; Fat: 0.1g; Sugar: 6.9g; Sodium: 1mg

Apple Strawberry Sauce

(Servings: 15|Cooking Time: 19 minutes)

Ingredients:

- 6 apples, peeled, cored and diced
- ¼ cup sugar
- 1 pear, peeled, cored and diced
- 2 tbsp. fresh lemon juice
- ¼ tsp. cinnamon
- 2 cups strawberries

Directions for Cooking:

1. Add all ingredients into instant pot and stir well.
2. Seal pot with lid and cook on manual high pressure for 4 minutes.
3. Allow pressure to release naturally for 15 minutes, then release using quick release method.
4. Mash the sauce until desired consistency.
5. Allow to cool completely and store.

Nutrition information per serving:
Calories: 71; Carbohydrates: 18.6g; Protein: 0.4g; Fat: 0.3g; Sugar: 14.5g; Sodium: 2mg

Pumpkin Apple Cinnamon Sauce

(Servings: 8|Cooking Time: 10 minutes)

Ingredients:

- 2 ½ lbs. apples, peeled, cored and diced
- 2/3 cup water
- 2 ½ tbsp. brown sugar
- 1 ½ tsp. cinnamon
- 2/3 cup pumpkin puree

Directions for Cooking:

1. Add all ingredients into instant pot and stir well.
2. Seal pot with lid and cook on manual high pressure for 5 minutes.
3. Allow pressure to release naturally for 5 minutes, then release using quick release method.
4. Allow to cool completely and transfer in a jar.
5. Store in the refrigerator.

Nutrition information per serving:
Calories: 55; Carbohydrates: 14.4g; Protein: 0.4g; Fat: 0.2g; Sugar: 10.7g; Sodium: 3mg

Chicken Bone Broth

(Servings: 4|Cooking Time: 70 minutes)

Ingredients:

- 1 chicken bones
- 6 cups water
- ¼ cup apple cider vinegar
- 1 tbsp. sea salt

Directions for Cooking:

1. Add all ingredients into instant pot.
2. Seal pot with lid and cook on manual mode for 60 minutes.
3. Allow pressure to release naturally for 10 minutes, then release using quick release method.
4. Strain the broth and store.

Nutrition information per serving:
Calories: 38; Carbohydrates: 0.9g; Protein: 4.9g; Fat: 1.4g; Sugar: 0.7g; Sodium: 763mg

Leftover Turkey Stock

(Servings: 4|Cooking Time: 70 minutes)

Ingredients:

- 1 lb. leftover turkey carcass
- 6 cups water
- 2 garlic cloves
- 1 cup carrots, sliced
- 1 cup celery, sliced
- 1 cup onion, diced

Directions for Cooking:

1. Add all ingredients into instant pot.
2. Seal pot with lid and cook on manual mode for 60 minutes.
3. Allow pressure to release naturally for 10 minutes, then release using quick release method.
8. Strain the stock and store.

Nutrition information per serving:

Calories: 10; Carbohydrates: 0.9g; Protein: 2g; Fat: 0g; Sugar: 0.9g; Sodium: 990mg

Bolognese Sauce

(Servings: 4|Cooking Time: 8 minutes)

Ingredients:

- 1 lb. ground beef
- 1 ½ tsp. garlic, minced
- 3 tbsp. fresh parsley, chopped
- 14 oz. marinara sauce

Directions for Cooking:

1. Add all ingredients into instant pot and stir well.
2. Seal pot with lid and cook on manual high pressure for 8 minutes.
3. Quick release pressure then open the lid.
4. Stir well and serve.

Nutrition information per serving:

Calories: 300; Carbohydrates: 14.2g; Protein: 36.3g; Fat: 9.8g; Sugar: 8.8g; Sodium: 483mg

Spicy Beef Stock

(Servings: 6|Cooking Time: 45 minutes)

Ingredients:

- 2 lbs. beef bones
- ½ tsp. red pepper flakes
- 2 tsp. chili pepper
- 3 tbsp. red wine vinegar
- ¼ cup onions, chopped
- ¼ cup celery, chopped
- ¼ cup celery stalk, chopped
- 3 garlic cloves
- 3 chili peppers
- 1 tsp. salt

Directions for Cooking:

1. Add all ingredients to the pot and pour enough water to cover.
2. Seal pot with lid and cook on manual high pressure for 35 minutes.
3. Allow pressure to release naturally for 10 minutes, then release using quick release method.
4. Strain stock and store.

Nutrition information per serving:

Calories: 17; Carbohydrates: 1.7g; Protein: 2g; Fat: 0.4g; Sugar: 0.6g; Sodium: 396mg

Chicken Thyme Stock

(Servings: 4|Cooking Time: 35 minutes)

Ingredients:

- 2 lbs. chicken necks
- 1 tsp. peppercorns
- 1 tsp. dried thyme
- ½ cup fresh parsley, chopped
- 2 chicken thighs
- 2 tsp. sea salt

Directions for Cooking:

1. Add all ingredients to the pot and pour enough water to cover.

2. Seal pot with lid and cook on manual high pressure for 25 minutes.
3. Allow pressure to release naturally for 10 minutes, then release using quick release method.
4. Strain stock and store.

Nutrition information per serving:

Calories: 12; Carbohydrates: 1g; Protein: 0.8g; Fat: 0.6g; Sugar: 0.1g; Sodium: 941mg

Spicy Lamb Stock

(Servings: 5|Cooking Time: 6 hours 10 minute)

Ingredients:

- 2 lbs. lamb bones
- ½ tsp. white pepper
- 1 tsp. red pepper flakes
- 2 tsp. chili powder
- ¼ cup red wine vinegar
- ¼ cup celery, chopped
- 5 garlic cloves
- 1 onion, sliced
- 1 tsp. salt

Directions for Cooking:

1. Add all ingredients into instant pot and pour enough water to cover.
2. Seal pot with lid and cook on Slow Cook mode for 6 hours.
3. Allow pressure to release naturally for 10 minutes, then release using quick release method.
4. Strain stock and store.

Nutrition information per serving:

Calories: 24; Carbohydrates: 4.2g; Protein: 2.5g; Fat: 0.7g; Sugar: 1.2g; Sodium: 620mg

Classic Beef Stock

(Servings: 4|Cooking Time: 45 minutes)

Ingredients:

- 2 lbs. beef bones
- ½ tsp. dried basil
- 1 tsp. peppercorns
- 4 garlic cloves
- ½ cup celery stalks, chopped
- 2 tbsp. red wine vinegar
- 1 tsp. sea salt

Directions for Cooking:

1. Add all ingredients into instant pot and pour enough water to cover.

2. Seal pot with lid and cook on manual high pressure for 35 minutes.
3. Allow pressure to release naturally for 10 minutes, then release using quick release method.
4. Strain stock and store.

Nutrition information per serving:

Calories: 18; Carbohydrates: 1.8g; Protein: 2.3g; Fat: 0.4g; Sugar: 0.2g; Sodium: 479mg

Celery Lamb Stock

(Servings: 4|Cooking Time: 15 minutes)

Ingredients:
- 2 lbs. lamb bones
- 1 tsp. dried thyme
- 2 tbsp. apple cider vinegar
- ½ cup celery leaves
- 2 celery stalks, chopped
- 2 onions, sliced
- 1 tsp. salt

Directions for Cooking:

1. Add all ingredients into instant pot and pour enough water to cover.
2. Seal pot with lid and cook on manual high pressure for 15 minutes.
3. Quick release pressure then open the lid.
4. Strain stock and store.

Nutrition information per serving:
Calories: 42; Carbohydrates: 6g; Protein: 3.4g; Fat: 0.6g; Sugar: 2.6g; Sodium: 773mg

Butter Cheese Sauce

(Servings: 8|Cooking Time: 8 minutes)

Ingredients:
- 1/3 cup butter
- ¼ tsp. dried basil
- 1 tsp. red chili flakes
- 1 cup vegetable stock
- 2 garlic cloves, crushed
- ¼ cup fresh parsley, chopped
- 2 tbsp. parmesan cheese, grated
- 1 cup cottage cheese
- 2 cups cream cheese
- ½ tsp. salt

Directions for Cooking:

1. Add butter, basil, red chili flakes and salt to the instant pot. Set on Sauté mode.
2. Once butter is melted then add garlic and sauté for a minute.
3. Add parmesan cheese, cottage cheese and cream cheese. Cook for 2 minutes.
4. Add parsley and stock. Stir well. Seal pot with lid and cook on manual mode for 6 minutes.
5. Quick release pressure then open the lid.
6. Once sauce is cool completely, store in a jar.

Nutrition information per serving:
Calories: 308; Carbohydrates: 3.2g; Protein: 9.2g; Fat: 29.3g; Sugar: 0.5g; Sodium: 617mg

Cheese Onion Sauce

(Servings: 5|Cooking Time: 35 minutes)

Ingredients:
- 1 onion, chopped
- 2 tsp. dried parsley
- 1 tsp. onion powder
- 2 tbsp. olive oil
- 1 cup vegetable stock
- 2 cups cream cheese

Directions for Cooking:

1. Add oil into instant pot and set on Sauté mode.
2. Add onion and sauté for 10 minutes.
3. Add remaining ingredients and stir well.
4. Seal pot with lid and cook on manual high pressure for 15 minutes.
5. Allow pressure to release naturally for 10 minutes, then release using quick release method.
6. Allow to cool completely then store.

Nutrition information per serving:
Calories: 385; Carbohydrates: 5.3g; Protein: 7.3g; Fat: 3804g; Sugar: 1.7g; Sodium: 420mg

Enchilada Sauce

(Servings: 8|Cooking Time: 20 minutes)

Ingredients:

- 14 oz. can roasted tomatoes, diced
- ½ cup water
- 1 tsp. red chili powder
- 2 chipotle chilies in adobo sauce
- 3 garlic cloves
- ½ jalapeno pepper, sliced
- ½ bell pepper, chopped
- ½ onion, chopped
- 1 tsp. salt

Directions for Cooking:

1. Add all ingredients except tomatoes into instant pot and stir well.
2. Add tomatoes on top. Seal pot with lid and cook on manual high pressure for 10 minutes.
3. Allow pressure to release naturally for 10 minutes, then release using quick release method.
4. Blend the sauce and store.

Nutrition information per serving:
Calories: 20; Carbohydrates: 4.2g; Protein: 0.7g; Fat: 0.1g; Sugar: 1.9g; Sodium: 408mg

Curry Tomato Sauce

(Servings: 8|Cooking Time: 13 minutes)

Ingredients:

- 28 oz. can tomatoes, crushed
- ½ cup can coconut milk
- ½ tsp. black pepper
- 1 tbsp. fresh thyme leaves
- ¼ tsp. ground cinnamon
- ¼ tsp. red pepper flakes
- ½ tsp. turmeric
- ½ tsp. garam masala
- 1 tbsp. ginger, minced
- 3 garlic cloves
- ½ onion, diced
- 1 tsp. sea salt

Directions for Cooking:

1. Add all ingredients into instant pot and stir well.
2. Seal pot with lid and cook on manual high pressure for 10 minutes.
3. Quick release pressure then open the lid.
4. Blend the sauce until smooth.
5. Transfer sauce in container and store.

Nutrition information per serving:
Calories: 58; Carbohydrates: 7.4g; Protein: 1.5g; Fat: 3.1g; Sugar: 3.7g; Sodium: 448mg

Parmesan Basil Sauce

(Servings: 5|Cooking Time: 15 minutes)

Ingredients:

- 1 tbsp. parmesan cheese
- ¼ tsp. dried thyme
- ¼ tsp. black pepper
- 1 tbsp. olive oil
- 1 garlic clove, crushed
- ½ cup fresh basil
- ½ cup feta cheese, crumbled
- 1 cup cream cheese
- ½ cup water
- ½ tsp. salt

Directions for Cooking:

1. Add all ingredients into a heat-safe bowl and stir well.
2. Pour water into instant pot then insert trivet.

3. Place bowl on top of the trivet. Seal pot with lid and cook on manual mode for 10 minutes.
4. Quick release pressure then open the lid.
5. Remove bowl from the pot and set aside to cool completely.

6. Place in refrigerator for an hour. Serve chilled.

Nutrition information per serving:
Calories: 232; Carbohydrates: 2.2g; Protein: 6.1g; Fat: 22.5g; Sugar: 0.7g; Sodium: 555mg

Tomato Goat Cheese Sauce

(Servings: 4|Cooking Time: 3 hours)

Ingredients:
- 1 cup goat cheese, crumbled
- ¼ tsp. chili powder
- 1 tsp. dried rosemary
- ¼ cup apple cider vinegar
- 3 tbsp. olive oil
- 3 garlic cloves, crushed
- 1 onion, chopped
- ½ cup mozzarella cheese, shredded
- 1 cup tomatoes, diced

Directions for Cooking:
1. Add all ingredients into instant pot and stir well to combine.
2. Seal pot with lid and cook on Slow Cook mode for 3 hours.
3. Quick release pressure then open the lid.
4. Allow to cool completely then serve.

Nutrition information per serving:
Calories: 207; Carbohydrates: 6.6g; Protein: 6.9g; Fat: 18.3g; Sugar: 2.4g; Sodium: 162mg

Marinara Sauce

(Servings: 8|Cooking Time: 17 minutes)

Ingredients:
- ¼ cup water
- ¼ tsp. red pepper flakes
- ½ tsp. oregano
- ½ tsp. thyme
- 3 tbsp. fresh basil
- 1 carrot, peeled and grated
- 1 ¼ lbs. tomatoes, crushed
- 3 garlic cloves, chopped
- 1 onion, chopped
- 1 tbsp. olive oil
- Pepper
- Salt

Directions for Cooking:

1. Add oil into instant pot and set on Sauté mode.
2. Add garlic and onion and sauté for 2 minutes.
3. Add remaining ingredients and stir well.
4. Seal pot with lid and cook on manual high pressure for 30 minutes.
5. Quick release pressure then open the lid.
6. Blend the sauce.
7. Allow to cool completely then store in a container.

Nutrition information per serving:
Calories: 39; Carbohydrates: 5.3g; Protein: 1g; Fat: 1.9g; Sugar: 2.8g; Sodium: 29mg

Onion Apple Sauce

(Servings: 8|Cooking Time: 55 minutes)

Ingredients:

- 1 onion, chopped
- 2 apples, chopped
- ¼ tsp. liquid stevia
- ¼ cup fresh cilantro, chopped
- 1 cup vegetable broth
- 2 tbsp. butter
- ¼ cup apple cider vinegar
- ½ tsp. salt

Directions for Cooking:

1. Add butter into instant pot and set on Sauté mode.
2. Add onion and apple to the pot and sauté for 10 minutes.
3. Add stevia, apple cider vinegar and salt. Stir well.
4. Add broth and cilantro. Seal pot with lid and cook on manual mode for 35 minutes.
5. Allow pressure to release naturally for 10 minutes, then release using quick release method.
6. Using blender puree the sauce until smooth.

Nutrition information per serving:
Calories: 66; Carbohydrates: 9g; Protein: 1g; Fat: 3.2g; Sugar: 6.5g; Sodium: 265mg

Pasta Sauce

(Servings: 12|Cooking Time: 33 minutes)

Ingredients:

- 8 cups tomatoes, diced
- 1 tsp. sugar
- 1 tsp. pepper
- 1 ½ tbsp. Italian seasoning
- 4 garlic cloves, minced
- 1 onion, diced
- 3 cups water
- 2 tbsp. olive oil
- 1 tsp. salt

Directions for Cooking:

1. Add oil into instant pot and set on Sauté mode.
2. Add garlic and onion and sauté for 2-3 minutes.
3. Add remaining ingredients and stir well. Seal pot with lid and cook on manual high pressure for 30 minutes.
4. Quick release pressure then open the lid.
5. Puree sauce.
6. Serve over pasta and enjoy.

Nutrition information per serving:
Calories: 54; Carbohydrates: 6.5g; Protein: 1.3g; Fat: 3.1g; Sugar: 4g; Sodium: 203mg

Chapter 12 Instant Pot Dessert Recipes

Delicious Baked Apples

(Servings: 6|Cooking Time: 14 minutes)

Ingredients:

- 6 apples, cored and cut into wedges
- ¼ tsp. nutmeg
- 1 tsp. cinnamon
- 1/3 cup honey
- 1 cup red wine
- ¼ cup pecans, chopped
- ¼ cup raisins

Directions for Cooking:

1. Add all ingredients into instant pot and stir well.
2. Seal pot with lid and cook on manual mode for 4 minutes.
3. Allow pressure to release naturally for 10 minutes, then release using quick release method.
4. Stir well and serve.

Nutrition information per serving:
Calories: 233; Carbohydrates: 52.7g; Protein: 1g; Fat: 1.3g; Sugar: 42.6g; Sodium: 5mg

Moist Pumpkin Brownie

(Servings: 16|Cooking Time: 40 minutes)

Ingredients:

- 3 eggs
- 1 tsp. pumpkin pie spice
- ¾ cup cocoa powder
- ¼ cup palm sugar
- ¼ cup maple syrup
- ½ cup pumpkin puree
- ¼ cup coconut oil
- Pinch of salt

Directions for Cooking:

1. Spray baking dish with cooking spray and set aside.
2. Add all ingredients into the large bowl and stir well to combine. Pour batter into the prepared baking dish.
3. Pour 1 cup of water into instant pot then insert trivet.
4. Place baking dish on top of the trivet.
5. Seal pot with lid and cook on manual high pressure for 40 minutes.

6. Quick release pressure then open the lid.
7. Remove dish from the pot and set aside to cool completely.
8. Cut into pieces and serve.

Nutrition information per serving:
Calories: 77; Carbohydrates: 9.3g; Protein: 1.9g; Fat: 4.8g; Sugar: 5.6g; Sodium: 32mg

Lemon Custard

(Servings: 4|Cooking Time: 11 minutes)

Ingredients:
- 4 eggs
- 1 tsp. lemon extract
- 2/3 cup sugar
- 2 tsp. lemon zest
- 2 cups water
- 2 ½ cups milk

Directions for Cooking:
1. In a saucepan, add lemon zest and milk and heat over medium heat. Bring to boil and stir constantly.
2. Once milk starts to boil, remove from heat. Set aside to cool for 15 minutes.
3. Pour milk through a strainer into a bowl.
4. In another bowl, beat together eggs and lemon extract for 2-3 minutes.
5. Slowly pour milk to the egg mixture. Mix until smooth and creamy.

6. Pour mixture into the 4 ramekins and cover each with foil.
7. Pour water into instant pot then insert trivet.
8. Place ramekins on top of the trivet.
9. Seal pot with lid and cook on manual high pressure for 8 minutes.
10. Quick release pressure then open the lid.
11. Remove ramekins from the pot and set aside to cool completely.
12. Place custard ramekins in the refrigerator for 2 hours.
13. Serve chilled and enjoy.

Nutrition information per serving:
Calories: 268; Carbohydrates: 41.5g; Protein: 10.6g; Fat: 7.5g; Sugar: 40.7g; Sodium: 134mg

Pumpkin Pudding

(Servings: 4|Cooking Time: 14 minutes)

Ingredients:
- 4 cups pumpkin, cubed
- 1 tbsp. raisins
- ½ tsp. cardamom powder
- ½ cup desiccated coconut
- 10 tbsp. brown sugar
- ½ cup almond milk
- 2 tbsp. ghee

Directions for Cooking:
1. Add ghee into instant pot and set on Sauté mode.
2. Add pumpkin and sauté for 2-3 minutes. Add almond milk and stir well.

3. Seal pot with lid and cook on manual high pressure for 5 minutes.
4. Quick release pressure then open the lid.
5. Mash pumpkin.
6. Add sugar and cook on Sauté mode for 2-3 minutes.
7. Add remaining ingredients and stir well to combine. Cook for 2-3 minutes.
8. Serve warm and enjoy.

Nutrition information per serving:
Calories: 301; Carbohydrates: 14.2g; Protein: 3.5g; Fat: 14.2g; Sugar: 32.3g; Sodium: 23mg

Easy Yogurt Custard

(Servings: 6|Cooking Time: 40 minutes)

Ingredients:
- 1 cup Greek yogurt
- 2 tsp. cardamom powder
- 1 cup milk
- 2 cups water
- 1 cup condensed milk

Directions for Cooking:
1. Add all ingredients into the heat-safe bowl and mix until well combined. Cover bowl with foil.
2. Pour water into instant pot then insert trivet.
3. Place bowl on top of the trivet. Seal pot with lid and cook on manual high pressure for 20 minutes.
4. Allow pressure to release naturally for 20 minutes, then release using quick release method.
5. Remove bowl from the pot and set aside to cool completely.
6. Place custard bowl in refrigerator for 1 hour.
7. Serve chilled and enjoy.

Nutrition information per serving:
Calories: 215; Carbohydrates: 33.1g; Protein: 7.8g; Fat: 5.8g; Sugar: 32.4g; Sodium: 113mg

Zucchini Pudding

(Servings: 4|Cooking Time: 20 minutes)

Ingredients:
- 2 cups zucchini, shredded
- ½ tsp. cardamom powder
- 1/3 cup sugar
- 5 oz. half and half
- 5 oz. milk

Directions for Cooking:
1. Add all ingredients except cardamom to the instant pot and stir well.
2. Seal pot with lid and cook on manual high pressure for 10 minutes.
3. Allow pressure to release naturally for 10 minutes, then release using quick release method.
4. Add cardamom and stir well.
5. Serve and enjoy.

Nutrition information per serving:
Calories: 136; Carbohydrates: 22g; Protein: 2.9g; Fat: 4.9g; Sugar: 19.3g; Sodium: 37mg

Delicious Pina Colada

(Servings: 8|Cooking Time: 12 minutes)

Ingredients:
- 1 cup Arborio rice
- 1 tbsp. cinnamon
- 5 oz. can pineapple, crushed
- 13.5 oz. coconut milk
- 1 cup condensed milk
- 1 ½ cups water

Directions for Cooking:
1. Add rice and water into instant pot and stir well.
2. Seal pot with lid and cook on manual low pressure for 12 minutes.
3. Quick release pressure then open the lid.
4. Add remaining ingredients and stir well.
5. Serve and enjoy.

Nutrition information per serving:
Calories: 330; Carbohydrates: 45.4g; Protein: 5.8g; Fat: 14.9g; Sugar: 24.2g; Sodium: 59mg

Apple Caramel Cake

(Servings: 8|Cooking Time: 35 minutes)

Ingredients:

- 21 oz. apple fruit filling
- ¼ cup caramel syrup
- ½ cup butter, cut into slices
- 1 cup water
- 15 oz. yellow cake mix

Directions for Cooking:

1. Spray baking dish with cooking spray. Spread apple fruit filling in the bottom of baking dish.
2. Add caramel syrup and stir to coat.
3. Top with yellow cake mix and butter slices.
4. Pour water into instant pot then insert trivet.
5. Place baking dish on top of the trivet.
6. Seal pot with lid and cook on manual high pressure for 35 minutes.
7. Quick release pressure then open the lid.
8. Serve and enjoy.

Nutrition information per serving:
Calories: 357; Carbohydrates: 57g; Protein: 2g; Fat: 13g; Sugar: 28g; Sodium: 596mg

Apple Rice Pudding

(Servings: 8|Cooking Time: 15 minutes)

Ingredients:

- ¾ cup Arborio rice
- 1 tsp. cinnamon
- 1 cinnamon stick
- 1 tsp. vanilla
- ¼ apple, peeled and chopped
- 2 rhubarb stalks, chopped
- ½ cup water
- 1 ½ cup milk

Directions for Cooking:

1. Add all ingredients into instant pot and stir well.
2. Seal pot with lid and cook on manual mode for 15 minutes.
3. Quick release pressure then open the lid.
4. Stir well and serve.

Nutrition information per serving:
Calories: 96; Carbohydrates: 18.3g; Protein: 2.8g; Fat: 1.1g; Sugar: 3g; Sodium: 24mg

Vegan Coconut Risotto Pudding

(Servings: 6|Cooking Time: 30 minutes)

Ingredients:

- ¾ cup Arborio rice
- ¼ cup maple syrup
- 1 ½ cups water
- ½ cup shredded coconut
- 1 tsp. lemon juice
- ½ tsp. vanilla
- 15 oz. can coconut milk

Directions for Cooking:

1. Add all ingredients into instant pot and stir well.
2. Seal pot with lid and cook on manual mode for 20 minutes.
3. Allow pressure to release naturally for 10 minutes, then release using quick release method.
4. Stir well and using blender blend pudding until smooth.
5. Serve and enjoy.

Nutrition information per serving:
Calories: 284; Carbohydrates: 30.8g; Protein: 3.3g; Fat: 17.5g; Sugar: 8.3g; Sodium: 15mg

Vanilla Avocado Pudding

(Servings: 2|Cooking Time: 3 minutes)

Ingredients:

- ½ avocado, cut into cubes
- 1 tsp. agar powder
- ¼ cup coconut cream
- 1 cup coconut milk
- 2 tsp. swerve
- 1 tsp. vanilla

Directions for Cooking:

1. Add coconut cream and avocado into the blender and blend until smooth. Set aside.
2. In a large bowl, whisk together coconut milk, vanilla, swerve and agar powder. Stir until well combined.
3. Add coconut cream and avocado mixture. Stir well.
4. Pour mixture into a heat-safe bowl.
5. Pour one cup of water into instant pot then insert trivet.
6. Place bowl on top of the trivet.
7. Seal pot with lid and cook on Steam mode for 3 minutes.
8. Quick release pressure then open the lid.
9. Remove bowl from the pot and set aside to cool completely.
10. Place bowl in refrigerator for 1 hour.
11. Serve and enjoy.

Nutrition information per serving:
Calories: 308; Carbohydrates: 27.9g; Protein: 2.1g; Fat: 21.8g; Sugar: 19.6g; Sodium: 32mg

Vanilla Almond Risotto

(Servings: 4|Cooking Time: 15 minutes)

Ingredients:

- 1 cup Arborio rice
- 1 cup coconut milk
- 2 cups unsweetened almond milk
- ¼ cup sliced almonds
- 2 tsp. vanilla extract
- 1/3 cup sugar

Directions for Cooking:

1. Add almonds and coconut milk into instant pot. Stir well.
2. Seal pot with lid and cook on manual high pressure for 5 minutes.
3. Allow pressure to release naturally for 10 minutes, then release using quick release method.
4. Stir in vanilla extract and sweetener.
5. Serve and enjoy.

Nutrition information per serving:
Calories: 432; Carbohydrates: 60.3g; Protein: 6.3g; Fat: 19.3g; Sugar: 19.2g; Sodium: 102mg

Ginger Orange Glaze Pears

(Servings: 4|Cooking Time: 20 minutes)

Ingredients:

- 4 firm pears, peel and leave stem intact
- 1 tsp. ginger
- 1/3 cup sugar
- 1 cinnamon stick
- 1 cup orange juice
- 1 tsp. nutmeg
- 2 tsp. cinnamon
- 1 dash whole cloves

Directions for Cooking:

1. Add orange juice and all spices into instant pot.
2. Place trivet into instant pot. Arrange pears in trivet.
3. Seal pot with lid and cook on manual high pressure for 7 minutes.

4. Allow pressure to release naturally for 10 minutes, then release using quick release method.
5. Remove pears from pot and set aside.
6. Remove trivet, cinnamon stick and cloves from the pot.
7. Add sugar into the pot and cook on Sauté mode until sauce thickens — about 3 minutes.
8. Pour sauce over pears and serve.

Nutrition information per serving:
Calories: 219; Carbohydrates: 56.5g; Protein: 1.3g; Fat: 0.7g; Sugar: 42.5g; Sodium: 4mg

Bread Pudding

(Servings: 3|Cooking Time: 25 minutes)

Ingredients:
- 4 cups bread cube
- ½ tsp. vanilla extract
- 3 eggs, beaten
- 1 tsp. ground cinnamon
- ½ cup raisins
- 1 cup milk
- 1 tsp. vegetable oil
- 2 cups water
- ¼ tsp. salt

Directions for Cooking:
1. Place bread cubes in casserole dish.
2. In a bowl, mix all remaining ingredients until combined.
3. Pour the mixture over the top of bread cubes and cover the dish with foil.
4. Pour water into instant pot then insert trivet.
5. Place dish on top of the trivet.
6. Seal pot with lid and cook on Steam mode for 15 minutes.
7. Allow pressure to release naturally for 10 minutes, then release using quick release method.
8. Serve and enjoy.

Nutrition information per serving:
Calories: 358; Carbohydrates: 51.8g; Protein: 15.2g; Fat: 10.9g; Sugar: 15.2g; Sodium: 653mg

Strawberry Cobbler

(Servings: 3|Cooking Time: 22 minutes)

Ingredients:
- 3/4 cup strawberries, sliced
- 1 ½ tsp. baking powder
- ½ cup granulated sugar
- 1 ¼ cup all-purpose flour
- 1 tsp. vanilla
- 1/3 cup butter
- 1 ½ cups water
- 3/4 cup milk

Directions for Cooking:
1. In a large bowl, add all ingredients except strawberries and mix well.
2. Add sliced strawberries and fold well.
3. Grease 3 ramekins with butter then pour batter into the ramekins.
4. Pour water into instant pot then insert trivet.
5. Place ramekins on top of the trivet. Seal pot with lid and cook on manual high pressure for 12 minutes.
6. Allow pressure to release naturally for 10 minutes, then release using quick release method.
7. Serve and enjoy.

Nutrition information per serving:
Calories: 544; Carbohydrates: 80.2g; Protein: 7.8g; Fat: 22.3g; Sugar: 38.2g; Sodium: 178mg

Cinnamon Peach Cobbler

(Servings: 6|Cooking Time: 20 minutes)

Ingredients:

- 21 oz. can peach pie filling
- 2 tsp. cinnamon
- ½ cup butter, melted
- 1 tsp. nutmeg
- 15 oz. vanilla cake mix

Directions for Cooking:

1. Add peach pie filling into instant pot.
2. In a large bowl, mix together all remaining ingredients and spread over peaches.
3. Seal pot with lid and cook on manual high pressure for 10 minutes.
4. Allow pressure to release naturally for 10 minutes, then release using quick release method.
5. Serve and enjoy.

Nutrition information per serving:

Calories: 459; Carbohydrates: 79.4g; Protein: 0.2g; Fat: 15.5g; Sugar: 49.7g; Sodium: 785mg

Hazelnuts Almond Brownies

(Servings: 6|Cooking Time: 25 minutes)

Ingredients:

- 4 eggs
- 1 tsp. vanilla
- ½ cup mascarpone
- ½ cup flaxseed meal
- 3/4 cup almond flour
- 3 tbsp. hazelnuts, chopped
- ¼ cup Swerve
- 1 cup water
- 2 tbsp. butter

Directions for Cooking:

1. In a large bowl, add all ingredients and beat until smooth.
2. Spray baking dish with cooking spray.
3. Pour batter into the prepared pan.
4. Pour water into instant pot then insert trivet.
5. Place dish on top of the trivet. Seal pot with lid and cook on manual high pressure for 25 minutes.
6. Quick release pressure then open the lid.
7. Cut into pieces and serve.

Nutrition information per serving:

Calories: 198; Carbohydrates: 4.8g; Protein: 8.9g; Fat: 15.5g; Sugar: 0.7g; Sodium: 90mg

Chocolate Brownies

(Servings: 6|Cooking Time: 25 minutes)

Ingredients:

- 3 eggs
- ¼ cup almonds, chopped
- 1/3 cup coconut cream
- ¼ cup cocoa powder
- 2 tsp. vanilla
- 2 tsp. baking powder
- ¼ cup Swerve
- 2 tbsp. butter, melted
- ¼ cup flaxseed meal
- 2 cups water
- 3/4 cup almond flour

Directions for Cooking:

1. In a large bowl, mix together almond flour, baking powder, swerve, cocoa powder and flaxseed meal.
2. Add eggs, coconut cream, almond, vanilla and butter. Blend on low until well combined.
3. Spray baking pan with cooking spray.

4. Pour batter into the pan and cover the pan with foil. Set aside.
5. Pour water into instant pot then insert trivet.
6. Place pan on top of the trivet. Seal pot with lid and cook on manual high pressure for 25 minutes.

7. Quick release pressure then open the lid.
8. Cut into the slices and serve.

Nutrition information per serving:
Calories: 177; Carbohydrates: 6.8g; Protein: 6.2g; Fat: 14.9g; Sugar: 1.2g; Sodium: 65mg

Chocó Mug Cake

(Servings: 1|Cooking Time: 5 minutes)

Ingredients:
- 3 tbsp. almond flour
- 2 tsp. swerve
- 1 tbsp. cocoa powder
- 3 tbsp. coconut oil
- ¼ tsp. vanilla
- ½ tsp. baking powder
- 1 cup water
- 1 tbsp. chocolate chips

Directions for Cooking:
1. In a small bowl, mix together all ingredients until well combined.

2. Pour batter into the heat-safe mug and cover mug with foil.
3. Pour water into instant pot then insert trivet.
4. Place mug on top of the trivet. Seal pot with lid and cook on manual high pressure for 5 minutes.
5. Quick release pressure then open the lid.
6. Serve and enjoy.

Nutrition information per serving:
Calories: 555; Carbohydrates: 19g; Protein: 6.3g; Fat: 55.1g; Sugar: 6.4g; Sodium: 12mg

Cinnamon Apple Pear Crisp

(Servings: 4|Cooking Time: 20 minutes)

Ingredients:
- 3 apples, peel and cut into chunks
- 1 tsp. cinnamon
- ¼ cup date syrup
- 1 cup steel cut oats
- 2 pears, cut into chunks
- 1 ½ cup water

Directions for Cooking:
1. Add all ingredients into instant pot and stir well.

2. Seal pot with lid and cook on manual high pressure for 10 minutes.
3. Allow pressure to release naturally for 10 minutes, then release using quick release method.
4. Serve warm and enjoy.

Nutrition information per serving:
Calories: 282; Carbohydrates: 69.3g; Protein: 5.5g; Fat: 1.8g; Sugar: 40.8g; Sodium: 7mg

Apple Crisp

(Servings: 4|Cooking Time: 17 minutes)

Ingredients:
- 4 apples, peeled and diced
- 1 tbsp. butter, melted
- 1 tbsp. cinnamon
- ½ cup brown sugar
- 1 cup rolled oats
- ½ cup water
- 1 tbsp. honey
- 1 tbsp. flour

Directions for Cooking:
1. Add apples, cinnamon and brown sugar in a large bowl. Mix well.
2. Mix together flour, honey and oats. Toss with apples.
3. Pour water into instant pot then drop apple mixture.
4. Seal pot with lid and cook on manual high pressure for 7 minutes.
5. Allow pressure to release naturally for 10 minutes, then release using quick release method.
6. Serve and enjoy.

Nutrition information per serving:
Calories: 315; Carbohydrates: 69.6g; Protein: 3.6g; Fat: 4.7g; Sugar: 45.4g; Sodium: 30mg

Blueberry Almond Cupcakes

(Servings: 6|Cooking Time: 10 minutes)

Ingredients:
- 2 eggs
- 1 tsp. vanilla
- ¼ cup blueberries
- ¼ cup Swerve
- 3 tbsp. yogurt
- ¼ cup cream cheese
- 1 cup shredded coconut
- 2 tsp. baking powder
- 3 tbsp. butter
- 2 tbsp. cocoa powder
- 1 cup water
- 1 ½ cups almond flour

Directions for Cooking:
1. In a large bowl, combine together butter and eggs. Beat gently using a blender until fluffy.
2. Add swerve, yogurt and cream cheese. Stir well.
3. Add almond flour, baking powder and shredded coconut. Mix well.
4. Add blueberries and fold well. Pour batter into the six-tray silicone mold and set aside.
5. Pour water into instant pot and insert trivet.
6. Place silicon mold on top of the trivet. Seal pot with lid and cook on manual high pressure for 10 minutes.
7. Quick release pressure then open the lid.
8. Serve and enjoy.

Nutrition information per serving:
Calories: 330; Carbohydrates: 11.8g; Protein: 9.9g; Fat: 29.4g; Sugar: 3.2g; Sodium: 100mg

Peanut Butter Fudge

(Servings: 12|Cooking Time: 90 minutes)

Ingredients:
- 1 cup chocolate chips
- 1 tsp. vanilla
- ¼ cup erythritol
- 8 oz. cream cheese
- ¼ cup peanut butter

Directions for Cooking:
1. Add all ingredients into instant pot and stir well.

2. Seal pot with lid and cook on Slow Cook mode for 1 hour.
3. Release pressure using quick release method.
4. Stir until smooth and cook for 30 minutes more on Sauté mode.

5. Pour mixture into the 8x8" baking pan and place in refrigerator for 2 hours, or until set.
6. Slice and serve.

Nutrition information per serving:
Calories: 173; Carbohydrates: 13.9g; Protein: 3.9g; Fat: 13.5g; Sugar: 7.8g; Sodium: 92mg

Tapioca Pudding

(Servings: 8|Cooking Time: 16 minutes)

Ingredients:
- 1 cup tapioca pearls
- ¼ cup honey
- 3 cups water
- 1 tbsp. vanilla
- 2 egg yolks
- 1 can coconut milk
- ½ tsp. sea salt

Directions for Cooking:
1. Add water and tapioca pearls into instant pot.
2. Seal pot with lid and cook on manual mode for 6 minutes.

3. Allow pressure to release naturally for 10 minutes, then release using quick release method.
4. Add honey and salt. Whisk well.
5. In a small bowl, whisk together egg yolks and coconut milk. Whisk into the pot.
6. Set pot on Sauté mode. Whisk pudding mixture constantly until boiling.
7. Turn off the instant pot. Add vanilla and stir well.
8. Serve and enjoy.

Nutrition information per serving:
Calories: 110; Carbohydrates: 20.6g; Protein: 0.7g; Fat: 2.6g; Sugar: 8.9g; Sodium: 124mg

Vanilla Cheesecake

(Servings: 8|Cooking Time: 30 minutes)

Ingredients:
- 2 eggs
- 1 tsp. vanilla
- 16 oz. cream cheese
- ½ cup Swerve
- 2 cups water

Directions for Cooking:
1. Spray 7-inch spring-form pan with cooking spray and set aside.
2. Add all ingredients into the blender and blend until smooth.
3. Pour batter into the prepared pan and cover the pan with foil.
4. Pour water into instant pot then insert trivet.

5. Place cake pan on top of the trivet. Seal pot with lid and cook on manual high pressure for 20 minutes.
6. Allow pressure to release naturally for 10 minutes, then release using quick release method.
7. Remove cake pan from the pot and set aside to cool completely.
8. Place in refrigerator for 2-3 hours.
9. Serve and enjoy.

Nutrition information per serving:
Calories: 215; Carbohydrates: 1.8g; Protein: 5.7g; Fat: 20.9g; Sugar: 0.3g; Sodium: 183mg

Vanilla Raspberry Pudding

(Servings: 6|Cooking Time: 35 minutes)

Ingredients:

- ½ cup heavy cream
- 1 cup Arborio rice
- 3 tbsp. raspberry jam
- ¼ cup sugar
- 2 cups milk
- 2 cups raspberries
- 1 tsp. vanilla
- 1 cinnamon stick
- 1 cup water

Directions for Cooking:

1. Set instant pot on Sauté mode.
1. Add water, jam, sugar and milk into the pot. Stir well and cook until sugar dissolves.
2. Add cinnamon stick, vanilla and rice. Stir well.
3. Seal pot with lid and cook on Porridge mode for 35 minutes.
4. Allow pressure to release naturally, then open lid.
5. Stir in cream and raspberries.
6. Serve and enjoy.

Nutrition information per serving:
Calories: 269; Carbohydrates: 49.3g; Protein: 5.5g; Fat: 5.8g; Sugar: 18.4g; Sodium: 46mg

Cranberry Pudding

(Servings: 8|Cooking Time: 40 minutes)

Ingredients:

- 1 cup Arborio rice
- 1/8 tsp. cloves
- ¼ tsp. cinnamon
- 1 ½ cups water
- ¼ cup cranberries, dried
- 2/3 cup half and half
- 14 oz. condensed milk
- 1/8 tsp. nutmeg
- 2 cups milk
- 1/8 tsp. salt

Directions for Cooking:

1. Add rice, nutmeg, cloves, cinnamon, salt, water, cranberries and milk into instant pot. Stir well.
2. Seal pot with lid and cook on Porridge mode for 30 minutes.
3. Allow pressure to release naturally for 10 minutes, then release using quick release method.
4. Stir in half and half and condensed milk.
5. Pour pudding into the airtight container and place in the fridge for 2 hours or until set.

Nutrition information per serving:
Calories: 304; Carbohydrates: 502g; Protein: 8.1 g; Fat: 8g; Sugar: 29.9g; Sodium: 138mg

Carrot Almond Cake

(Servings: 8|Cooking Time: 50 minutes)

Ingredients:

- 3 eggs
- ¼ cup coconut oil
- 1 ½ tsp. apple pie spice
- 1 tsp. baking powder
- 2/3 cup Swerve
- 1 cup almond flour
- ½ cup walnuts, chopped
- 1 cup carrot, shredded

- ½ cup heavy whipping cream
- 2 cups water

Directions for Cooking:

1. Spray 6-inch baking dish with cooking spray and set aside.
2. Add all ingredients into the large mixing bowl and mix with electric mixer until well combined.
3. Pour batter into the prepared dish and cover dish with foil.
4. Pour water into instant pot then insert trivet.
5. Place baking dish on top of the trivet.
6. Seal pot with lid and cook on manual high pressure for 40 minutes.
7. Allow pressure to release naturally for 10 minutes, then release using quick release method.
8. Remove dish from the pot and set aside to cool completely.
9. Serve and enjoy.

Nutrition information per serving:
Calorie: 184; Carbohydrates: 3.9g; Protein: 5 g; Fat: 17.6g; Sugar: 1.1g; Sodium: 38mg

Indian Rice Pudding

(Servings: 6|Cooking Time: 35 minutes)

Ingredients:

- 1 cup basmati rice, rinsed and drained
- 1 ½ cups sugar
- ½ cup walnuts
- 1 cup water
- 5 cups milk

Directions for Cooking:

1. Add rice, 2 cups milk and ¾ cups sugar into instant pot. Stir well.
2. Seal pot with lid and cook on manual mode for 30 minutes
3. Meanwhile, soak walnut into the water for 15 minutes.
4. Add walnuts and ½ cup water into the food processor. Process until consistency of a coarse paste.
5. Quick release pressure then open the lid.
6. Mash rice with a ladle.
7. Set instant pot on Sauté mode. Add remaining milk, walnut paste and sugar.
8. Stir well and simmer for 3 minutes.
9. Serve and enjoy.

Nutrition information per serving:
Calorie: 466; Carbohydrates: 85.7g; Protein: 11.4g; Fat: 10.5g; Sugar: 59.3g; Sodium: 99mg

Coconut Cake

(Servings: 8|Cooking Time: 50 minutes)

Ingredients:

- Dry ingredients:
- 1 tsp. apple pie spice
- 1/3 cup Swerve
- ½ cup shredded coconut
- 1 cup almond flour
- 1 tsp. baking powder
- Wet ingredients:
- ¼ cup butter, melted
- 2 eggs, lightly beaten
- ½ cup heavy whipping cream

Directions for Cooking:

1. In a large bowl, mix together all dry ingredients until well combined.
2. Add all wet ingredients into the dry mixture and beat until well combined.
3. Spray 6" baking dish with cooking spray. Pour batter into the prepared baking dish.
4. Pour 2 cups water into instant pot then insert trivet.
5. Place baking dish on top of the trivet. Seal pot with lid and cook on manual high pressure for 40 minutes.

6. Allow pressure to release naturally for 10 minutes, then release using quick release method.
7. Remove baking dish from the pot and set aside to cool completely.

8. Serve and enjoy.

Nutrition information per serving:
Calorie: 192; Carbohydrates: 4.6g; Protein: 4.8; Fat: 18.3g; Sugar: 0.9g; Sodium: 61mg

Brown Rice Pudding

(Servings: 4|Cooking Time: 35 minutes)

Ingredients:
- 1 cup brown rice
- 1 tbsp. butter
- 1 cinnamon stick
- 1 tbsp. vanilla extract
- 1 ½ cup water
- ½ cup heavy cream
- 3 tbsp. honey
- 1 cup raisins

Directions for Cooking:
1. Add rice, cinnamon stick, vanilla, butter and water into instant pot. Stir well.

2. Seal pot with lid and select manual. Set timer for 20 minutes.
3. Allow pressure to release naturally for 10 minutes, then release using quick release method.
4. Discard cinnamon stick from the pot.
5. Stir in cream, honey and raisins. Set pot on Sauté mode and simmer for 5 minutes.
6. Serve and enjoy.

Nutrition information per serving:
Calorie: 415; Carbohydrates: 78.7g; Protein: 5.1g; Fat: 9.9g; Sugar: 34.8g; Sodium: 36mg

Egg Custard

(Servings: 6|Cooking Time: 17 minutes)

Ingredients:
- 6 eggs
- 3/4 cup Swerve
- 4 cups cream
- 1 tsp. vanilla
- 1 ½ cups water

Directions for Cooking:
1. In a large mixing bowl, beat eggs. Add cream, vanilla and swerve. Bend until well combined.
2. Pour blended mixture into the baking dish and cover with foil.

3. Pour water into instant pot then insert trivet.
4. Place baking dish on top of the trivet. Seal pot with lid and cook on manual high pressure for 7 minutes.
5. Allow pressure to release naturally for 10 minutes, then release using quick release method.
6. Serve and enjoy.

Nutrition information per serving:
Calorie: 168; Carbohydrates: 5.7g; Protein: 6.8g; Fat: 13.3g; Sugar: 3.6g; Sodium: 114mg

Sweet Potato Pudding

(Servings: 8|Cooking Time: 8 minutes)

Ingredients:
- 1 medium sweet potato, peeled and shredded
- 1 tsp. cinnamon
- 1 ½ cups water
- ½ cup honey
- 12 oz. milk
- 1 can coconut milk
- 2/3 cup raisins
- 1 cup Arborio rice
- ½ tsp. cardamom

- 1 tsp. vanilla
- 1 tbsp. butter
- 1 tsp. salt

Directions for Cooking:
1. Add butter into instant pot and set on Sauté mode.
2. Add honey, water, milk and coconut milk. Stir well.
3. Add cinnamon, vanilla, cardamom and salt. Stir well and simmer.

4. Add rice and sweet potato. Stir well.
5. Seal pot with lid and cook on manual high pressure for 8 minutes.
6. Quick release pressure then open the lid.
7. Stir in raisins and serve.

Nutrition information per serving:
Calorie: 251; Carbohydrates: 51.7g; Protein: 3.9g; Fat: 4g; Sugar: 27.5g; Sodium: 335mg

Coconut Custard

(Servings: 4|Cooking Time: 40 minutes)

Ingredients:
- 3 eggs
- 1 cup coconut milk
- 1 tsp. vanilla extract
- 1/3 cup Swerve2 cups water

Directions for Cooking:
1. Spray 6-inch baking dish with cooking spray and set aside.
2. In a large mixing bowl, blend together eggs, vanilla, swerve and coconut milk.
3. Pour blended mixture into the baking dish and cover dish with foil
4. Pour water into instant pot then insert trivet.

5. Place baking dish on top of the trivet. Seal pot with lid and cook on manual high pressure for 30 minutes.
6. Allow pressure to release naturally for 10 minutes, then release using quick release method.
7. Remove dish from the pot and set aside to cool completely.
8. Place in refrigerator for 3-4 hours.
9. Serve and enjoy.

Nutrition information per serving:
Calorie: 189; Carbohydrates: 3.9g; Protein: 5.5g; Fat: 17.6g; Sugar: 2.4g; Sodium: 55mg

Creamy Pecan Pudding

(Servings: 8|Cooking Time: 30 minutes)

Ingredients:
- 1 cup arborio rice
- 1 tbsp. butter
- 1 cup brown rice
- 1 cup water
- 1 cup half and half
- ½ cup pecans, chopped
- 2 tsp. vanilla
- ½ cup heavy cream
- 1 tsp. salt

Directions for Cooking:
1. Add butter into instant pot and set on Sauté mode.

2. Add pecans into the pot and stir until toasted.
3. Add remaining ingredients except for heavy cream and vanilla. Stir well.
4. Seal pot with lid and select manual mode for 20 minutes.
5. Allow pressure to release naturally for 10 minutes, then release using quick release method.
6. Stir in vanilla and heavy cream.
7. Serve and enjoy.

Nutrition information per serving:
Calories: 265; Carbohydrates: 38.9g; Protein: 4.6g; Fat: 9.7g; Sugar: 0.3g; Sodium: 320mg

Pumpkin Pudding

(Servings: 6|Cooking Time: 30 minutes)

Ingredients:

- 2 eggs
- 1 tsp. vanilla
- 3/4 cup Swerve
- ½ cup heavy whipping cream
- 1 tsp. pumpkin pie spice
- 15 oz. can pumpkin puree
- 1 ½ cups water

Directions for Cooking:

1. In a large mixing bowl, whisk eggs with remaining ingredients until well combined.
2. Spray 6x3" baking dish with cooking spray and set aside.
3. Pour batter into the prepared baking dish.
4. Pour water into instant pot then insert trivet.
5. Place baking dish on top of the trivet. Seal pot with lid and cook on manual high pressure for 20 minutes.
6. Allow pressure to release naturally for 10 minutes, then release using quick release method.
7. Remove baking dish from the instant pot and set aside to cool completely.
8. Place in refrigerator for 4-5 hours.
9. Serve and enjoy.

Nutrition information per serving:
Calories: 164; Carbohydrates: 25.9g; Protein: 4.6g; Fat: 5.2g; Sugar: 10.2g; Sodium: 37mg

Indian Saffron Rice Pudding

(Servings: 6|Cooking Time: 27 minutes)

Ingredients:

- ½ cup rice
- 4 tbsp. almonds, chopped
- 4 tbsp. walnuts, chopped
- 1 tsp. cardamom powder
- ½ cup sugar
- 1 tbsp. shredded coconut
- ½ tsp. saffron
- 2 tbsp. raisins
- 4 cups milk
- 1 tbsp. ghee
- 1/8 tsp. salt

Directions for Cooking:

1. Add ghee into the pot and set on Sauté mode.
2. Add rice and sauté for 30 seconds.
3. Add 3 cups milk, coconut, raisins, saffron, nuts, cardamom powder, sugar, ½ cup water and salt into the pot. Stir well.
4. Seal pot with lid and cook on manual high pressure for 10 minutes.
5. Allow pressure to release naturally for 15 minutes, then release using quick release method.
6. Add remaining milk and stir well. Cook on Sauté mode for 2 minutes.
7. Serve and enjoy.

Nutrition information per serving:
Calories: 287; Carbohydrates: 41.2g; Protein: 8.7g; Fat: 10.9g; Sugar: 26.1g; Sodium: 129mg

Mini Chocolate Cake

(Servings: 2|Cooking Time: 9 minutes)

Ingredients:

- 2 eggs
- ½ tsp. baking powder
- 2 tbsp. heavy cream
- 2 tbsp. swerve
- ¼ cup cocoa powder
- 1 tsp. vanilla
- 1 cup water

Directions for Cooking:

1. In a bowl, mix together all dry ingredients until well combined.

2. Add all wet ingredients to the dry mixture and whisk until smooth.
3. Spray two ramekins with cooking spray.
4. Pour batter into the prepared ramekins.
5. Pour water into instant pot then place trivet to the pot.
6. Place ramekins on top of the trivet. Seal pot with lid and cook on manual high pressure for 9 minutes.
7. Quick release pressure then open the lid.
8. Remove ramekins from the pot and set aside to cool completely.
9. Serve and enjoy.

Nutrition information per serving:
Calories: 151; Carbohydrates: 9.5g; Protein: 7.8g; Fat: 11.3g; Sugar: 0.8g; Sodium: 71mg

Moist Almond Pumpkin Brownie

(Servings: 4|Cooking Time: 35 minutes)

Ingredients:
- 2 eggs
- 1 tbsp. vanilla
- ¼ cup coconut milk
- 1 cup maple syrup
- 1 cup pumpkin puree
- ½ tsp. baking powder
- 1/3 cup cocoa powder
- ½ cup almond flour
- 2 cups water

Directions for Cooking:
1. Add all ingredients into the large bowl and mix well to combine.
2. Grease spring-form pan with butter.
3. Pour batter into the pan and cover the pan with foil.
4. Pour water into instant pot and place trivet into the pot.
5. Place pan on trivet. Seal pot with lid and cook on manual mode for 35 minutes.
6. Quick release pressure then open the lid.
7. Cut into pieces and serve.

Nutrition information per serving:
Calories: 338; Carbohydrates: 64.2g; Protein: 5.8g; Fat: 8.8g; Sugar: 50.2g; Sodium: 47mg

Almond Chocolate Mousse

(Servings: 5|Cooking Time: 6 minutes)

Ingredients:
- 4 egg yolks
- 1 cup heavy whipping cream
- ¼ cup cocoa powder
- ¼ cup water
- ½ cup Swerve
- ½ tsp. vanilla
- ½ cup almond milk
- 1 ½ cups water

Directions for Cooking:
1. In a bowl, add egg yolks and whisk until well beaten.
2. In a medium saucepan, add swerve, cocoa powder and water. Whisk until well combined.
3. Add almond milk and heavy whipping cream to the saucepan. Whisk to combine. Heat over medium-low heat until just hot.
4. Add vanilla and salt. Stir well.
5. Slowly add saucepan mixture to the eggs and whisk until well combined.
6. Pour batter into the ramekins.
7. Pour water into instant pot then insert trivet.
8. Place ramekins on top of the trivet. Seal pot with lid and cook on manual mode for 6 minutes.
9. Quick release pressure then open the lid.
10. Remove ramekins from the pot and set aside to cool completely.
11. Place ramekins in the refrigerator for 3-4 hours,Serve and enjoy.

Nutrition information per serving:
Calories: 192; Carbohydrates: 5.1g; Protein: 4g; Fat: 18.8g; Sugar: 1g; Sodium: 20mg

Made in the USA
Columbia, SC
06 July 2020